THE FRAGRANCE OF SWEET-GRASS

THE FRAGRANCE OF SWEET-GRASS

L.M. Montgomery's Heroines and the Pursuit of Romance

ELIZABETH ROLLINS EPPERLY

UNIVERSITY OF TORONTO PRESS
Toronto Buffalo London

© University of Toronto Press Incorporated 1992
First paperback edition 1993
Toronto Buffalo London
Printed in Canada
ISBN 0-8020-7461-8

Printed on acid-free paper

Canadian Cataloguing in Publication Data

Epperly, Elizabeth R.
The fragrance of sweet-grass : L.M. Montgomery's
heroines and the pursuit of romance
Includes index.
ISBN 0-8020-5999-6 (bound) ISBN 0-8020-7461-8 (pbk.)
1. Montgomery, L.M. (Lucy Maud), 1874–1942 –
Criticism and interpretation. I. Title.
PS8526.O57Z63 1992   C813'.52   C91-095692-8
PR9199.2.M65Z63   1992

This book has been published with the help of a grant from the Canadian
Federation for the Humanities, using funds provided by the Social Sciences
and Humanities Research Council of Canada.

To the memory of my father,
John David Epperly,
who loved Montgomery's books and introduced me to them,
and to the memory of my cousin
Nancy Weddle Goodman,
a rare and beautiful spirit

Contents

Acknowledgments

Quotations from the novels of Lucy Maud Montgomery are published with the permission of Ruth Macdonald, David Macdonald, and John G. McClelland. I am grateful to them for this permission and also for their encouragement with this project. I am also much indebted to Mary Rubio and Elizabeth Waterston, whose joint and separate works on Montgomery are essential to us all. They have been unfailingly generous with their knowledge and energy. Thanks to the E. Stuart Macdonald Estate and the L.M. Montgomery Collection, University of Guelph Library and Oxford University Press for permission to quote from L.M. Montgomery's journals. My thanks to the Confederation Centre of the Arts in Charlotte-town – and most especially to Moncrieff Williamson, Mark Holton, and Kevin Rice – for permission to examine and make use of L.M. Montgomery's manuscripts. My thanks also to Karen Walsh, with whom I have enjoyed many delightful conversations about Montgomery and imagination. I would also like to thank George and Maureen Campbell of Silver Bush on Prince Edward Island for involving me with their L.M. Montgomery newsletter, *Kindred Spirits of P.E.I.*, and for welcoming me into a very personal dimension of the Montgomery world.

Abbreviations

THE FRAGRANCE OF SWEET-GRASS

Introduction

'You jest have to stumble on it – you're walking along on the sand-hills, never thinking of sweet-grass – and all at once the air is full of sweetness – and there's the grass under your feet. I favour the smell of sweet-grass ... I don't like these boughten scents – but a whiff of sweet-grass belongs anywhere a lady does.'
(Captain Jim, *Anne's House of Dreams* 138)

L.M. Montgomery's writing changes people's lives. To those accustomed to thinking of her as a writer for children, who presumably forget her when they grow up, or as a complacent and dismissible scribbler of romances, to hear that Montgomery's writing profoundly affects the way people think about themselves will sound absurd. But it is true: thousands of readers identify with and are inspired by Montgomery's characters, descriptions, and romanticized realism. Why?

Montgomery crosses cultural and generational lines in her phenomenal, continuing popularity. Polish soldiers in the Second World War were issued copies of *Anne of the Island* to take to the front with them (Wachowicz 10); a post-war Japan turned to *Anne of Green Gables* for lessons in cheerfulness and optimism (Katsura 57–60; Epperly, 'Greetings' 5). Recently a musical based on *The Blue Castle* has been a smash hit in Poland (Wachowicz 7–35), and thousands of Japanese tourists come to Prince Edward Island to see for themselves the land of Green Gables, and then at home import Anne memorabilia and attend large professional exhibitions of Montgomery materials. Montgomery's twenty novels and volumes of short stories and poems are appearing in new, handsome, illustrated editions. Montgomery's journals have gained a solid readership. Several of the novels have been translated into half a dozen languages, and a recent series of Canadian television movies has made *Anne* a household word all over again in North America. Sophisticated writers such as Alice Munro (Afterword 357–61) and Jane Urquhart (Afterword 330–4) talk about the important influence of Montgomery on their understanding of themselves as females and as writers. I know personally numbers of people who have read and loved Montgomery and have subsequently left other provinces or countries behind to move permanently to Prince Edward Island. What makes Montgomery's stories so powerful and her characters and landscapes so beloved?

When Montgomery first started writing short stories, she had her eye on the market. She probably read stories in the *Family Herald and Weekly Star*, as Nellie McClung did (Roper 279), and she read stories in magazines imported from the States, among them the popular *Godey's Lady's Book* (Montgomery, *Alpine* 48). From the standards and patterns set by periodicals such as these Montgomery fashioned her early pieces in the 1890s.

Her own literary taste had been formed by her reading of nineteenth-century fiction and poetry – whatever volumes she could borrow from the Cavendish Literary Society or from friends and relatives. She had studied literature at Prince of Wales College while she took a teacher's licence (1893–4) and at Dalhousie University where she was a student for one year (1895–6). She read, among others, Scott, Dickens, Thackeray, the Brontës, Trollope, George Eliot, and – her beloved for years – Bulwer Lytton; among the poets she relished Keats, Shelley, Byron, Scott, Wordsworth, Tennyson, and both Brownings. From the best literature of the nineteenth century – and some introduction to Shakespeare as well as to Milton – Montgomery drew her ideas about narration, description, dialogue, dialect, and moral rectitude. But she shaped her stories to sell to the periodicals she knew or heard about, and she carefully crafted her own pieces to conform to the formula a particular journal favoured.

From reading early examples of Montgomery's stories, we see how thoroughly she imitated the patterns of the day – dramatic reversals of fortune, suddenly discovered long-lost relatives, sentimental love scenes, and purple patches of description. But if the pieces are formulaic, they are also often very clever, suggesting the gift behind the conformity, the artistic powers barely tapped by the marketable tale.[1] A sharp eye for detail and a keenly developed sense of humour and irony show even in some of the most stylized pieces. Montgomery, in short, was successful early in her career for many of the same reasons that she remained popular in her own lifetime and beyond – she wrote what people wanted to read. She adapted material to the form or formula that would sell.

When Montgomery's grandfather died in 1898, the twenty-four-year-old Maud gave up teaching and returned to Cavendish so that she could take care of her aging grandmother. There she read or reread whatever she could find – perhaps a classic, invaluable to a writer of girls' stories, such as Louisa May Alcott's *Little Women*, or a startlingly unconventional work such as Olive Schreiner's *The Story of an African Farm*. The Cavendish lending library kept a thin stock of new books, and she read Kate Douglas Wiggin's *Rebecca of Sunnybrook Farm* (published in 1903)[2] and Elizabeth von Arnim's *Elizabeth and Her German Garden* (published in 1898, but read by Montgomery in 1905), which may have inspired Montgomery's use of the phrase 'kindred spirit.'[3] Within a few years of returning to Cavendish and after a brief stint in Halifax on a newspaper, her arduous apprenticeship paid off, and she began to earn a fairly comfortable living by her pen. Poetry never made much money, but she enjoyed writing it and thought she touched 'a far higher note in my verse than in prose' (*Letters* 3). She decided to expand an idea for a serial into a novel, and in 1905 she began what was to become *Anne of Green Gables*. It was rejected by five publishing houses, and then, when she had almost given up on it completely, she took it out of the hatbox where she had stored it and sent it off to the L.C. Page Company in Boston. The rest is a publishing success story. The Page Company not only wanted it, but wanted her to prepare a sequel right away. *Anne of Green Gables* was published in July 1908, and by October of that year the book had gone through five printings. The success continued, and Montgomery became world famous, receiving fan mail from prime ministers and great writers, from young and old, and from as far away as Tibet and Australia.

Montgomery had obviously gone beyond the formula of her early, smart little stories; she had touched what T.D. MacLulich calls a 'universal nerve' ('Portraits' 459) and what her bibliographers call 'the deepest places in the heart of childhood' (Russell, Russell, and Wilmshurst xix). She continued to touch that nerve in almost all her writing.

Montgomery's detractors like to say that she stumbled onto a lucky formula in *Anne of Green Gables* (MacLulich, 'Portraits' 459) and continued to exploit it in all her subsequent fiction. And there is some truth in this, but only some. There is something of formula in all her novels, since she was writing within the safe and fairly predictable boundaries of children's stories or domestic romance. But just as there was a glimmer of irony and wit in many of those very early magazine pieces that she wrote to order, so in even the most predictable of scenes in her novels we find the twist of irony or humour that transforms the expected into the surprising. And, more importantly, what Montgomery often did exploit was archetype rather than mere formula – the fundamental themes of life rather than just superficial social interchanges. As Elizabeth Waterston explains in her landmark essay on Montgomery in *The Clear Spirit*, Montgomery's fiction deals with the deepest anxieties about growing up (198–220). And, Mary Rubio would add, growing up includes confronting the power relations implicit not only in Avonlea community life but in the relations of the sexes themselves ('Canada's' 2).

Much of Montgomery's lasting appeal, Mary Rubio explains, has to do with the way Montgomery played with the expectations of her audience. She invited her female readers in particular to enjoy in the stories assaults against their own confinement, under the guise of ironic and humorous deflations of authority. The same confinement and oppression that women readers may feel in the culture surrounding them is also felt by other downtrodden groups and cultures – and they, too, read Montgomery and feel the thrill of getting the better of authority in sly, witty, safe ways. Mary Rubio outlines eight 'strategies' Montgomery used for including social criticism in apparently innocuous stories: (1) choosing the women's genres of domestic romance and children's fiction, (2) writing happy endings for her stories but undercutting those happy endings all along the way with shifts in the tone or form of the writing, (3) undercutting her own subversive elements by using humour, (4) making subversive comments through characters of 'no-importance' so that no one takes responsibility for such comments in the fiction, (5) using feelings and thoughts rather than tight plots or straight chronologies, (6) using the narrator to intrude with comments on a heroine's refusal to conform to convention or expectation, (7) presenting patriarchs as women, thus making behaviour and attitudes that would have been acceptable in a man seem grotesque, (8) using literary allusions and references to reinforce subversive messages for those who know the original literary works ('Canada's' 3–7). Rubio ends her interesting assessment with these words: 'In summary, L.M. Montgomery's little romances are more complicated than appear on the surface. We can see that she, like many other female writers of her day, played the literary game with superb finesse, remaining within the confines of genteel female respectability, while incorporating serious social criticism into her novels' ('Canada's' 8).

Montgomery had learned in the early years of her apprenticeship to write for the market; she wanted to sell what she wrote and to become a successful 'worker,' as she put it, since she did not regard herself as a genius who could ignore money for the sake of art. But Montgomery also learned in those early days to inject something of herself into the writing – to infuse her sense of fun or her own perspective into some of the surprises of dialogue or event. And thus when she did write her first novel, she was already adept at writing within boundaries and yet liberating her own poetic and humorous bents. The impulses behind her descriptions and her irony keep her novels popular even yet.

Montgomery's books are primarily about female characters. Her heroines range in age from young to old. Eleven of her novels are focused on child or young adolescent heroines, and nine are focused on older adolescent or adult heroines. Each of the heroines[4] learns to value herself in relation to the surrounding community and culture; each heroine learns to love and create a home for herself. In discovering or appreciating or creating 'home,' the heroines are creating or strengthening interconnections between themselves and the value or beauties of the spiritual or material culture around them. In other words, Montgomery's heroines act out what Carol Gilligan describes (*In a Different Voice*) as the essentially female valuation of interconnectedness and interrelatedness, as opposed to the male valuation of competition and separation. Anne Shirley wants everyone to love her, and she celebrates the joyous beauty of the natural world; even though she is less obviously sociable, Emily Byrd Starr prizes her connections with the traditions of the women of her clan and cultivates her gifts for recreating the beauty she sees.

For each of Montgomery's heroines a recognition of her own distinctive voice is a crucial step to self-awareness; talking back is sometimes a measure of self-confidence or self-worth; love of place is a way of celebrating the centred, whole personality. For Montgomery's heroines 'home' includes an awareness of the centred self; 'home' is an attitude as well as a place. Through ingenious – and perhaps often necessarily unconscious – subversions of the various systems and codes around them, Montgomery's heroines learn to hold their own in a culture that will give them a very limited framework in which to live respectably and comfortably. Not a single one of Montgomery's heroines loses respectability. Even Valancy's real break with 'the Stirlings of Deerwood' in *The Blue Castle* is made only after she gets married; her nursing of the consumptive outcast, Cissy Gay, was a cracking of rather than a clear breaking from code, since selfless acts of mercy were still acceptable for the unmarried female. Valancy's early defiance of the rules of proper daughterly conduct includes saying what she thinks at a clan gathering and viciously pruning a rose-bush. In the world scheme these peccadilloes are minor indeed, but Montgomery and the reader know that within the context of Valancy's restricted and beleaguered life, these outbreaks are flamboyant.

What can we learn by looking closely at Montgomery's writing? We can learn what confinement to genre means in terms of the compromises she had to make with character or narrative development. We can also appreciate how Montgomery used and reused certain subjects and themes to suggest intricacies of personality or ironic implications of a scene. We can see how far Montgomery was willing to stretch the boundaries of romance and children's fiction. In looking carefully at her heroines and their literary context, we can understand something more about our own expectations for female characters and their possibilities for growth, change, and independence.[5] We must read carefully if we are to discern what assumptions underlie the humour and the pathos, the indignation and the joy. We will find that Montgomery's writing is filled with apparently unexamined prejudices – if her writing is in any way a just reflection of her own thinking, she was sometimes racist, classist, ageist, weight-prejudiced, and chauvinistic. It will be impossible for many readers of the 1990s to see the concluding lines of either *Magic for Marigold* or *A*

Tangled Web, for example, without dismay or shock at the values they suggest. Montgomery's stories often support not only the white, English-speaking status quo but also stereotypes about men and women and the supposed battle of the sexes.

Nevertheless, despite the chosen limitations of her genre and the perhaps unconscious prejudices of her background and/or times, Montgomery has a great deal to offer the careful reader. Her idealized, late-Romantic, occasionally transcendentalist nature descriptions, for example, are wonderfully attractive and versatile. Montgomery makes considerable use of what Annis Pratt calls the 'green-world archetype,' a 'special world of nature' that is a continuing source of joy, beauty, and power for the female hero (16). The most pervasive and conspicuous preoccupation is with romance, partly defined by her chosen genres and involved constantly in her own depictions of human foibles and interactions as well as in her descriptions. In every book she wrote, the main characters grapple consciously or unconsciously with their conception of the romantic. The best-drawn heroines struggle openly to define romance and the romantic, and in so doing challenge readers to assess their own assumptions and prescriptions. Montgomery knew what she was doing when she made the child Anne Shirley wrestle with Tennyson's code of chivalry in Avonlea and years later made Anne's son Walter set out for the First World War, convincing himself that he must be Tennyson's Galahad. Romance involves the heroine's most intimate thoughts about herself as well as the most stringent cultural expectations for her. In Montgomery's career-long preoccupation with romance and chivalry we find every culture's debate over its highest ideals and its most practical distribution of labour.

Montgomery's heroines' estimations of and responses to romance – in love stories, in the idealizing of nature, in acts of courage – invite our most careful self-analyses and honesty. What do we make of the fact that Montgomery's novels invert some forms of romance only to reinstate and reinforce them ultimately? Are the freedom and possibilities suggested in the inversion what attract readers or is the restoration of expectations what attracts readers? Or is it that readers, even in the 1990s, want the flouting of authority and the established rules to be subliminal – indirect – so that they can enjoy it without having to think about its implications for their own lives? Do readers of Montgomery's fiction delude themselves about the cultural forces in their own lives and, in fact, perpetuate their own confinement and oppression? In her book on romance fiction, Janice Radway says: 'By reading the romance as if it were a realistic novel about an individual's unique life ... the reader can ignore the fact that each story prescribes the same fate for its heroine and can therefore unconsciously reassure herself that her adoption of the conventional role, like the heroine's, was the product of chance and choice, not of social coercion' (17). Is Radway's argument inappropriate for Montgomery's novels, since Radway is talking about formula romance fiction such as Harlequin romances? Are Montgomery's domestic romances really different from Harlequins, themselves phenomenally popular?

Let me offer here a word about romance and the way I have used the term and the concept in this book. The writer who tries to define rigidly either *romance* or *romantic* will come to grief quickly (Fowler 37–53). The terms have reasonably precise boundaries when we speak of the Romantic movement or medieval romance literary conventions, but blur when we begin to talk colloquially, as Montgomery's characters do, about 'how romantic' some thing or person is. Confusion could set in when we refer to formula romance (of the kind that John Cawelti, Kay J. Mussell, Janice Radway, or Bonnie Kreps talk about) and at the same time compare it with romantic fairy-tale endings and/or Tennysonian chivalry, itself a Victorian-Romantic remaking of medieval romance. Montgomery's own thinking, and that of her characters, is influenced by nineteenth-century concepts of romance and valour, themselves much influenced by the Romantics and of course by Sir Walter Scott, and also by the Romantic and then the Victorian-Romantic revaluing of medieval romance; Montgomery's nature descriptions are strongly influenced by the Romantic poets and by late-Victorian romanticism. *And* Montgomery's ideas about love and male-female love relations are heavily marked by nineteenth-century conventional and radical literary thinking. *Jane Eyre*, a formative text for Montgomery, is both traditionally romantic in supporting passionate love relationships between men and women and radical in challenging in the love story customary barriers of class, age, and gender. I have tried to avoid confusion in my use of the words *romance* and *romantic* by using them in their popular – and not strictly literary – senses. At the same time, I try to suggest the rich history behind our popularizing of the terms and concepts.

With Montgomery's heroines we see several forms of romance at work simultaneously and continuously.[6] As children, the heroines romanticize the natural world – trailing Wordsworthian clouds of glory, they thrill to the beauty and splendour in the hills and fields and woods and shore and sky. They thrill to tales of chivalry. As they grow older, they continue to enjoy nature, which continues to be described in rhapsodic language, and they face the romance of a love relationship, with all the juggling of self and roles that this kind of romance suggests. They are called on to perform acts of courage and honour. Meanwhile, the heroines are often reading and rereading Victorian-Romantic poems or stories and/or current magazine formula romances and are shaping themselves and their conceptions of roles and love in response to this romantic reading.[7] Ultimately, each heroine defines herself through a highly idealized perception of natural beauty, which is given to us in Montgomery's romantic descriptions, and through some reconciliation between what the heroine sees as her talents and her concept of home.

Each heroine pursues romance – whether through love of nature or home or person or code – all her life. Romance is, in Montgomery's wonderfully evocative writing, seen as an individual and collective preoccupation. Yet persistent as this search for beauty or love or honour may be, Montgomery would have us believe that for healthy girls and women, romance is merely woven into a larger pattern of everyday human interactions. Genuine romance, she suggests, will not be permanently realized, but will waft in and out of a heroine's life, as overpowering and elusive as the fragrance of the sweet-grass Captain Jim brings to Anne for her handkerchiefs (*AHD* 138).[8] In pursuit of one kind of romance, the heroines are frequently surprised by another, sweeter kind. Montgomery's stories and characters and descriptions suggest that mature romance is wholesome and beautiful. This endorsement of, and perhaps vagueness about, romance is one of the fundamental assumptions I would like to explore in Montgomery's work.

In the following chapters I talk about Montgomery's books as literary creations that present believable heroines who make difficult choices and seek to answer complex questions and who find life full of beauty and surprise. Montgomery makes uneven use of her talents for humour, irony, description, dialogue, and scene in the novels, and I explore in the following chapters her use of symbol, repetition, literary echo, changes in voice and perspective, shifts in genre and form, narrative asides, sentimentality, realism and idealism, and time. I concentrate on the heroines, and on their struggles wth self and celebrations of home, and connect these with the overt and covert assumptions about romance. In exploring the romanticized interconnections between self and home, I believe we will come close to the essence of Montgomery's appeal.

This book is divided into three parts, giving the greatest amount of attention and space to the Anne books, which are Montgomery's best-known works. Though I talk about all eight Anne novels, I concentrate on the original six. In the first three Anne books Montgomery establishes Anne's voice through nature description and comic episode and relies on a number of types of romance to suggest Anne's power. By the time Anne gets to college, the reader is accustomed to assuming Anne's perspective without having to hear much of Anne's voice. The next three books, which act as a second trilogy, respond to the Great War, and encode in Anne's idyllic honeymoon and early married life Montgomery's hopes for her own culture – of which Anne is now emblematic. Heroism and romance take on wholly new meanings in the context of war, and Montgomery's indirect and then direct treatment of the war show how far the heroines of a culture reflect its values (Edwards 4). The two late Anne books, treated together in a short chapter, suggest Montgomery's difficulties in thinking her way back into a romanticized realism she had been changing over the years.

Part II, dealing with the Emily trilogy, offers Montgomery's most detailed study of the female artist and the constraints upon her. Montgomery uses emotionally charged works – Charlotte Brontë's *Jane Eyre*, Olive Schreiner's *The Story of an African Farm*, and Elizabeth Barrett Browning's *Aurora Leigh* – to suggest parallels for the struggles and forces in Emily's life and to rationalize Emily's responses to romance. Emily's knowledge of literature and her experiments with various kinds of writing provide rich intertextual material. Montgomery suggests that the writer's life can be read as the way she reads herself writing and reading herself. With Emily we are most aware of the techniques of autobiography and biography.

In Part III, I examine the two Pat books and *Jane of Lantern Hill* together, arguing that a passion for place that goes sadly awry in the Pat books, and makes Pat obsessed with her physical home, is balanced by Jane Stuart's healthy self-discoveries and celebrations. Then, in a brief overview of each of the six remaining Montgomery novels, I examine how each heroine responds to various kinds of romance and speculate on some of the cultural expectations Montgomery may have been addressing.

It is a complicated business nowadays to write about 'the reader' and 'we,' but I have persisted in doing so for several reasons: (1) as a Montgomery fan for more than thirty years, I have talked with many other readers, and I have tried to represent their responses along with my own in 'the reader' and 'we'; (2) as a reader trained in criticism of the nineteenth-century novel (Montgomery's own reading background), I also believe in an imaginary and idealized reader as a convention of narration, in the same way as I believe in the role of the narrator; (3) I believe that, as Jonathan Culler suggests in discussing Stanley Fish, 'the reader' comes up with interpretations that may explain or account for emotions no specific reader may have had (67) – but I also like the possibility for an indefinitely expanding text and readership; (4) Rachel Brownstein suggests that many of us read about heroines because we want to become the heroine (xix), and my 'reader' is at times a member of this band of adventurers; (5) ultimately I use 'the reader' and 'we' because I like to think that many of 'us' may truly share perspective or values or questions – alongside our radical differences in interpretations – in assessing a woman writer's assessment of women.

Montgomery has commanded a large audience since the publication of *Anne of Green Gables* in 1908. These hundreds of thousands of readers love Montgomery's writing for the way she makes them think about themselves and their connections with the world around them. And now a new readership is speaking up. One edited collection of essays about Montgomery's writing appeared in 1976 (Sorfleet). With the publication of the letters and journals, more and more people – including academic critics, traditionally the most disdainful of all Montgomery's readers (Epperly, 'Changing' 177–85) – are giving serious attention to her writing. A recent doctoral thesis in Sweden examines feminist elements of Montgomery's fiction.[9] These new readers, together with the traditional Montgomery fans, are comparing the gripping self-dramatizations of her private life with her determinedly positive fiction. And those who did not already know Montgomery are beginning to suspect that the supposedly simple romances are indeed encoded with multiple messages and miscuings, and that the apparent concessions to convention usually involve shrewd reassessments of the familiar. Although Montgomery's heroines are far from free from cultural biases, restraints, and expectations, many of them do learn to analyse themselves and do question some of the conceptions that shape them. As we explore Montgomery's ways of presenting her heroines and themes, perhaps we will gain insight into what she chose to say and what she chose to leave unsaid for a reading public she credited with being analytical, but only up to a point. 'What point?' we ask.

I have written this book for Montgomery enthusiasts as well as for those who, whether they know her writing or not, are curious about how a perennially popular female novelist challenges a diverse, growing readership. If we read the heroines carefully, and try to understand Montgomery's various intensities and types of romance, we may be startled to find how often we *are* – in limitations and in freedom – the heroines of her novels.

PART I

Anne

Romancing the Voice:
Anne of Green Gables

The most successful and best-loved[1] of Montgomery's twenty novels has been her first, *Anne of Green Gables* (1908). In creating the story of the irrepressible redhead, Montgomery also established the pattern for all her novels and their heroines: the love for/creation of home and the exploration/declaration of self are themes Montgomery pursues in the eight Anne novels as well as with Kilmeny, the King children, Emily, Valancy, Marigold, Pat, the Dark and Penhallow clans, and Jane. At their best, Montgomery's heroines outface misunderstanding and underestimation; they learn to follow their own voices; they challenge constraint and expectation; they strive to distinguish between false and genuine (though not necessarily liberating) romance. Yet since Montgomery was not a radical, and herself chose to fit into respectable society and take on the responsibilities her culture designated for her, she created heroines who also embrace traditions. Anne Shirley rebels, but only up to a point.

Montgomery's heroines may resist cultural repression, but they ultimately choose to accept many of the roles and attitudes they have apparently earned the right to defy. Anne Shirley's story is retold in many different ways during Montgomery's career. Anne's vocal self-dramatizations and spontaneity charm the stodgy establishment of Avonlea, but then, having won her right to speak, Anne gives up passionate articulation in favour of a conventional, maidenly dreaminess and reserve. Without her exuberance at the outset readers would not have cared about Anne; yet without her restraint at the end of the book, there could be no promised romance with Gilbert. Readers who insist on conventional romance are especially eager to believe that Anne is responsible for as well as satisfied with her own choices. These readers have no problems reconciling Anne's original, fiercely independent spirit with her later willingness to conform.

No matter how we respond to the cultural pressures on Anne or Anne's evident capitulation to them, we can enjoy the ways Montgomery's novels call into question and play the concepts that continue to shape the female of the 1990s as much as the female of the turn of the century: sense of self, love of/quest for home, power of romance.

The delightful, young Anne Shirley is a self with a most distinctive voice; in fact, the whole of *Anne of Green Gables* is charged with the rhythm and energy of Anne's voice and personality. Anne's determined romanticism enriches her own spoken language and informs/complements the narrator's nature descriptions. Appropriately, important events in beauty-loving Anne's life are marked by nature descriptions that reflect her own rapture over her surroundings. We become a part of the world of Avonlea as the powerfully imaginative Anne sees and loves it. Seeing with Anne's eyes and hearing her voice, we too are heroines as we read the novel.

But before we hear Anne, we hear the narrator, and the narrator prepares us for Anne's energy and also for the quality of world Anne will herself intensify, explore, and join. In the very first sentence of the novel, the narrator, supposedly describing Mrs Lynde and the course of a brook in Avonlea, invites us to engage with Avonlea life. The brook has personality and conscious will – and knows how to regulate its rushing and murmuring to evade the community busybody, Rachel Lynde. Montgomery pairs up nature and human emotions so that we take sides: it's the brook against Rachel Lynde, just as it will soon be Anne Shirley against unimaginativeness. Even before we meet Anne, we too have experienced how the guardians of Avonlea expect conformity and quiet from Avonlea inhabitants – be they brooks or people – and we suspect that defying such vigilance will be great fun. As we accept the restraint and the secrets of the brook, we are really entering into a complex arrangement between reading about and participating in Anne's story. Look at how Montgomery encourages the reader to respond to (at least) four different positions in reading the first sentence of *Anne of Green Gables*. Here is the sentence:

Mrs Rachel Lynde lived just where the Avonlea main road dipped down into a little hollow, fringed with alders and ladies' eardrops and traversed by a brook that had its source away back in the woods of the old Cuthbert place; it was reputed to be an intricate, headlong brook in its earlier course through those woods, with dark secrets of pool and cascade; but by the time it reached Lynde's Hollow it was a quiet, well-conducted little stream, for not even a brook could run past Mrs Rachel Lynde's door without due regard for decency and decorum; it probably was conscious that Mrs Rachel was sitting at her window, keeping a sharp eye on everything that passed, from brooks and children up, and that if she noticed anything odd or out of place she would never rest until she had ferreted out the whys and wherefores thereof. (1–2)

The energetic one-hundred-and-forty-eight-word-long sentence,[2] divided by three semi-colons, involves several viewpoints and sets of values: (1) Rachel Lynde and her demand for propriety and knowledge, (2) the brook's secret, free, and then regulated movements and its consciousness of Mrs Rachel's vigilance, (3) the narrator's view of Mrs Rachel's demands on the brook and inhabitants of Avonlea and the brook's and inhabitants' apparent conformity, (4) the reader's invited understanding of Mrs Rachel's vigilance, the brook's apparent conformity, and the narrator's amusement over Mrs Rachel, the brook, and the inhabitants who conform with or defy Mrs Rachel Lynde. Thus in one loaded, laughing sentence Montgomery's narrator introduces the expectations of the Avonlea establishment and at the same time suggests both the delight of rebelling against such conformity and the satisfaction of living in a community where conformity and independence have places and seasons.

This very first sentence, with its introduction of different points of view, is itself a lengthy imitation of the twists of the road and stream it describes and also a mimicry of Rachel Lynde's relentless questionings and vigilance. More than half the sentence pretends to be about the brook that runs by Mrs Lynde's place, but is also a comic imitation of Mrs Lynde's projected self-image: she believes that all in Avonlea should behave – in front of her at least – with 'decency and decorum,' whatever they may do beyond her ken. Much of the first chapter of the novel plays with Mrs Lynde's way of thinking. The narrator and Mrs Lynde even use some of the same words, as though the narrator's imitation of Mrs Lynde's mental rhythms is almost identical with Mrs Lynde's own speech. Notice, for example, how the phrase 'to be sure' is used in a summary of Mrs Lynde's thoughts (given by the narrator) and then repeated in Mrs Lynde's own words. First the narrator describes Mrs Lynde's going to Green Gables: 'Accordingly after tea Mrs Rachel set out; she had not far to go; the big, rambling, orchard-embowered house where the Cuthberts lived was a scant quarter of a mile up the road from Lynde's Hollow. *To be sure*, the long lane made it a good deal further' (3–4, emphasis added). In the very next paragraph, Mrs Lynde is evidently talking to herself about Matthew and Marilla: 'I'd rather look at people. *To be sure*, they seem contented enough' (4, emphasis added). This kind of echoing between the narrator and a character invites the reader to hear in the narrator's words an extension of the character's thoughts.

A blurring of the borders between imitation and commentary here in chapter one with Mrs Lynde encourages the reader, in chapter two, to recognize Anne's perspective in the narrator's poetic interpretations of sky and landscape. The narrator continues throughout the novel to use playful echoes between commentary and speech with characters other than Anne. With Anne, the fun is of a different kind, and the imitations of Anne's thinking are the serious, poetic descriptions of nature. Any fun the narrator wants to have with Anne is done with direct comment, ironic interjection, or comic chronicle – any imitation of Anne's tone of mind is offered as seriously as Anne would want herself to be taken (and, by obvious extension, as Anne's participant-readers would also want to be taken). In other words, every role the narrator plays in the novel enhances the focus on Anne and appreciation of her; other characters may be mimicked comically, but Anne belongs either with serious poetry or with straightforward comedy where she is an actor.

Apart from the comic tension the narrator establishes between vigilance and rebellion in the initial sentence of the novel, we also know from the opening descriptive phrases that the 'eye' of the story is an appreciator of beauty. The road 'dipped' into a 'hollow, fringed with alders and ladies' eardrops'; back in the woods we imagine the brook's 'dark secrets of pool and cascade.' Clearly the narrator of the story will note the beauties of nature while sharing with the reader the comic struggles between those who would regulate behaviour and those who would be free.

Before Anne is introduced, in chapter two, the narrator treats us to two apparently fanciful descriptions of nature. In both, the narrator is describing the pleasures of the June day. In Mrs Lynde's kitchen: 'The sun was coming in at the window warm and bright; the orchard on the slope below the house was in a bridal flush of pinky-white bloom, hummed over by a myriad of bees' (2). On Matthew's trip to Bright River: 'It was a pretty road, running along between snug farmsteads, with now and again a bit of balsamy fir wood to drive through or a hollow where wild plums hung out their filmy bloom. The air was sweet with the breath of many apple orchards and the meadows sloped away in the distance to horizon mists of pearl and purple' (10). The 'bridal flush' of the orchard, the 'snug' farms, the hollows where wild plums shyly 'hung out their filmy bloom' all suggest the welcoming personality of the countryside and the season; Anne is due to arrive in a world that is more than ready for her. We will shortly find out that she belongs here – she belongs (as does the reader) because she can see and feel the loveliness around her.

With Anne, the narrator is frequently a careful stage director. It is easiest to appreciate this directing by looking closely at Anne's five confession/apology scenes, ranging from the early fury with Mrs Lynde, to the last embarrassed thank-you to Gilbert Blythe. In each, the narrator quietly bolsters sympathy with Anne and Anne's voice. When Anne apologizes to Mrs Lynde, the narrator concentrates on Marilla's dismay and Anne's obvious sincerity. When Anne makes up a story about the amethyst brooch, since Marilla told her she must confess, the narrator does not tell us Anne is innocent – we should have learned to trust Anne already – but the narrator tells us that Anne confesses 'as if repeating a lesson she had learned' (105). Anne's apology to Mrs Barry about accidentally giving Diana currant wine instead of raspberry cordial is a failure, and we judge Mrs Barry by the narrator's cue: 'Her face [Mrs Barry's] hardened. Mrs Barry was a woman of strong prejudices and dislikes, and her anger was of the cold, sullen sort which is hardest to overcome' (137). Miss Josephine Barry capitulates to Anne's charm when Anne apologizes to her, and the narrator describes the change in Miss Barry's eyes. The scene focuses on Anne's speech, but the narrator tells us that Miss Barry's eyes were initially 'snapping through her gold-rimmed glasses' (167); then Anne talks, and 'Much of the snap had gone' (167). When Anne finishes explaining, 'All the snap had gone by this time' (168). The narrator's small touches complement Anne's energetic speeches.

At the very end of the novel, we find the fifth confession. When Anne thanks Gilbert for giving up the Avonlea school for her so that she can board at home with Marilla, she also has to confess that she has long ago forgiven him and was sorry for her earlier stubbornness. The narrator's role here is to suggest Gilbert's delight and Anne's pleasure in becoming friends. The narrator tells us that with 'scarlet cheeks' Anne thanks him and extends her hand; 'Gilbert took the offered hand eagerly' (328). After Gilbert speaks, 'Anne laughed and tried unsuccessfully to withdraw her hand,' and the reader sees that instead of being offended by Gilbert's warmth, it prompts Anne to confess: 'I've been – I may as well make a complete confession – I've been sorry ever since' (328). The small scene is meant to tie together the last of the novel's threads and prepare the way for a romance between Anne and Gilbert. As the expected culmination of the novel's preoccupation with romance, the scene will work only if the comic rejection of romance used throughout the book is here displaced by the narrator's gentle but insistent revelation of Anne's discomfort and pleasure.

In each of the five confession scenes the narrator describes others' motivations or changes, but Anne's own words are the primary stimulators of reader sympathy. We will probably remember Anne's – not the narrator's – own persuasive, colourful language: 'I'm a dreadfully wicked and ungrateful girl, and I deserve to be punished and cast out by respectable people for ever ... Oh, Mrs Lynde, please, please, forgive me. If you refuse it will be a lifelong sorrow to me. You wouldn't like to inflict a lifelong sorrow on a poor little orphan girl, would you, even if she had a dreadful temper?' (78); 'I never took the brooch out of your room and that is the truth, if I was to be led to the block for it – although I'm not very certain what a block is' (102); 'Oh, Mrs Barry, please forgive me. I did not mean to – to – intoxicate Diana. How could I? Just imagine if you were a poor little orphan girl that kind people had adopted and you had just one bosom friend in all the world. Do you think you would intoxicate her on purpose?' (138); 'Have you any imagination, Miss Barry? If you have, just put yourself in our place. We didn't know there was anybody in that bed and you nearly scared us to death. It was simply awful the way we felt. And then we couldn't sleep in the spare room after being promised. I suppose you are used to sleeping in spare rooms. But just imagine what you would feel like if you were a little orphan girl who had never had such an honour' (168); 'I want to thank you for giving up the school for me. It was very good of you – and I want you to know that I appreciate it ... I forgave you that day by the pond landing, although I didn't know it. What a stubborn little goose I was' (328). In the first four of these, when Anne is still a young girl, we hear her self-dramatization in the confession. She pictures herself as the heroine of a glamorized story of her own orphanhood – or as willing to be led to the block for honour and truth. Anne creates herself as the romantic heroine of her own adventures, and the narrator provides the setting and reinforcement for her self-drama.

The narrator helps to orchestrate a book-length, comic deconstruction and reconstruction of romance. While Anne's own notion of romance is carefully deflated or inverted, another form of romance is created from the substance of what is supposed to be real life. The story of Gilbert's interest in Anne and hers in him is the conventional plot-line version of romance. In the book itself this one kind of romance is a far less prominent feature of Anne's discovery of self, and of her sense of home, than is Anne's own exploration of beauty and harmony and her consequent rejection of exaggeration and impossible intensity.

Catherine Sheldrick Ross says that the whole of *Anne of Green Gables* plays with romance and that Montgomery turns Anne's notion of romance on its head while at the same time creating in Avonlea a place every bit as romantic as anything Anne has imagined. Thus while readers laugh at Anne's unreal concept of the romantic and the ideal, they are encouraged to accept the beauties of Avonlea with all the breathlessness and wonder that romance invites. Further, Anne is encouraged to reject the unreal romantic stories she reads, while all the while her own attachment to Gilbert is developing for the reader into a species of romance. Ross sees Montgomery's novel as a very sophisticated handling of genre and an inversion and restoration of genre (43–58). Certainly what Ross describes can be heard in Anne's own voice and seen in the nature descriptions that we are encouraged to believe are often offered from Anne's perspective.

Anne creates herself the heroine of a romance she discovers to be false, while the reader sees Anne as a genuine heroine of a romantic world that the book conspires to make us believe is real. Anne's imagination may need curbing, but Anne's perception of and joy in her surroundings is romantic enough for any of Anne's readers. Prince Edward Island itself is a part of Anne's identity, the bedrock of her love of home, and the romance surrounding its beauties is powerful enough to make the passages describing them stand apart from and yet related to Anne's most ingenious and delightful speeches. Montgomery's/Anne's/the narrator's love affair with Prince Edward Island is what counterbalances Anne's self-conscious speeches and what offers us hope that even a mature Anne, who has dropped the endearing verbal eccentricities of her childhood, will have a loving vitality great enough to sustain continued reading about her.

Anne's own words show us how thoroughly romantic she is, how she has been shaped by early reading of sentimental and chivalric poems and stories. Her very first words to Matthew, on the Bright River platform, show how she has learned to imagine herself as the heroine of her own continuing private fiction, created to counteract the dullness or harshness of the real world around: 'I had made up my mind that if you didn't come for me tonight I'd go down the track to that big wild cherry-tree at the bend, and climb up into it to stay all night. I wouldn't be a bit afraid, and it would be lovely to sleep in a wild cherry-tree all white with bloom in the moonshine, don't you think? You could imagine you were dwelling in marble halls, couldn't you?' (13). Rea Wilmshurst points out that 'dwelling in marble halls' is probably an allusion to the popular romantic song 'I Dreamt that I Dwelt in Marble Halls' from Alfred Bunn's sentimental *The Bohemian Girl* (17). In any case, the image and the picturing of herself in a romantic setting is clearly what has sustained the orphan Anne Shirley in her neglected eleven years. She tells Matthew that she spent time in the orphanage creating stories for her otherwise dismal life: 'It *was* pretty interesting to imagine things about them – to imagine that perhaps the girl who sat next to you was really the daughter of a belted earl, who had been stolen away from her parents in her infancy by a cruel nurse who died before she could confess' (14). We recognize in this hackneyed plot a host of popular (and often inferior) romances and Gothic tales of the kind Henry Fielding parodies with such zest in *Joseph Andrews*. Anne has been reading romances and has learned their addictive appeal: creating yourself the heroine makes all the adventures your own

(Brownstein). Anne continues to tell herself stories about her surroundings, even insisting on giving human names to plants and places since they, too, have personalities and parts in her ceaseless internal drama. (Certainly the personification in Montgomery's opening sentence and in the nature descriptions seems a ready-made part of Anne's drama.) Though she is enraptured with the real surroundings of Avonlea, Anne feels that the predictability of life in general could still use help from her romantic story-telling and retelling. She acknowledges on her first morning at Green Gables, when she thinks she will have to return to the orphanage, that romances don't exactly square with life and are not really preferable to it: 'It's all very well to read about sorrows and imagine yourself living through them heroically, but it's not so nice when you really come to have them, is it?' (36).

Nevertheless, once established at Green Gables, she continues to embroider life with romance, and usually comes to grief in the process. She imagines herself a raven-haired beauty, and dyes her hair – green, by accident; she pictures herself a nun, romantically renouncing life and taking the veil, and forgets to cover the pudding sauce so that a mouse drowns in it; she imagines herself dishonoured in front of Josie Pye, accepts a dare to walk the ridge-pole of the Barry kitchen, falls, and breaks her ankle. Even her separation from Diana, whom Mrs Barry believes Anne has made drunk deliberately, is turned into a romantic and 'tragical' beauty: ' "Fare thee well, my beloved friend. Henceforth we must be as strangers though living side by side. But my heart will ever be faithful to thee." ... Then she turned to the house, not a little consoled for the time being by this romantic parting. "It is all over," she informed Marilla ... "Diana and I had such an affecting farewell down by the spring. It will be sacred in my memory forever. I used the most pathetic language I could think of and said 'thou' and 'thee' " ' (141–2). When a distraught Diana comes to Anne to rescue her baby sister from an attack of croup, Anne, who shows great practicality in remembering to take the ipecac with her, is actually transported by excitement: 'Anne, although sincerely sorry for Minnie May, was far from being insensible to the romance of the situation and to the sweetness of once more sharing that romance with a kindred spirit' (151). A sense of chivalric bravery uplifts her when she faces Miss Barry and begs her to forgive her for jumping on her in the spare-room bed. And, as we have seen, it is this bravery and Anne's quaint phraseology that win Miss Barry's heart, just as sincere melodrama had won Mrs Lynde's earlier when Anne apologized to her for losing her temper.

Anne's imagination seriously betrays her twice, and as a result of these two incidents, she recognizes a need to change her attitude to romance, though she is not sure until later what such a change will mean. Anne gets carried away imagining gruesome creatures, and the innocent spruce grove becomes the sinister Haunted Wood with a vengeance. When an unsympathetic Marilla makes Anne walk through the wood in the dark, Anne learns that she must constrain her imagination. Nevertheless, we find that Anne's reading continues to feed her morbid fancies, until Miss Stacy makes her promise to give up Gothic horror. Nearly eighty pages after the Haunted Wood episode, Anne confesses to Marilla: 'She found me reading a book one day called, "The Lurid Mystery of the Haunted Hall." It was one Ruby Gillis had lent me, and, oh, Marilla, it was so fascinating and creepy. It just curdled the blood in my veins. But Miss Stacy said it was a very silly, unwholesome book, and she asked me not to read any more of it or any like it' (257). Obviously Anne has not made the connection between reading material and development of imagination that the reader of Montgomery's book is encouraged to make at every turn in the understanding of Anne.

The second episode in which Anne's imagination betrays her – indeed, threatens her very life – is with the game based on Tennyson's 'Lancelot and Elaine,' a book in the epic-length Arthurian poem *Idylls of the King*.[3] Anne and her friends have studied Tennyson's romantic poem in school, and it is certainly a perfect example of the blighted-love and pure-sacrifice story Anne's childhood reading and imagining have prepared her to embrace. Montgomery's use of the poem is a brilliant stroke in the novel. When Elaine/Anne's barge/dory springs a leak, Anne is truly in need of rescue, and, as life would have it, the boy to do this knightly deed is none other than Gilbert Blythe for whom Anne has sworn eternal enmity. In this one comic inversion of romance, Tennyson's idealized story is overthrown and the prosaic Gilbert rescues Anne in his father's dory (Ross 46–8). Quick to see romance almost anywhere but in Avonlea, and certainly not with Gilbert as the hero, Anne scorns Gilbert's attempt at reconciliation. With truly queenly dignity she rejects him – and thus Montgomery brings into clash the imagined romance of the story with the real-life romance of Gilbert's timely rescue and eager appeal. A sucker for book romance (and natural beauty), Anne cannot recognize a new kind of romance behind school rivalry or even behind friendship and camaraderie. (Interestingly, Anne dotes on the pathetic Elaine, who can only choose to die when Lancelot will not love her, and yet finds satisfaction in her own powers to reject a potential suitor.)

The nearly fatal imitation of Tennyson reminds us how thoroughly Anne has been indoctrinated by literary romances. The scanty catalogue of her early childhood reading suggests the quality of contrivance, exaggeration, and idealization Anne has revered. She has been tutored in heroic battle and in (hopeless) loves: Thomas Campbell's 'The Battle of Hohenlinden' and 'The Downfall of Poland,' William Edmonstoune Aytoun's 'Edinburgh after Flodden,' Thomson's *The Seasons*, Henry Glassford Bell's 'Mary Queen of Scots,' Sir Walter Scott's *The Lady of the Lake* and later *Marmion* and *Rob Roy*, Mrs Hemans' 'The Woman on the Field of Battle.' Anne early tells Marilla, 'I read in a book once that a rose by any other name would smell as sweet' (42) and does not realize she is quoting from Shakespeare, evidently lumping *Romeo and Juliet* together with many other tragic love stories. Anne's early speeches especially are liberally sprinkled with archaisms, romantic clichés, or quaint turns of phrase ('depths of despair' [28], 'My life is a perfect graveyard of buried hopes' [40]), and we learn to recognize in her outlandish sentences ('I am well in body although considerably rumpled up in spirit, thank you, ma'am' [90]) products of a romance-fed imagination and an instinctive ear for poetry. It is this instinct for the grand or beautiful turn of phrase, after all, that makes so effective the combination of Anne's perspective and the narrator's words.

But Anne gradually outgrows the odd language and self-dramatization, even if she has more trouble reconciling herself to a world shorn of its earlier romantic glory. Anne grows to value the beauty around her and understands better than Diana why Avonlea is preferable to Charlottetown, or why an artificial romance is inferior to consciousness of belonging to a world of solid values and lasting but humble pleasures. When Miss Barry asks Anne which place she would prefer, the city or the country, Anne thoughtfully replies: 'It's nice to be eating ice-cream at brilliant restaurants at eleven o'clock at night once in awhile; but as a regular thing I'd rather be in the east gable at eleven, sound asleep, but kind of knowing even in my sleep that the stars were shining outside and that the wind was blowing in the firs across the brook' (250). Having learned the true romance of nature and belonging, Anne is almost ready to give up the artificial speech that before separated her from an uncaring environment. Miss Barry herself notices a change in her own response to Anne's spirit: 'But Miss Barry found herself thinking less about Anne's quaint speeches than of her fresh enthusiasms, her transparent emotions, her little winning ways, and the sweetness of her eyes and lips' (251).

Everything in the novel conspires to make us hear Anne's voice and to understand her point of view. We watch her as she has 'pruned down and branched out' (293), and we come to identify her with the broader, thoughtful view of the narrator's descriptions, just as we hear in their poetry her rapture with beauty. Anne's self-deluding reliance on romantic stories may have to give way, but Anne's love of beauty will be a lifelong romance Montgomery constantly supports.[4]

Montgomery's nature descriptions are full of poetry. She uses the conventions of poetry – appeal to the senses, personification, simile, metaphor – and chooses her words with the intention of transporting the reader both into and beyond the elements she describes. As in her poems, in the prose-poetry Montgomery favours flowers both as subjects and for comparison (skies of crocus or saffron or rose or marigold or violet); she delights in precious stones, metals, or wood largely for their colour and shine (crystal, pearl, diamond, emerald, sapphire, amethyst, ruby, gold, silver, ebony); she loves brilliant colours of all kinds (particularly scarlet and yellow) and especially enjoys the qualifiers 'misty' 'filmy' 'ethereal' in front of colours (notably purple and green); she has a passion for sunsets and twilight just after sunset. Despite the obvious preoccupation with colour, Montgomery's descriptions also appeal to touch and hearing and taste and smell – the 'satin-smooth roads with the snow crisping under the runners' (162), the spicy scent of ferns, the fragrance of trampled mint, and the tang of the sea are never far away. Montgomery celebrates the four seasons, the wind in the leaves and boughs of trees, sunshine, shadow, starlight, moonlight. The sea does not play a prominent part in the descriptions, and there is probably more emphasis on sky than on earth; on flowers and trees than on fields.

What characterizes all the descriptions is their humanness, their invitation to participate in a kind of communion. The descriptive passages are not just vivid ornaments to the narrative, but are instead expressions of attitude, indexes of the observers' ability to join the spirit of love and the pursuit of beauty that characterize Anne's quest for identity and home. The humanness of the descriptions is evident not only in personification (as we saw in the opening sentence of the novel), but in the tenderness of appreciation (young ferns are not just young ferns, but are 'little curly ferns' [170] struggling to grow). Enjoying the descriptions involves accepting or at least entertaining a way of being in relationship to the world around. And when we realize that three-quarters of the novel's nature descriptions (by my count, twenty-six out of thirty-five descriptions) are offered as though through Anne's eyes, we see that Montgomery was using poetry as a means to initiate the reader into a way of seeing the world, to express Anne's delight in beauty, to suggest the hidden possibilities for seeing and feeling in the most commonplace of things, to celebrate the feeling of 'coming home' that a communion with beauty offers to all who share in it, and to punctuate Anne's story with appropriate reminders of her spirit's capabilities and growth.

Shortly after Anne is introduced and we hear her nimble imagination startling the shy Matthew with insight and story, we find the narrator's words and Anne's point of view joined together. Anne is staggered by the blossom-embowered lane she later names the White Way of Delight, and the narrator provides a description of what Anne's otherwise undaunted tongue cannot utter. Mid-sentence Anne breaks off and the narrator takes over: ''' – oh, Mr. Cuthbert! Oh, Mr. Cuthbert!! Oh, Mr. Cuthbert!!!'' ... Overhead was one long canopy of snowy fragrant bloom. Below the boughs the air was full of a purple twilight and far ahead a glimpse of painted sunset sky shone like a great rose window at the end of a cathedral aisle. Its beauty seemed to strike the child dumb' (19). We find that for the rest of the book, when the narrator describes the beauty of nature, Anne is usually looking at it, and we are thus encouraged to read the words as though they capture her feelings. In those few times when Anne is not present, we still hear (or are free to hear) Anne's quality of mind, for the narrator and Anne share the same spirit.

Within four pages of Anne's rapture over the White Way of Delight, the narrator reinforces this identification between Anne's mind and narrative words. She has just confessed to Matthew a 'pleasant ache ... just to think of coming to a really truly home' (20–1) when she looks out over Barry's Pond. Anne calls it 'pretty,' and then the narrator launches into a description that is quintessential Montgomery – full of colour, personification, metaphor, and simile:

They had driven over the crest of a hill. Below them was a pond, looking almost like a river so long and winding was it. A bridge spanned it midway and from there to its lower end, where an amber-hued belt of sand-hills shut it in from the dark blue gulf beyond, the water was a glory of many shifting hues – the most spiritual shadings of crocus and rose and ethereal green, with other elusive tintings for which no name has ever been found. Above the bridge the pond ran up into fringing groves of fir and maple and lay all darkly translucent in their wavering shadows. Here and there a wild plum leaned out from the bank like a white-clad girl tip-toeing to her own reflection. From the marsh at the head of the pond came the clear, mournfully-sweet chorus of the frogs. There was a little gray house peering around a white apple orchard on a slope beyond and, although it was not yet quite dark, a light was shining from one of its windows. (21)

This rhapsody of light, colour, and sound is the poetic wish-fulfilment of the beauty-starved, love-starved orphan. It is also an invitation to the reader to 'come home,' as well. In responding to the images, as Anne responds to the scene itself, we participate in the lush beauty of 'home,' a place where the commonplace is revealed to be compounded of the richest colours and the miracle of sentient trees and houses. The elements of the place belong together, interact in harmony with each other, and the charm Montgomery offers her readers – through the narrator and Anne – is that we, too, belong whenever we can see and feel the power of this beauty.

In the narrator's description of Barry's Pond, we feel the humanness of the landscape (wild plums 'tip-toeing' to their own reflections; a house 'peering around a white apple orchard'), and on the very next page, Anne says to Matthew about the Lake of Shining Waters: 'I always say good night to the things I love, just as I would to people. I think they like it. That water looks as if it was smiling at me' (22). We are encouraged to believe that the girl who considers the feelings of water would be the one to imagine wild plum trees looking at their own reflections. The joining of Anne's fancy and the narrator's fanciful descriptions is completed within a few pages of our introduction to Anne.

Interestingly, the narrator's romanticizing of the general landscape translates into very specific appreciations: of Anne Shirley and Prince Edward Island. Montgomery's generic elements – sand, trees, water, lights – seem to be special because they are on Prince Edward Island, not simply because they are beautiful in themselves and can be appreciated elsewhere in the world. After all, Anne herself has come 'from away' (as local P.E.I. dialect dubs it) to this place; she was starved for beauty when she was not on P.E.I. Evidently, the whole novel conspires to convey, Prince Edward Island is an enchanted place where orphans suddenly find the home they have longed for and beauty and magic fairly leap from the sky and earth and sea. Children of all ages have long loved islands, and Montgomery gives us an island that is geographically undeniable and is at the same time almost incredibly, exquisitely lovely. The mixture of magic and fact is personified in Anne herself – we can believe in Anne the girl with the vivid imagination and heightened awareness because Anne is also prone to mishap and full of temper. In other words, Montgomery's use of a real place, P.E.I., helps us to believe in the beauty of it, just as Anne's normal problems and conflicts help us to believe in the powers of her imagination. Eventually, with the constant reinforcement of the identification of narrator and Anne, we identify Anne herself with Prince Edward Island and with all the enchantment of its moods and features.

The novel's thirty-odd other descriptive passages broaden our view of Prince Edward Island and enrich our understanding of Anne. And even when the narrator speaks about Anne and not as though (partly) through her eyes, the scene described merely confirms our faith in what Anne sees. For example, when the narrator describes the Birch Path that Diana and Anne use to walk to school, we know that though Anne is not looking at it at this particular moment, she has seen all of what the narrator is describing: 'Other people besides Anne thought so [that it was the 'prettiest place in the world'] when they stumbled on it. It was a narrow, twisting path, winding down over a long hill straight through Mr. Bell's woods, where the light came down sifted through so many emerald screens that it was as flawless as the heart of a diamond. It was fringed in all its length with slim young birches, white-stemmed and lissom boughed; ferns and starflowers and wild lilies-of-the-valley and scarlet tufts of pigeon berries grew thickly along it; and always there was a delightful spiciness in the air and music of bird calls and the murmur and laugh of wood winds in the trees overhead' (113). The humanness, the metaphor using emerald and diamond, the joyous luxuriance of the very plants and trees, all work together to affirm our view of Anne as the incarnation of and the interpreter within a fecund and benign natural world. Anne's energy is reflected in and is charged by nature even when Anne is not there.

Montgomery also uses the nature descriptions to mark events in Anne's life. Montgomery's favourite image in the novel is sunset; splendid sunsets celebrate or herald changes. Elizabeth Waterston and Mary Rubio draw our attention to the first sunset passage (quoted above), where Anne is struck dumb by the beauty of the White Way of Delight; in their analysis, sunsets and roses are bound together in the novel to suggest Anne's transformation and maturity (Afterword 312). In all, there are some eleven sunset or just post-sunset descriptions in the novel, and each of these punctuates some important event: the recognition of beauty almost beyond words (mentioned above 19); the first sight of Barry's Pond and the setting for Green Gables (21, 23); after Anne rescues Minnie May and Mrs Barry relents ('Afar in the southwest was the great shimmering, pearl-like sparkle of an evening star in a sky that was pale golden and ethereal rose over gleaming white spaces and dark glens of spruce' 155); the celebration of Diana's birthday before the catastrophic jumping on Miss Josephine Barry ('There was a magnificent sunset, and the snowy hills and deep blue water of the St. Lawrence Gulf seemed to rim in the splendour like a huge bowl of pearl and sapphire brimmed with wine and fire' 162); Anne's triumphant tea with Mrs Allan, the new minister's wife who is both role model and kindred spirit (Anne 'came home through the twilight, under a great, high-sprung sky gloried over with trails of saffron and rosy cloud, in a beatified state of mind and told Marilla all about it happily, sitting on the big red sandstone slab at the kitchen door with her tired curly head in Marilla's gingham lap' 191); after Anne's sobering lily-maid episode with Gilbert Blythe and just before Diana tells her they have been invited by Miss Barry to come to Charlottetown for the Exhibition ('It was a September evening and all the gaps and clearings in the woods were brimmed up with ruby sunset light. Here and there the lane was splashed with it, but for the most part it was already quite shadowy beneath the maples, and the spaces under the firs were filled with a clear violet dusk like airy wine' 243); relishing the thought of home after the dissipations of the Exhibition ('Beyond, the

Avonlea hills came out darkly against the saffron sky. Behind them the moon was rising out of the sea that grew all radiant and transfigured in her light' 251); the pass list is out for the examinations ('The eastern sky above the firs was flushed faintly pink from the reflection of the west, and Anne was wondering dreamily if the spirit of colour looked like that' 279); just before her recitation at the White Sands Hotel ('twilight – a lovely yellowish-green twilight with a clear blue cloudless sky. A big round moon, slowly deepening from her pallid lustre into burnished silver, hung over the Haunted Wood' 281); preparing for the final examinations at Queen's (Anne looked out on 'the glorious dome of sunset sky and wove her dreams of a possible future from the golden tissue of youth's own optimism' 305); at the very end of the novel, just before Anne apologizes to Gilbert ('Beyond lay the sea, misty and purple, with its haunting, unceasing murmur. The west was a glory of soft mingled hues, and the pond reflected them all in still softer shadings' 328). In many of Anne's key moments, we are invited to share the intensity of nature with her and to equate beauty with the multiple experiences of being, discovering, and reading.

In each of the sunset-marked experiences Anne learns something about herself and grows. Anne and the descriptions themselves change as Anne's story develops. The quality of poetic images is consistent throughout the novel, but the quality of perspective changes as Anne becomes more mature. Two-thirds of the way through the novel, in the chapter entitled 'Where the Brook and River Meet,' when Anne is fifteen, we see that the girl Anne has become the young woman. Marilla notices that 'You don't chatter half as much as you used to, Anne, nor use half as many big words. What has come over you?' (271). Anne's reply marks the end of the child's most spontaneous and whimsical speeches, and suggests a new conformity and consciousness of restraint: 'Anne coloured and laughed a little, as she dropped her book and looked dreamily out of the window ... "I don't know – I don't want to talk as much," she said, denting her chin thoughtfully with her forefinger. "It's nicer to think dear, pretty thoughts and keep them in one's heart, like treasures. I don't like to have them laughed at or wondered over. And somehow I don't want to use big words any more"' (271). After this there is a subtle change in the narrator and an obvious change in Anne. Anne goes off to Charlottetown to get a teacher's licence, and the narrator makes room for more of Anne's own comments on her surroundings. The childhood exuberance is now replaced by more mature (and, alas, far less interesting) comments made to her friends or even to herself. For example, in the sunset scene that includes the penultimate quotation given above, where Anne and her friends are preparing for examinations at Queen's, Anne makes the first observations about the sunset sky and then the narrator kicks in and completes the description, the commentary, and the chapter. Anne says, rather sententiously, to Josie and Jane and Ruby: 'Next to trying and winning, the best thing is trying and failing. Girls, don't talk about exams! Look at that arch of pale green sky over those houses and picture to yourselves what it must look like over the purply-dark beechwoods back of Avonlea' (304). The three other girls, understandably, ignore Anne's sky and her abjuration and begin to talk about fashions; but Anne herself, with clasped hands, gazes out the window and the narrator offers the 'glorious dome of sunset sky' (305) as what she sees. We have only to think back to the first sunset description to realize how different Anne is now. There the narrator offered the rose window of the cathedral and shortly after described Barry's Pond and the setting for Green Gables; here Anne characterizes the scene in her own words, and the narrator offers a brief, somewhat philosophical postscript. As with the earlier passages, we recognize in the narrator's description Anne's own vision, but now Anne's words are actually echoed by the narrator.

Because of the blurring between Anne's consciousness and the narrator's and also because of this newer development of the echoing of Anne's words by the narrator, it is hard to say who is responsible for a quotation from Tennyson in the last sunset scene in the novel. Since Anne has been an avid reader of Tennyson, as the lily-maid episode illustrates, she could herself be thinking of Tennyson's phrase when she is admiring the tranquil beauty of the countryside just before she meets up with Gilbert Blythe. But the Tennyson quotation is ironically appropriate to the situation, too, in a way Anne could not possibly have realized – since she did not know she was going to meet Gilbert – and so the irony of the words seems also to be a product of the omniscient narrator's broader view of the significance of Anne's determination to be friends with Gilbert.

Let us look at the passage itself and see what use it makes of Tennyson's famous phrase from 'The Palace of Art':

She lingered there [at Matthew's grave] until dusk, liking the peace and calm of the little place, with its poplars whose rustle was like low, friendly speech, and its whispering grasses growing at will among the graves. When she finally left it and walked down the long hill that sloped to the Lake of Shining Waters it was past sunset and all Avonlea lay before her in a dreamlike afterlight – 'a haunt of ancient peace.' There was a freshness in the air as of a wind that had blown over honey-sweet fields of clover. Home lights twinkled out here and there among the homestead trees. Beyond lay the sea, misty and purple, with its haunting, unceasing murmur. The west was a glory of mingled hues, and the pond reflected them all in still softer shadings. The beauty of it all thrilled Anne's heart, and she gratefully opened the gates of her soul to it. (327–8)

In the context of the passage, and to anyone not familiar with Tennyson's poem, the phrase 'a haunt of ancient peace' seems innocently descriptive, and could belong to either Anne or the narrator; troubling to make the distinction between the two points of view would seem like hair-splitting. And, indeed, perhaps Anne and/or the narrator merely liked the phrase out of its context and thought of it where its words, not irony, suited. But to ignore the original context of Tennyson's phrase makes no more sense here than it does in Anne's final quotation of the novel (only one page later) 'God's in his heaven, all's right with the world' (329). This final line is from Browning's verse drama *Pippa Passes*, which Anne would surely have read in its entirety. In it the young factory girl Pippa, unaware that there is a plot afoot to abduct her on this one day's holiday and sell her into prostitution in Rome, passes through the streets of the village of Asolo, singing about love and kindness and, ironically, working against evil simply by being so cheerful and innocent herself. The line is often quoted as though it is a purely ecstatic expression of well-being – and it is – but it is meant to be appreciated in the context of the danger around the unsuspecting Pippa. The line is a reminder to readers and to those who hear Pippa within the poem that good may be powerful, but it is constantly threatened by evil. To those who know Browning's poem (as Montgomery did) and his complex suggestions, Anne's quotation expresses Anne's determination as well as her happiness. Anne is choosing to believe in harmony and joy, not just chirruping over a pretty evening. A knowledge of the original work enriches our understanding of Anne's spirit.[5] And so it is here, too, with Tennyson's phrase from the allegorical debate 'The

Palace of Art.' In this early poem, Tennyson shows the futility of art's trying to live separate from people, from human life. At the outset of the poem the artist determines to build a palace high on a crag, to be the dwelling place of his soul (called 'she'). Each room is furnished for a different mood, and each mood suggests some place on the earth – among others, a rock-bound coast with violent waves, a broad moonlit sandshore where a solitary figure walks,

> And one, an English home – gray twilight poured
>   On dewy pastures, dewy trees,
> Softer than sleep – all things in order stored,
>   A haunt of ancient Peace. (85–8)

Tennyson's lines suggest the quality of peace and tranquillity Anne has just been experiencing by Matthew's grave and in the mellow afterglow of the sunset. But Anne is not meant to live forever in appreciation of scenery and tranquillity alone; she is destined to interact with many others, and most intimately with Gilbert Blythe. In the poem, the palace of art becomes a prison, and the soul eventually is horrified by the isolation and self-centredness she before thought to be contented seclusion. The soul 'shrieked' (258) in her agony and later fled down to a 'cottage in the vale' (291) where she could learn to live with others. Similarly, Anne decides that enmity against Gilbert Blythe has separated her from a richer, fuller life. When, a few moments later, she meets him on the hill, she extends her hand in friendship and puts behind her forever a mistaken loftiness and self-sufficiency.

Knowing the context for Tennyson's line, as Montgomery did, suggests a subtle and ironic depth to the choice of it in this description of twilight. Whether it is the narrator's or Anne's there is irony involved – though not quite the same irony – and either way Montgomery's choice of the phrase offers a wonderful subtextual commentary on the pastoral serenity of Avonlea life and on Anne's preference for a peopled rather than a peopleless landscape. Sadly, of course, there is the further (unconscious?) suggestion that Anne has indeed forsaken the palace of art when she accepts Gilbert's friendship. Perhaps the covert suggestion is that in deciding to explore a friendship with Gilbert, Anne has chosen to live in a conventional emotional and intellectual 'cottage' when her nature has fitted her for variety and experiment on a far more splendid scale. Tennyson's soul's dilemma is very like the dilemma of the intelligent and artistic woman of Montgomery's own time (his choice of female gender for the soul has never seemed accidental). But, of course, this subversive subtext is well below the surface, and what most obviously greets the reader with the choice of Tennyson's phrase is a pleasant consciousness of a lovely line used to grace a lovely scene.

The Tennyson quotation and the Browning one are, at least superficially, consistent with Anne's language throughout the novel. Their unexamined use might also be consistent with Anne's earlier love of romance and could suggest that the narrator and Montgomery are using Anne's uncritical identification with the poems to comment ironically on the incompleteness of Anne's self-knowledge. In any case, as with the sunset passages, these late allusions remind us to reconsider the novel's revaluing of romance.

Romanticized nature and romantic allusions are parts of Anne's identity, self-discovery, and love of home and of the novel's overall preoccupation with romance. Anne's own language, after all, is shown from the first to be saturated with romance. Free though the young Anne's imagination seems to be, it is actually constrained by the expectations of romance, honour, and chivalry. And yet the older, supposedly wiser Anne is probably equally constrained by a different kind of romance. In giving up ecstatic identification with Tennyson's Elaine and the other romantic poems and stories of her childhood and adapting to 'real' male-female relations, Anne may merely be conforming to a romanticized stereotype of her times. Anne's quieting down, two-thirds of the way through the book, suggests her tentative leanings towards the stereotypical image of womanhood that favours reserve, tolerance, self-sacrifice, domesticity, and dreamy-eyed abstraction. A reader of the 1990s may well wonder if Anne puts aside her early love of romance fiction only to take on a fiction her culture creates, one that includes rigid gender roles and the promise of happily-ever-after family life.[6] In thinking about Anne's early self-dramatizations and Montgomery's later imposition of a conventionally romantic ending on Anne's story, we may uncover in the text and in ourselves startling assumptions about love and roles and alternatives. We may come to recognize Anne's dilemma as a useful warning against any form of romance that sentimentalizes, restrains, diminishes, or subordinates.

The conventional, audience-pleasing end of *Anne of Green Gables* suggests that the way has now been cleared for Anne to get on with the real romance – the loving of Gilbert. Yet while Montgomery may even have believed such a union to be good, she did not let Anne succumb to all the conventions and stereotypes at once. We read through two more novels – six years of Anne's life – before Anne recognizes her love for Gilbert. Anne goes to college and graduates and then, faced with Gilbert's possible death, realizes her love for him. Anne does not instantly swap the old tortured, chivalric romance ideal for the equally prescriptive romance of love and marriage, nor does she immediately bury her identity in Gilbert's. That immolation comes, but Montgomery delays it for as long as she can.

And perhaps the love story was inevitable, as was the eventual marriage and possibly the disappearance of Anne, considering the time in which and the audience for whom Montgomery wrote.[7] But providing the expected conclusion does not mean Montgomery erased Anne's possibilities at the end of this novel. What Gilbert and perhaps the reader see as romance, Anne still chooses to interpret as friendship. Readers truly 'akin to Anne' can choose to imagine that a continuing independence and self-knowledge will take Anne to a happy self-sufficiency.[8] That is, until they read *Anne of Avonlea*.

No matter how we are tempted to read beyond the ending of *Anne of Green Gables*, what we do find in the book itself is an undeniably 'real' girl and young woman whose speech and thoughts encourage us to re-examine, even yet, our public and private voices and values, and our complex involvements with romance.

Romance Awry:
Anne of Avonlea

When the L.C. Page Company accepted *Anne of Green Gables*, it requested a sequel immediately. Under enormous private pressure from her grandmother and from her life in the community, Maud Montgomery blocked out her story and then wrote doggedly, suffering a form of nervous breakdown when she had finished it. She was surprised at the popularity of this sequel, *Anne of Avonlea* (1909), because she felt that the second book was unequal to the first.

Fans didn't seem to notice – so long as they got more of Anne they didn't care how the patterns of *Anne of Green Gables* were exploited or distorted or even undercut. In the second book they were gratified to find Anne's enthusiasm and occasional outspokenness; there is even a flash of red temper in the very first chapter. Anne wins as a teacher and tests her theories about life and people against experience. She feeds her imagination with reading and is always on the look-out for kindred spirits. The books seemed similar enough to satisfy fans' passion to have more of Anne. But there are huge, disturbing differences between *Anne of Green Gables* and *Anne of Avonlea*. Montgomery was gloomy while writing the book (*Journals* 1: 333–4), and, as Mary Rubio and Elizabeth Waterston point out, the new novel 'suggested Anne's lin-

gering immaturity, and showed resentment over male/female roles ... '
(Afterword 280).

L.M. Montgomery capitulated to reader expectation at the end of *Anne of Green Gables* and gave Anne's story a conventionally romantic resolution. What was she to do with Anne in a sequel? Would she show Anne as a romantic heroine, and concentrate on the budding love between Anne and Gilbert, or would she restore Anne to the common-sense world of Avonlea and share with readers some comic reversals of romance? Montgomery did not choose either of these options. Instead she struck a middle course that takes more of the weaknesses than the strengths from the alternatives. Anne does not actually dwindle into a romance heroine, but falls into stereotype of another kind and cherishes a domestic world she believes is fairy tale in camouflage. Correspondingly, Avonlea is not the believably conservative place it was in Anne's earlier days. Instead, despite the setbacks of the Avonlea Village Improvement Society, Avonlea conspires to support Anne's belief in romance.

Romance takes over – not necessarily in the prominence of the love story of Anne and Gilbert, but in the very foundations of Avonlea. Montgomery reinforces cultural stereotypes about male/female differences and in so doing relegates Anne to domesticity and fairy tale. Gone is much of the delicious, thoughtful irony of *Anne of Green Gables*.

Anne of Green Gables is about being and seeing; *Anne of Avonlea* is about doing and reacting. More importantly, the Anne of the first book is an individual noticeably different from those around; the Anne of the second book wants to fit in with everything and everybody. The mottoes for the two novels suggest these differences. The motto for *Anne of Green Gables* is taken from Browning's 'Evelyn Hope,' a eulogy on a sixteen-year-old who was all innocence and beauty. The short poem is about Evelyn Hope's spirit, just as the novel itself is about Anne's personality and our growing knowledge of her and her surroundings. On the title page of *Anne of Green Gables* we find Browning's two lines: 'The good stars met in your horoscope, / Made you of spirit and fire and dew.' The motto for *Anne of Avonlea* is taken from Whittier's poem 'Among the Hills': 'Flowers spring to blossom where she walks / The careful ways of duty, / Our hard, stiff lines of life with her / Are flowing curves of beauty.' Whittier's poem describes a city man's chance look at a graceful, cultured woman who has chosen to marry a farmer and live a life of frugal pleasures in the hills. The obvious lesson of the poem is that grace and beauty in the contented woman will enrich her surroundings and elevate the spirit of those with whom she has chosen to live. The woman is not so much a person as an instructive symbol – her activities teach others to accept their lot. As this motto suggests, the novel is about Anne's actions, her daily (but day-dream glamorized) round of school and home and community duties. *Anne of Green Gables* is about Anne; *Anne of Avonlea* is more about what Anne does.

Many children like this second Anne book because 'a lot happens.' They like the stories woven into the narrative itself; they like the eccentric minor characters such as Charlotta the Fourth with her face-splitting smile and enormous blue hair bows. They like the fact that Anne sells Mr Harrison's cow, dyes her nose red, falls through a roof-top, whips Anthony Pye, and discovers two enchanted gardens within walking distance of Green Gables. They like Davy, who relishes mischief, and they dislike his twin, Dora, who never does anything wrong, and they especially like the fact that Anne and Marilla both like Davy better than Dora, too. As a general rule, they dislike Paul Irving and share Davy's jealousy of Anne's treatment of Paul. They enjoy the outings and the trials of the Avonlea Village Improvement Society. With so much activity going on, they can ignore the speeches by Anne and Gilbert about their ambitions, and they can follow the fairy tale of Lavendar Lewis's rescue by a middle-aged prince charming, without wondering how these square with Anne's own realizations about truth and romance in the earlier story. In other words, as an active frolic that continues the good times of *Anne of Green Gables*, the sequel is a success; as an exploration of Anne's development and thinking, the book is a qualified failure.

So *Anne of Avonlea* is busy. Its first chapter suggests the hustle of the whole story. In those opening pages we are introduced to all the main story lines and treated to liberal dashes of Mr Harrison's and Rachel Lynde's peppery speeches. We are riveted to hear Mr Harrison call Anne a 'red-headed snippet' (7) and amused to hear Mrs Lynde characterizing new neighbors: 'his wife is a slack-twisted creature that can't turn her hand to a thing. She washes her dishes *sitting down*' (11). Anne daydreams about distant greatness for some imagined male student of hers (evidently having decided, as the novel's motto suggests, to shed warmth and light without stepping out of the round of duty and routine herself), but such dreaminess is quickly interrupted by Mr Harrison's 'irruption into the yard' (2). The narrator is an independent and lively commentator on all around, and we suspect that Anne's point of view will not be the one we see with in the story as a whole. And it is not. The story is given to us by the narrator and quantities of characters. The encouraged participation with long descriptive passages we enjoyed in *Anne of Green Gables* is not a big part of this novel. Here Anne Shirley is a quirky, engaging adolescent in a whirl of other people and their comings and goings and sayings. Her voice is not even the most interesting one we hear. Anne's doings are the substance of the book, but her thinking? Her ambitions? Her visions? What has happened to them?

Though it is a far less meditative book than *Anne of Green Gables*, *Anne of Avonlea* spends much time preaching and teaching. The narrator seems to have caught Marilla's disease from the first novel – one Marilla herself has lost here – and inculcates morals wherever she can. The irony of the first chapter, when discussing Mr Harrison's eccentricity ('Mr Harrison was certainly different from other people ... and that is the essential characteristic of a crank, as everybody knows' 3), becomes lesson-giving shortly afterwards in summing up a debate between Anne and Jane on corporal punishment: 'Gilbert, having tried to please both sides, succeeded, as is usual and eminently right, in pleasing neither' (36).

In fact, everything seems bent on teaching, though not necessarily learning, in this novel; it is even dedicated to one of Montgomery's teachers. Anne teaches Davy about being a gentleman; Mr Harrison teaches Anne not to trust appearances; Mrs Allan tries to instruct Anne about friendship and love; Mrs Morgan's fictional heroines teach Anne and Diana how to behave in crises. Anne is Paul Irving's teacher but, interestingly, Paul teaches Anne the lore of fairy tale all over again. Miss Lavendar looks upon Anne as a friend but teaches her (as Mr Harrison does) that life is not what it seems – is, in fact, far more romantic than it appears. The whole book conspires to teach the reader that romance is all around, but disguised. So much instruction is bound to wear on the reader even if Montgomery is skilful enough to season the lessons with humour.

The narrator's comments, asides, and little nudges eventually lead to an incredibly pedantic and moralizing stance about male and female and the powerful image of the Good Girl. Gilbert evidently keeps himself out of the 'fast set' where he teaches by holding up the image of Anne to himself.

As he plans his future life, with Anne in the picture, he wants to be sure he keeps himself 'worthy of its [the future's] goddess' (220–1). The narrator steps in. In the earlier book a line or two would have sufficed to cap Gilbert's feelings and to suggest Anne's response, but in this second novel about the teacher, the narrator moralizes to reinforce all the cultural stereotypes of Montgomery's time: 'She held over him the unconscious influence that every girl, whose ideals are high and pure, wields over her friends; an influence which would endure as long as she was faithful to those ideals and which she would as certainly lose if she were ever false to them' (221). One would like to think that this is a gratuitous piece of preaching and is not supported in Anne's conscious development of attitude, but it comes, in fact, as a narrative echo and moral embellishment of Anne's discussion of her own life's ambition.

At the end of *Anne of Green Gables*, when she has given up the Avery scholarship and is determined to teach in Avonlea and keep up with her own studies, Anne is still full of zest and direction, though the novel's concluding romantic overtones may make some of this direction doubtful. Early in their teaching days, Anne shows that she has now, like Whittier's heroine, embraced a domesticated romance instead of her former bold striving for excellence. Gilbert has decided to be a doctor so that he can add to knowledge and thus 'get square with his obligations to the race' (70). Anne's reply shows how far Montgomery has gone in squeezing the independence and individuality out of her spirited redhead. Anne sounds like a romantic guiding spirit rather than a flesh-and-blood adolescent: '"I'd like to add some beauty to life," said Anne dreamily. "I don't exactly want to make people *know* more ... though I know that *is* the noblest ambition ... but I'd love to make them have a pleasanter time because of me ... to have some little joy or happy thought that would never have existed if I hadn't been born"' (70). The narrator follows up with an appreciative Biblical allusion: 'Anne was one of the children of light by birthright' (70). In keeping with her first-page day-dream of inspiring some male pupil who will later recall and praise her, Anne's life ambitions have become quiet and small and harmless and the narrator invokes the Bible (Luke 16:8) to applaud Anne's circumscription.

Notice how Montgomery here reinforces traditional gender roles and their strict separation: Gilbert is a man; Gilbert chooses real, serious work that will contribute to world development and address the destiny of the race. He expects to strive and struggle in the great world. Anne 'chooses' the small, the pleasant, the pretty. She as much as admits that she is frivolous and decorative. She doesn't aspire to create knowledge; she just wants to be lovely and shower blessings. Montgomery seems to be endorsing the culturally approved, inevitably repressive oppositional thinking (that Jonathan Culler describes so well throughout *On Deconstruction*) where one thing is pitted against another and subordinated to another. Gilbert stands for what is supposedly superior: the world, work, knowledge, struggle, advancement, honour, strength, action, *male*; Anne stands for their supposedly inferior opposites: domesticity, pleasure, feeling, effortlessness, complacency, self-indulgence, weakness, reaction, *female*. Montgomery's largely unchallenged stereotypes are at the root of the book's problems because prescriptions and conventional romance seem so often to go together. If conventional romance did not require such rigid boundaries for gender, Gilbert and Anne could together explore the collective values they here split unevenly (see Moi 172–3).

Six-year-old Davy's attitude to male privilege is evidence that the divisions and confinements of the sexes are fostered in the young. Davy scorns what he perceives as feminine weakness – saying of Dora's response to his hair pulling, 'she just cried 'cause she's a girl.' He then tells Marilla that she should let him drive the buggy, 'since I'm a man' (77). Towards the end of the book, when Mr Harrison's wife has sought him out (and while we are wondering over Miss Lavendar's romance), Davy gives a child's-eye view of the division of power in marriage. He is discussing Mr Harrison's having left his wife: 'I wouldn't leave *my* wife for anything like that. I'd just put my foot down and say, "Mrs Davy, you've just got to do what'll please *me* 'cause I'm a *man*." *That'd* settle her pretty quick I guess' (290). In the story no one responds to Davy's philosophy – and we are free to laugh at it as a childishly simple misunderstanding of the complexity of things, or, perhaps, we see that Montgomery is using a child to voice the views of the presiding culture.[1] Perhaps we are encouraged to see Davy's attractive, free, bad-boy behaviour and his proud self-image as essential parts of the culture that promotes conventional romance. Certainly the conception of romance the book favours seems supportive of Davy's view of things. There would be little clash of wills between wife and husband, woman and man, if each accepted her or his sphere as Anne and Gilbert seem eager to do.

Anne-the-teacher is a confirmed romantic whose world affirms her romanticism. The inverted comedy of much of *Anne of Green Gables* is given the lie. Whereas in the young Anne's career we are encouraged to see that exaggerated romanticism leads to mishap and embarrassment, in the adolescent Anne's world, Prince Charming (even called that) arrives to take his bride from the enchanted palace that has not changed since he left it twenty-five years before. Lavendar Lewis's story, one of the most appealing in the book, of the stone house and its elfish echoes and Wonderland housemaid and Lady of Shalott-like prisoner of shadows suggests that Anne's belief in romance is supported by the actual world of Avonlea and environs. Similarly, the story of Hester Gray and her splendid, secluded garden tells us that Avonlea has its own secret romances. Hester, like the woman in Whittier's poem, gave up city life to marry a simple man and glory in the rustic beauty and wholesome toil of a backwoods homestead. Her early death from consumption makes her sound like a heroine of one of the stories Anne wept over as a child. Anne finds the romance around her – not because her active imagination manufactures it, but because it is there to be discovered. Anne is an interpreter, not a creator, of romance. Even the apparent woman-hater, Mr Harrison, turns out to be married to a loving wife. The Harrison reunion proves that virtually everything in Avonlea supports mating and pairing and some form of romance.

Towards the end of the book even Marilla wonders if Anne's poetic view of life isn't preferable to her own prose. When Marilla and Anne compare versions of the Lewis-Irving romance, Anne 'wins.' The old established Avonlea would be tempted to see the story much as Marilla does at first: 'I can't see that it's so terribly romantic at all ... In the first place two young fools quarrel and turn sulky; then Steve Irving goes to the States and after a spell gets married up there and is perfectly happy from all accounts. Then his wife dies and after a decent interval he thinks he'll come home and see if his first fancy'll have him. Meanwhile, she's been living single, probably because nobody nice enough came along to want her, and they meet and agree to be married after all. Now, where is the romance in all that?' (349–50). This commonsensical way of looking at the 'romance' is exposed as cynical, bald, and inadequate by the descriptions and dialogue in the Lewis story. But it is Anne who makes Marilla doubt her common-sense version with her response to 'where is the

romance in all that?': "'Oh, there isn't any, when you put it that way,''
gasped Anne, rather as if somebody had thrown cold water over her. "I
suppose that's how it looks in prose. But it's very different if you look at
it through poetry ... and *I* think it's nicer ...'' Anne recovered herself and
her eyes shone and her cheeks flushed ... "to look at it through poetry"'
(350). This argument is ingenious. It is perfectly consistent with Anne's
early idealism and romanticism, and at the same time affirms that the way
of interpreting actually determines what *is* there. Anne does not try to
argue with Marilla, but prefers her own interpretation because it is 'nicer.'
This statement of preference is virtually unarguable – Anne is not denying
any truth; she is making a choice about interpretation. This preference for
poetry argues in favour of the entire book's support of fairy tale – the
narrator reinforces Anne's bias for the poetic.

After Anne declares her allegiance to poetry, Marilla, that incarnation
of plain truth, capitulates: 'Marilla glanced at the radiant young face and
refrained from further sarcastic comments. Perhaps some realization came
to her that after all it was better to have, like Anne, "the vision and the
faculty divine" ... that gift which the world cannot bestow or take away,
of looking at life through some transfiguring ... or revealing? ... medium,
whereby everything seemed apparelled in celestial light, wearing a glory
and a freshness not visible to those who, like herself and Charlotta the
Fourth, looked at things only through prose' (350). Marilla's love for
Anne suddenly gives her faith that there is another way to see the world
– a way foreign to her, but evidently uplifting to Anne. Since Marilla
cannot ever be expected to see poetry herself (we are certain here that the
narrator, not Marilla, is echoing Wordsworth[2] in describing the sudden
shift in Marilla's thinking), this expression of faith is the closest the book
can come to declaring Avonlea's unqualified endorsement of Anne's
perception.

Even though Anne loves and talks about her love for poetry in this
novel, we actually find less poetry here than in the first book. *Anne of
Green Gables* and *Anne of Avonlea* do have roughly the same number of
poetic descriptions, but the length and quality of the descriptions is
markedly different. The poetic descriptions in *Anne of Avonlea* are often
shorter than those in *Anne of Green Gables*, and they rely on catalogues
of things and careful use of verbs rather than on vivid images and colours.
Often Anne herself will supply the quality of expression that the narrator

used in the early parts of *Anne of Green Gables*. The role reversal and role sharing between character and narrator (discussed in the previous chapter), which began at the end of *Anne of Green Gables*, are continued in *Anne of Avonlea* in the descriptive passages. But here while the narrator subsides, she also moralizes. Notice this early description and the lesson it offers:

A September day on Prince Edward Island hills; a crisp wind blowing up over the sand dunes from the sea; a long red road, winding through fields and woods, now looping itself about a corner of thick set spruces, now threading a plantation of young maples with great feathery sheets of ferns beneath them, now dipping down into a hollow where a brook flashed out of the woods and into them again, now basking in open sunshine between ribbons of golden rod and smoke-blue asters; air athrill with the pipings of myriads of crickets, those glad little pensioners of the summer hills; a plump brown pony ambling along the road; two girls behind him, full to the lips with the simple, priceless joy of youth and life. (51)

Notice how 'blowing,' 'winding,' 'looping,' 'threading,' 'dipping,' 'basking,' 'flashed,' 'ambling' dominate the mood. Glad activity characterizes the scene – but the narrator is sure to point the lesson that youth and life are precious things to be grateful for. And then it is Anne herself who takes up the fancifulness we before expected from the narrator or from the narrator and Anne together: ' "Oh, this is a day left over from Eden, isn't it, Diana?" ... and Anne sighed for sheer happiness. "The air has magic in it. Look at the purple in the cup of that harvest valley, Diana. And oh, do smell the dying fir! ... Bliss is it on such a day to be alive; but to smell dying fir is very heaven. That's two thirds Wordsworth and one third Anne Shirley" ' (51–2). Here we find the favourites of the *Anne of Green Gables* narrator – purple and cup and poetic allusion – used by Anne herself.

There are some places in the book where Anne picks up directly where the narrator leaves off in a description and gives a fanciful embellishment, perhaps a quotation. Watching a sunset, following Davy's question 'where is sleep?', Anne is inspired to quote from Poe's romantic 'Eldorado': 'Anne was kneeling at the west gable window watching the sunset sky that was like a great flower with petals of crocus and a heart of fiery yellow. She turned her head at Davy's question and answered dreamily, "Over the mountains of the moon, / Down the valley of the shadow''' (197). The familiar flower imagery reminds us of the younger Anne, and the quotation from Poe suggests her continuing love of the romantic and dreamy.

We see another type of embellishment of the narrator by Anne just before Anne and Diana stumble onto Miss Lavendar's romantic stone house. The girls are enjoying the ramble: 'the following afternoon they set out, going by way of Lover's Lane to the back of the Cuthbert farm, where they found a road leading into the heart of acres of glimmering beech and maple woods, which were all in a wondrous glow of flame and gold, lying in a great purple stillness and peace.' As though speaking aloud what she had only moments before thought silently, Anne picks up the colours and says, 'It's as if the year were kneeling to pray in a vast cathedral full of mellow stained light, isn't it? ... I just want to drink the day's loveliness in ... I feel as if she were holding it out to my lips like a cup of airy wine and I'll take a sip at every step' (239). The favourite images of cathedral window and cup of colour work to remind us that this is the same Anne Shirley we have known since the Bright River train left her on the station platform, but now it is Anne who gives the similes.

At other times, when we see the parts echoing or interchanging, the narrator's may be the more familiar: 'Early oats greened over the red fields; apple orchards flung great blossoming arms about the farmhouses and the Snow Queen adorned itself as a bride for her husband. Anne liked to sleep with her window open and let the cherry fragrance blow over her face all night' (272). Anne picks up the joyous strain: 'Thanksgiving should be celebrated in the spring ... I think it would be ever so much better than having it in November when everything is dead or asleep. Then you have to remember to be thankful ... I feel exactly as Eve must have felt in the garden of Eden before the trouble began. *Is* that grass in the hollow green or golden? It seems to me, Marilla, that a pearl of a day like this, when the blossoms are out and the winds don't know where to blow from next for sheer crazy delight must be pretty near as good as heaven' (273). The use here again of the garden of Eden reminds us of Anne's earlier speech about September (quoted above) and, of course, reinforces the paradise quality of Prince Edward Island itself.

The echoing back and forth between narrator and Anne is a standard feature of *Anne of Avonlea*, but the voice of the narrator is not always or even usually the voice or the perception of Anne. Primarily the narrator instructs. Notice, for instance, how the narrator combines in this passage allusion and paraphrase and then tacks on a moral. Anne is responding to Paul's fancies, and he has just asked her if it is not splendid to be one of the ones who can see imaginary people:

'Splendid,' Anne agreed, gray shining eyes looking down into blue shining ones. Anne and Paul both knew

> 'How fair the realm
> Imagination opens to the view,'

and both knew the way to that happy land. There the rose of joy bloomed immortal by dale and stream; clouds never darkened the sunny sky; sweet bells never jangled out of tune; and kindred spirits abounded. The knowledge of that land's geography ... 'east o' the sun, west o' the moon' ... is priceless lore, not to be bought in any market place. It must be the gift of the good fairies at birth and the years can never deface it or take it away. It is better to possess it, living in a garret, than to be the inhabitant of palaces without it. (167)

Either Anne or the narrator could be responsible for the quotation and for the virtual medley of allusions,[3] but the narrator alone insists on the moral at the end. In changing from child to adolescent Anne may have lost something of her irreverent spontaneity, but the narrator has become positively preachy.

Yet even the narrator is never so preachy as Anne is herself in the one dreadful chapter of this book, 'A Golden Picnic.' Anne's behaviour is distressingly precious, and the narrator seldom interjects to counterbalance her. She leads a picnic expedition into the woods and fields, insisting that she should be able to celebrate her birthday in blessed June since it is not her fault she was born in chilly March. The decidedly prosaic Diana Barry and Jane Andrews are there to offer a flattering contrast for the whimsical Priscilla Grant and the entirely fanciful Anne Shirley. Montgomery strains to reproduce realistic conversation of girls in their late teens while also endorsing Anne as special teacher. The episode begins poorly. Trusty. friend Diana, who has usually been the happy chorus for Anne's schemes, here sounds like a miniature Marilla. She thinks Anne's idea for a picnic sounds good, but she feels 'distrust of Anne's magic of words' (133) and is not enthusiastic. Since the days of abusing the imagination with the Haunted Wood nightmares, Diana has been a little afraid to share Anne's flights, but she has never been so stodgy as this. When all four girls are together, Anne gushes, 'Oh, girls, girls, see that patch of violets! There's something for memory's picture gallery' (134). This is not so bad, perhaps, until Priscilla adds, 'If a kiss could be seen I think it would look like a violet.' Anne 'glow[s]' and exclaims; 'I'm so glad you *spoke* that thought, Priscilla, instead of just thinking it and keeping it to yourself. This world would be a much more interesting place ... although it *is* very interesting anyhow ... if people spoke out their real thoughts' (134). Is this the girl who told Marilla in *Anne of Green Gables* that she had learned to keep dear thoughts to herself like treasures (*AGG* 271)?

Perhaps we are meant to feel that with friends Anne should be able to be herself. But the trouble is that Anne does not let the others be themselves. She actually commands them to be fanciful, is dismayed by their lack of poetry, and generally shows herself to be condescending. In this same scene, practical Jane objects to speaking out real thoughts – 'It would be too hot to hold some folks' (134) – and Anne sets her straight by moralizing and commanding: 'I suppose it might be, but that would be their own faults for thinking nasty things. Anyhow, we can tell all our thoughts to-day because we are going to have nothing but beautiful thoughts. Everybody can say just what comes into her head. *That* is conversation. Here's a little path I never saw before. Let's explore it' (134–5). When they come to a little pool Anne insists they dance around it 'like wood-nymphs' (135), but, the narrator tells us mildly, their rubbers come off and they give that up. When Anne makes them select names for the little pond she is aghast at the unimaginativeness of Diana's choice, 'Birch Pool.' (We remember that it was Diana who named Birch Path in *Anne of Green Gables* – would she really be so repetitive? Well, perhaps that is the point.) Jane's 'Crystal Lake' also fails to please. Anne 'implore[s] Priscilla with her eyes not to perpetrate another such name,' and Priscilla comes up with 'Glimmer-glass,' while Anne herself contributes (a fairly dull) 'The Fairies' Mirror.' When 'Crystal Lake' is chosen from the hat, the narrator tells us Anne probably 'thought that chance had played the pool a shabby trick' (136).

Anne's offences go on. Perhaps most revealing is Anne's editing of her wishes. When asked to tell what each would wish for, Anne obviously violates her own rule for the day that they speak their thoughts. Jane wants to be 'rich and beautiful and clever' and Diana 'tall and slender' and Priscilla 'famous,' but 'Anne thought of her hair and then dismissed the thought as unworthy. "I'd wish it might be spring all the time and in everybody's heart and all our lives"' (137). So much for honesty and originality! Can this missish tyrant be the same Anne Shirley who spoke so freely in most of *Anne of Green Gables*? Even Anne's subsequent words about wearing pink dresses in heaven cannot fully offset the high tone she has taken with her friends. If Montgomery were showing this older Anne to be a heroine of her own inner drama, a drama we are supposed to see as misguided and self-deluding, we could perhaps sympathize with Anne's immaturity. We could believe that the older girl/woman has chosen mistakenly a new kind of romance to replace the equally misguided courtly one of childhood. Instead, the contrasts with the other girls seem to support the narrator's belief in Anne's high-mindedness. The book suggests that there is nothing comical or wrong in Anne's criticism of others or in the self-editing of her ideals. Maybe this is the fault of the book in a nutshell: it does not laugh at itself enough.

At the end of the chapter we have another concentration of Anne's voice. First Anne instructs Jane and Diana about poetry and the narrator conspires to make the two literal-minded girls seem almost dim-witted compared with Anne. When Anne cries out 'Look, do you see that poem?' Diana and Jane look around 'expecting to see Runic rhymes on the birch trees' and Anne patiently corrects. Notice Anne's consciously instructive and poetic 'athwart': 'There ... down in the brook ... that old green, mossy log with the water flowing over it in those smooth ripples that look as if they'd been combed, and that single shaft of sunshine falling right athwart it, far down into the pool. Oh, it's the most beautiful poem I ever saw' (143). Jane objects that poetry is written in 'lines and verses,' but Anne dismisses her easily: 'The lines and verses are only the outward garments of the poem and are no more really it than your ruffles and flounces are *you*, Jane' (144). A short while later Anne and Priscilla discuss the colour of souls, and Diana and Jane are clearly mystified by such an imaginative flight. We are encouraged by the narrator, unkindly I think, to feel that Jane and Diana are laughable because they cannot see what Anne and Priscilla see. Would the Anne Shirley who knew how much it hurt to be misunderstood and excluded really treat her dearest friend so insensitively?

The narrator does not desert us entirely in the chapter, however, and we are invited to be amused by one of Anne's excesses: 'Anne had brought glasses and lemonade for her guests, but for her own part drank cold brook water from a cup fashioned out of birch bark. The cup leaked, and the water tasted of earth, as brook water is apt to do in spring; but Anne thought it more appropriate to the occasion than lemonade' (143). We can smile at Anne's insistence on drinking earthy water, and yet even our amusement here is qualified. Is there not a touch of conscious superiority in Anne's choice – and in the fact that she does not even try to persuade her less discerning friends that spring water is more 'appropriate' to the occasion than lemonade? The moralizing narrator of the rest of the book and this complacent Anne evidently share values.

The climax of 'A Golden Picnic' is the finding of Hester Gray's garden, that romantic overgrown Eden where Hester was happy and died. The narrator we knew in *Anne of Green Gables* sets the tone for the discovery of the garden: 'Past the spruces the lane dipped down into a sunny little open [sic] where a log bridge spanned a brook; and then came the glory of a sunlit beechwood where the air was like transparent golden wine, and the leaves fresh and green, and the wood floor a mosaic of tremulous sunshine' (138). The other three exclaim out loud at the beauty, but 'Anne only gazed in eloquent silence' (139). The fact that the prosaic Diana tells the story of Hester Gray is meant to confirm what the whole book seems bent on showing – that Anne's brand of romance is evident in the actual world around Avonlea. Having Diana speak here is rather like having Marilla corroborate Anne's preference for poetry in the interpretation of Lavendar Lewis's story. Anne's faith in romantic love stories is supported by the narrative.

Anne of Avonlea is a busy story, almost as though Montgomery is trying to distract us from the fact that Anne is not learning or growing or really thinking. We welcome the activities of other characters. It's more fun to listen to Mr Harrison and his parrot and to Mrs Lynde, or even to Davy, than it is to listen to Anne.[4]

Yet even though Anne's intense energy is refracted into minor characters and into subplots, there is enough of Anne's enthusiasm and sense of wonder to glue the book together and let it pass as a story about her. The main story with Anne is the love story with Gilbert, and this thread runs through the narrative as a whole. Inevitably, this story is linked to the other romances of the book and to the novel's overall privileging of sentiment over thought. While the narrator in *Anne of Green Gables* encourages our recognition of Anne's misguided idealization of chivalry, in *Anne of Avonlea* the narrator establishes Gilbert as a knight. Trying to have it both ways – highlighting romance and fairy tale and at the same time suggesting that Anne could settle for a real young man of her own community – is a neat narrative trick. The story of Lavendar Lewis is a handy reinforcer of romance and works at the same time to suggest that romance lives in the everyday world if you know how to look for it because Lavendar Lewis is intelligent and clear-sighted about herself and her situation. Lavendar Lewis is fond of verbal quips, plays with biblical passages in ironically characterizing her own isolated life,[5] and is even prone to depression – and yet she is the princess of a fairy tale. The romance of the stone house is a miniature, fanciful prefiguring of Anne's own story with Gilbert Blythe. Montgomery very cleverly uses Anne's and the narrator's words together to fuse the two stories and to bring her own novel to its formula conclusion.

The narrator interprets or rather transcribes for us Anne's thoughts about Steven Irving's request through Anne to meet with Lavendar Lewis. In a chapter entitled 'The Prince Comes Back to the Enchanted Palace,' Anne and Irving meet and Anne responds thus: 'Yes, this was romance, the very, the real thing, with all the charm of rhyme and story and dream. It was a little belated, perhaps, like a rose blooming in October which should have bloomed in June; but none the less a rose, all sweetness and fragrance, with the gleam of gold in its heart' (339). At the very end of the novel after the Lewis-Irving wedding, Anne waits in Lavendar Lewis's garden for Gilbert to return. The enchanted garden is the obvious place for Anne to reconsider how she feels about Gilbert. A question from Gilbert elicits a comment from the narrator and then a transcription of Anne's thoughts. The narrator's words here echo Anne's earlier thoughts about the late-blooming rose: 'Perhaps, after all, romance did not come into one's life with pomp and blare, like a gay knight riding down; perhaps it crept to one's side like an old friend through quiet ways; perhaps it revealed itself in seeming prose, until some sudden shaft of illumination flung athwart its pages betrayed the rhythm and the music; perhaps ... perhaps

... love unfolded naturally out of a beautiful friendship, as a golden-hearted rose slipping from its green sheath' (366). Into this one passage Montgomery has distilled the message of her book and, in a sense, excused the apparent support of fairy tale by suggesting that real life is better than fairy tale. We recognize in the image of the 'gay knight riding down' Anne's younger passion for Lancelot[6] and her stated preference here for a lover-friend. The rose, as the symbol of passion and romance, is associated in Anne's mind with the fairy-tale of Miss Lavendar and her own changing friendship with Gilbert. While Anne apparently eschews courtly, chivalric romance in favour of real life, she is merely turning away from medieval romance (or a Victorian version of it) and towards the traditional romance of which the rose is the emblem. If we thought Anne at the end of *Anne of Green Gables* had moved beyond chivalry, we are told here at the end of *Anne of Avonlea* that Anne only now sees that perhaps the knight is not so powerful as the friend. And, at the same time, friendship-love is given the very emblem associated with courtly and passionate love. To add to this mixing of reversals and apparent reversals, we find on the last page of the novel, in what appears to be a transcription of Gilbert's thoughts, Gilbert's identification of himself as a knight errant winning a princess: 'Gilbert wisely said nothing more; but in his silence he read the history of the next four years in the light of Anne's remembered blush. Four years of earnest, happy work ... and then the guerdon of a useful knowledge gained and a sweet heart won' (367). The poetic, archaic 'guerdon' aligns Gilbert with Camelot, with the chivalry and romance of quest and reward. Whether or not Montgomery intends the echoes and reversals to be ironic, we do know that she is cleverly conforming to the dictates of her genre (domestic romance) and yet at the same time withstanding pressure for a complete, stereotypical capitulation of the yielding damsel to the worthy knight. She has saved Anne's reconsideration, as she did in *Anne of Green Gables*, until the very last pages of the book.

The closing of the novel is a fascinating instance of Montgomery's care to stay within her chosen prescriptions and yet to flirt with reversals of the expected. If Anne can give up the image of the knight and turn to a friend-lover, how will Gilbert feel if he has imagined himself a knight winning a guerdon? Could Montgomery just possibly be hinting at the confusion of expectations and roles we experience when we insist that the script of our inner private drama is really the script of another's drama? In any case, the novel's repeated play with poetry versus prose is an indication that Anne's hidden and divulged scripts for her own drama will continue to be liberally glossed with romantic images and expressions. Anne's preference for poetry over prose ensures that she will continue to find romance in life just as she found romance in the woodland pool. The repetition of the very word 'athwart' suggests a persistent romanticism. Here, the narrator says, 'some sudden shaft of illumination flung athwart' (366) the prose will show the poetry of life in the apparently commonplace, just as Anne earlier saw in the pool the 'single shaft of sunshine falling athwart' (143) an old log and making poetry out of nature. At this very late stage in the narrative, the narrator and Anne together return to the book-length lesson of *Anne of Green Gables*: the real world is the place of beauty and romance.

Perhaps this echo of Montgomery's earlier book and the repetition here of the possibility that Anne will see Gilbert differently help to make *Anne of Avonlea* sound as though it is not really unlike *Anne of Green Gables*. And to a remarkable extent Montgomery was able in *Anne of Avonlea* to tap the energy and fun that made the first book vibrate with life. If 'A Golden Picnic' is jarring, there are still chapters such as 'An Adventure on the Tory Road' that capture the 'old' Anne flavour right down to the quality of mishap and the interaction of Diana and Anne.

In truth, *Anne of Avonlea* is a chequered book. But Montgomery is a skilful writer, and she eventually turns a fairy-tale subplot into a touchstone for the romantic possibilities of everyday life. If Anne's voice is sometimes irksome it is also at other times genuinely entertaining; if the narrator's moralizing is irritating, the descriptions of Charlotta the Fourth and the episodes at the stone house are related with superb comic timing. The apparent book-length endorsement of stereotypical divisions between male and female is undercut at the end, perhaps, by the fact that Gilbert and Anne will set off to college together. The book lacks ease and assurance, but Montgomery manages to keep even very critical readers wondering what sort of dream world that 'red-headed snippet' will perceive in Kingsport.

Recognition:
Anne of the Island

In 1913, four years after the publication of *Anne of Avonlea*, the L.C. Page Company persuaded L.M. Montgomery to write a third Anne novel. In the meantime she had expanded a short story, 'Una of the Garden,' into *Kilmeny of the Orchard* (1910), written her own personal favourite of all her novels, *The Story Girl* (1911), and its sequel, *The Golden Road* (1913), and had refashioned some already-published short stories so that they sometimes included Anne Shirley and Avonlea families and published them under the title *Chronicles of Avonlea* (1912). But it was a full-length story of Anne that fans clamoured for, and Montgomery finally succumbed to pressure and conjured up the third Anne book – a task for which, she complained to her journal, she felt wholly unequal (*Journals* 2: 133).

Between the publication of the second Anne book in 1909 and the publication of *Anne of the Island* (1915), Montgomery's life went through dramatic changes that were bound to affect her private and public philosophies: she married Presbyterian minister Ewan Macdonald in 1911 and moved away from Prince Edward Island to Ontario; she gave birth to one healthy boy (1912) and suffered through the stillbirth of another (1914); war broke out in Europe, and the young men in her parish were enlisting. During the months of composing *Anne of the Island* (*Anne of Redmond* she called it), the peaceful life of a Green Gables home became, indeed, a thing of fiction.

Montgomery was loath to write the book, and complained that her forte was humour and that youth's love stories should be sacred from humour.[1] This attitude coupled with the bleak conditions of the time in which she wrote may have encouraged Montgomery to turn back to some of the original impulses and comic patterns of *Anne of Green Gables* for inspiration. Or perhaps the heavily sentimental and formulaic story of Kilmeny and the frolic-filled writing of (most of) the other three intervening books enabled Montgomery to recover imaginative balance in her sixth book. For *Anne of the Island* is filled with humour and yet contains the love story of Gilbert and Anne. Gone is the moralizing narrator of the overtaxed *Anne of Avonlea*; instead we find in *Anne of the Island* a story that relies on comedy but finds its strength in symbol and symmetry. Anne matures.

Anne's voice in this novel seldom lapses into the dreamy sentimentality of *Anne of Avonlea*; instead, this Anne shows herself sometimes sarcastic, sometimes ironic, sometimes outraged, embarrassed, or downright angry. She can stoop to sparring with Mrs Harmon Andrews; she can write sentimental trash; she can mistake infatuation for love; she can get depressed and feel alienated from home and spiritual kinship. Even if the genre Montgomery chose (domestic romance) and the audience for which she wrote predetermined that the novel would be preoccupied with marriage and fully exploring the right man rather than finding the individual self, Anne Shirley is frequently here a believable and fairly independent person.

To fault the story for its lack of alternatives for the female is certainly a reasonable reading of the 1915 novel in the 1990s, but such a critical rereading must also look at the ways Montgomery uses humour to stretch the sentiment of formula into a comic evaluation of the cultural inevitability of marriage. Unlike the far less flexible *Anne of Avonlea*, *Anne of the Island* suggests that while marriage may be inevitable for somebody like Anne, her happiness is by no means inevitable, and her choice of mate is dependent on her knowledge of self. The novel echoes with the alarm of danger-only-averted-by-a-hair's-breadth. The minor illustrative stories remind us that wrong choices for wrong reasons are constant temptations:

Phil could have stayed in Bolingbroke, as her mother wanted, to choose Alec or Alonzo – but instead she comes to college and thus finds Jonas Blake; Janet Sweet could have despaired of the silent John Douglas and turned him away; Amelia Crowe could have been tempted by the mansion of William Obadiah Seaman to give up the honest and poor Thomas Skinner. Anne Shirley is herself courted by the dark, melancholy hero of her early dreams and realizes only at the brink of accepting his proposal that he is humourless and boring. As in *Anne of Green Gables*, in *Anne of the Island* romance must accommodate reality, and that reality demands careful scrutiny of the self.

Anne of the Island supposedly begins one week after Miss Lavendar's wedding at the end of *Anne of Avonlea*. But the Anne of this new book is a lifetime beyond the earlier miss in her understanding of fun and human nature. And Diana, too, is not the dumpy dumbbell of the earlier book, who couldn't seem to understand anything on the famous Golden Picnic. Here Diana and Anne laugh at the smug Charlie Sloane, and Diana even takes poetic flight – just as we are sure the childhood best friend of Anne would be capable of doing: '"What a beautiful sunset," said Diana. "Look, Anne, it's just like a land in itself, isn't it? That long, low bank of purple cloud is the shore, and the clear sky further on is like a golden sea"' (106). Anne is not always day-dreaming and is even given to human self-protection. Of the ubiquitous Charlie: '"I am very glad that all the Sloanes get seasick as soon as they go on water," thought Anne mercilessly' (25); of Christine Stuart: '"She looks just as I've always wanted to look," thought Anne miserably. "Rose-leaf complexion – starry violet eyes – raven hair – yes, she has them all. It's a wonder her name isn't Cordelia Fitzgerald into the bargain! But I don't believe her figure is as good as mine, and her nose certainly isn't"' (226). This Anne says thought-provoking things. For example, when Paul's grandmother remarks that Anne and Paul 'talk as much foolishness as ever,' Anne baffles her by replying: 'Oh, no, we don't ... We are getting very, very wise, and it is such a pity. We are never half so interesting when we have learned that language is given us to enable us to conceal our thoughts.' The sympathetic narrator reinforces Anne's sagacity by pretending to excuse Mrs Irving's ignorance: 'She [Mrs Irving] had never heard of Tallyrand [*sic*] and did not understand epigrams' (205). This Anne is not merely a starry-eyed believer in fairy tales; she is alive and learning.

The Anne of this book is well read and quick witted and has friends who can appreciate what she says and how she says it. She quotes, mostly playfully but sometimes seriously, from the Bible, Shakespeare, William Cowper, Byron, Scott, Wordsworth, Poe, Dickens, Browning, Lewis Carroll, William Cullen Bryant, Charles Hadden Spurgeon, and Daniel O'Connell, among others (Wilmshurst 22–6). When Stella quotes from Byron's *Don Juan* to ease the tension of burying the chloroformed Rusty, Anne immediately caps and counters – as Montgomery herself was fond of doing (Epperly 'Greetings') – when showing that Rusty is still alive: ' "We've got the grave ready. 'What, silent still and silent all?' " [Stella] quoted teasingly. " 'Oh, no, the voices of the dead / Sound like the distant torrent's fall' " promptly counter-quoted Anne, pointing solemnly to the box' (162). Priscilla, too, has some witticisms and is responsible for a comic use of Whittier's sentimental poem 'Maud Muller.' When Roy Gardner's mother and two sisters have left after their surprise visit to Anne, Priscilla lifts the luckless cushion where she had hurriedly hidden a chocolate cake, now a flattened mess, and quotes, 'Of all sad words of tongue or pen / The saddest are it might have been' (287). And Priscilla's quotation is not only funny but also ironic – perhaps the rich Gardners' visit to the poor Anne may have inspired Priscilla's comic reference to the poem, whose wealthy unmarried lawyer forever must lament that he did not marry the beautiful and poor peasant girl, Maud Muller. In any case, to use Whittier spontaneously to bewail the loss of the cake is in keeping with the book's literary fun.

The cleverest of Anne's friends – the only one to scold Anne over Gilbert and Roy and to give Gilbert hope that Anne has changed her mind – is Philippa Gordon, who quotes from or adapts from as full a range of literary sources as do Anne and the narrator.[2] One of her clever puns will give an idea of her quick-wittedness. She plays with Othello's respectful words of address to the Venetian elders. Othello calls them 'Most potent, grave and reverend signiors' (I.ii.76) and Phil solemnly borrows the address to characterize the final-year students at Redmond: 'Potent, wise, and reverend Seniors' (289).

Anne's voice is believably imaginative and playful, and she is surrounded by friends who are studying as hard as she is and who are also well-read and witty. To amplify and echo the young women's literary dialogues and repartee and also to suggest the quality of Anne's education and friendships, the narrator uses the Bible, Shakespeare, Wordsworth, Keats, Thackeray, Poe, Thomas Campbell, and Tennyson, among others. Their learning and their fun make the young women special, but Anne is always the most special of all. Her biggest lessons must come not from books or college but from facing herself. One way or another, everything in the book is related to Anne and to her recognition of the importance of knowing herself so that she can understand what romance really involves.

Everything in the book seems geared to a consideration of marriage or partnership or the possibilities of partnership. In writing this third Anne novel Montgomery carefully preserves the internal chronology of her series by referring here in 1915 to stories she published in *Chronicles of Avonlea* in 1912. Appropriately, the stories she chooses to mention from the short story collection are about courtship and the difficulties of making accommodations for partnership. In *Anne of the Island* Mrs Lynde refers (55) to the MacPhersons who have bought her farm ('Aunt Olivia's Beau' in *Chronicles of Avonlea*); Anne and Marilla discuss (73) and the narrator mentions (205) the apparently interminable courtship of Ludovic Speed and Theodora Dix ('The Hurrying of Ludovic'); Anne tells Gilbert (320) she is going to a Penhallow wedding ('The Winning of Lucinda'). In 'Aunt Olivia's Beau' a single woman's ingrained neatness and primness make her rebel against the hearty, blustering masculinity of Malcolm MacPherson. Aunt Olivia learns at the last minute that she will have to give up some of her primness if she is going to have a husband, and she realizes that loving Malcolm MacPherson is more important than a swept rug or tidy antimacassars. In 'The Hurrying of Ludovic' Ludovic Speed is hurried up by Anne's introducing a rival for him; Lodovic has to face up to the possibility of losing through his own complacency the woman he loves. In 'The Winning of Lucinda' a small accident gives two stubborn people an excuse to speak and patch up the fifteen years' silent feud that prevented their marriage. In each piece mistakes and misunderstandings could all too easily have spoiled people's chances for married happiness – these episodes turn out well, but only because some desperate resolution or freakish accident turns near-disaster into triumph. The possibility of missed opportunity or misunderstanding also makes the novel suspenseful and instructive. The reminders of others' difficulties emphasize Anne's necessity for soul-searching and recognition so that she can make the 'right' choice.

Most of the stories in this novel also deal with or end with marriage. Lavendar and Steven Irving return with Paul to the stone house from which they were married; Diana marries Fred; Jane marries a Winnipeg millionaire; Phil marries Jonas Blake; Mrs Skinner tells her courtship story; Janet Sweet marries John Douglas; widowers make 'sheep's eyes' at Aunt Jamesina; Anne receives six proposals. Even nine-year-old Davy shows the preoccupation of the culture, as well as the carefully instilled attitudes to gender and roles. We remember that it was a six-year-old Davy in *Anne of Avonlea* who revelled in male privilege. Here Davy sends Anne his composition 'The kind of a wife Id like to Have':

She must have good manners and get my meals on time and do what I tell her and always be very polite to me. She must be fifteen years old. She must be good to the poor and keep her house tidy and be good tempered and go to church reglarly. She must be very handsome and have curly hair. If I get a wife that is just what I like Ill be an awful good husband to her. I think a woman ought to be awful good to her husband. Some poor women havent any husbands. (170)

In the confused and confusing context of fairy tale in *Anne of Avonlea*, the intended response to Davy's learned assumptions is ambiguous at best, but here in *Anne of the Island*, Davy's summation of male/female roles in marriage is evidently intended to be (no matter how irritating we may find it) an adorably naïve, comical over-simplification of the truth. And yet, 'Some poor women havent any husbands' is definitely the prevailing attitude of the world within the book, the Spofford women and Marilla notwithstanding.

At any rate, the presence of the essay reinforces the focus of the book as a whole on marriage and romance and expectations for men and women. When Anne visits Phil in Bolingbroke and discovers the tiny little yellow house where she was born twenty years before, she recovers her parents through a small bundle of their love letters the owner had discovered in a closet. Even in recovering her own parents, Anne is faced with their courtship and early wedded struggles and happiness. There simply seems to be little worth finding out about that does not include the all-important issue of mating appropriately. We note that neither Stella nor Priscilla seems to have a steady beau – and they are forever shadow figures, witty voices that echo Anne's and Phil's apparently larger wit and experience of life. Even on the brink of death Ruby Gillis regrets she has to die now when she has at long last found 'Mr. Right.'

But if Montgomery's focus is relentless, it is not humourless. We find here the same quality of comedy and comic reversal of romance we experienced in *Anne of Green Gables*, and we can laugh at and with Anne's misunderstanding of romance. Montgomery enjoys a comic romp with literary romance and the ambitions of a budding writer. She will treat the subject of authorship seriously when she writes the story of Emily Byrd Starr, but here Anne's winsome notions of popular fiction provide a comic commentary on writing and, simultaneously, on misplaced sentimentality. Montgomery uses what happens to Anne's beloved story as emblematic of what should happen to Anne's ideas of romance.

The creating of a character who writes stories is a wonderful, often comic literary device Montgomery had herself enjoyed in such books as Louisa May Alcott's *Little Women* (with Jo March). The young author-in-the-novel inevitably exposes her own immaturity and sentimentality in the kind of story she creates. And so it is with Anne. She of course chooses idealized names and language – Averil Lester and Perceval Dalrymple. (No wonder Diana wants to name the hired boy of the story Raymond Fitzosborne, though Anne does say finally, 'I'm afraid that is too aristocratic a name for a chore boy, Diana' 116.) Mr Harrison's ruthlessly matter-of-fact criticisms sound like the later Mr Carpenter of *Emily of New Moon*, and could certainly be criticisms levelled at Montgomery's own early short stories (and even some of the lush descriptions in *The Golden Road*): ' "Cut out all those flowery passages" he said unfeelingly ... "I've left out *all* the descriptions but the sunset," she said at last. "I simply *couldn't* let it go. It was the best of them all." "It hasn't anything to do with the story," said Mr. Harrison' (119). Montgomery has fun with the trials of the young, misguided author who must face the expectations of a prosaic audience. She uses the blunt, ungrammatical Harrison to ridicule Anne's evident penchant for purple prose: 'But your folks ain't like real folks anywhere. They talk too much and use too high-flown language. There's one place where that *Dalrymple* chap talks even on for two pages, and never lets the girl get a word in edgewise. If he'd done that in real life she'd have pitched him' (120). Anne's spoken and unspoken responses to Mr. Harrison show just exactly how little of life's passion and suffering she has yet endured as an adult. She is still enchanted by the fairy-tale world Montgomery has coddled her in in *Anne of Avonlea*, but the good-humoured, truthful narrator of *Anne of the Island* exposes Anne's idealism for what it is. Anne replies to Mr Harrison's criticism: '''I don't believe it,'' said Anne flatly. In her secret soul she thought that the beautiful, poetical things said to *Averil* would win any girl's heart completely. Besides, it was gruesome to hear of *Averil*, the stately, queen-like *Averil*, ''pitching'' any one. *Averil* ''declined her suitors''' (120). When Anne refuses five proposals herself, she finds out with a vengeance how inadequate this lofty detachment is to describe the incredulity or embarrassment or anger or pain she experiences.

But Anne does not have to wait for larger experience to cure her of the high-flown style of 'Averil's Atonement.' After the story has been rejected several times and Anne has given up on it, Diana secretly edits it slightly for a baking powder contest and Anne wins the prize. Her 'queen-like Averil' and the peerless Perceval are now used to promote Rollings Reliable baking powder, and the story is printed in coloured leaflets and distributed to each customer of the local general store. Without realizing it, Anne has hit the formula style of the magazine romance, and this is why her story – even altered – is such a success. Montgomery is careful to make us see that Anne is shamed by the baking-powder prize into giving up a style that she has not yet learned through personal experience to be wholly inadequate to depict truth and the richness of life. She moans to Gilbert: 'I feel as if I were disgraced forever. What do you think a mother would feel like if she found her child tattooed over with a baking powder advertisement?' (153). Even before Anne finishes college and suffers fully for her recognition of her love for Gilbert, she knows how false 'Averil's Atonement' is to real-life experience. The Anne who agonizes over the editing of her story is still very much the little girl clinging to the slimy pilings while Elaine's funeral barge sinks beneath her. We are invited to laugh at her innocent (but not harmless) support of the wrong kind of romance.

Interestingly, while Anne is imagining herself in love with Roy Gardner, she comes to terms with her own true writing voice. Going through hilariously melodramatic old Story Club pieces, she finds the fanciful sketch she wrote while caught in the roof of the Cobb duckhouse (a mishap chronicled in that excellent chapter in *Anne of Avonlea* entitled 'An Adventure on the Tory Road'). Anne now recognizes the value of the little spirit-dialogue, rewrites it, and sends it off. It is accepted for publication in *Youth's Friend* and we know that Anne's imagination and her literary voice are finally mature. It is a shame that in subsequent books Anne's writing never goes beyond sketches and pieces for children, as though she is later thoroughly and unhealthily transfixed in the domestic world she has here chosen as a healthful alternative to sentimental excess.

In keeping with the book's preoccupation with marriage, Anne's most bracing lessons in disillusionment come through five of her proposals. Just as Jane Andrews and Anne are drifting off to sleep one stormy night, Jane proposes on behalf of her brother Billy. When a startled Anne refuses and says she hopes Billy won't 'feel very badly over it,' Jane coolly replies: 'Oh, he won't break his heart. Billy has too much good sense for that. He likes Nettie Blewett pretty well, too, and mother would rather he married her than any one' (80–1). After Jane leaves the next day Anne cries over this first disillusionment, and we hear in the summary of her self-consolation about the future the misguided romanticism that will inspire 'Averil's Atonement' and the later affair with Royal Gardner: 'and the "some one" was to be very handsome and dark-eyed and distinguished-looking and eloquent, whether he were Prince Charming to be enraptured with "yes," or one to whom a regretful, beautifully worded, but hopeless refusal must be given' (82). This Anne still cherishes the knights and chivalry and poetry that inspired the child Anne in Green Gables days. As with the early story, here, too, we can laugh at Anne's false romanticism while sympathizing with her surprise and anguish.

Charlie Sloane's proposal, right on the heels of Jane's for Billy, makes Anne angry. They quarrel, and Charlie 'flung himself out of the house with a very red face' while Anne 'threw herself on her bed, in tears of humiliation and rage ... Oh, this was degradation, indeed – worse even than being the rival of Nettie Blewett!' (85). The third comic proposal comes from the lank-haired, raggedy hired man, Sam Tolliver, whose favourite word is 'yep' and who offers himself with nonchalant simplicity: 'Wall, I've been thinking some of gitting a place of my own ... But ef I rents it I'll want a woman ... Will yeh hev me?' (266) By this time in the narrative 'Anne's illusions concerning proposals had suffered so much of late years that there were few of them left. So she could laugh whole-heartedly over this one, not feeling any secret sting' (267). Anne learns to steel herself to the evidently universal preoccupation with finding a mate.

Billy's and Charlie's and Sam's proposals are the comic relief for the serious problems Gilbert and Roy Gardner represent. At the end of *Anne of Green Gables* Anne accepts friendship with Gilbert, and there is a deliberate foreshadowing of romance in the description of their new relationship. Then in *Anne of Avonlea* Anne stays militantly unconscious of Gilbert's appeal until the very last pages of that narrative. The skilful story-teller, like Scheherazade, was spinning out the story, but she was also postponing an inevitability she dreaded. Montgomery confided to her journal that in writing this third Anne book she knew she would have to give in to the pressure to get Anne and Gilbert engaged, but 'I am not good at depicting sentiment – I can't do it well. Yet there *must* be sentiment in this book. I must at least engage Anne for I'll never be given any rest until I do' (*Journals* 2: 133). True to the pattern of the first two books, Anne does not realize her love for Gilbert until the very last pages of this third novel. Before Anne can accept Gilbert, she must confront her own concept of romance and learn to recognize and value her true feelings. She must endure Gilbert's first proposal to her, and then she must be able to withstand Prince Charming, Royal Gardner.

Montgomery deliberately sets the stage for Gilbert's heartfelt, no-nonsense proposal to Anne. The chapter carries the simple title 'Gilbert Speaks,' and it begins with Phil calling it a 'dull, prosy day' (184). Anne's reply to Phil is characteristically idealized, showing Anne to be uninitiated in genuine heartache: 'It has been a prosy day for us ... but to some people it has been a wonderful day. Some one has been rapturously happy in it. Perhaps a great deed has been done somewhere to-day – or a great poem written – or a great man born. And some heart has been broken, Phil' (184). When Phil complains that Anne has spoiled her pretty thought by tacking on heart-break, Anne rebukes her with words she will, in a very few moments, be tasting bitterly herself: 'Do you think you'll be able to shirk unpleasant things all your life, Phil' (184). Dreamy and self-contained, Anne goes out for a walk and is found by Gilbert. His proposal is direct and sincere: 'Will you promise me that some day you'll be my wife?' (188), and her own answer is also eloquently simple: 'No, I can't' (188). Anne and Gilbert both suffer; no romantic flights can ease either of them: 'Gilbert's face was white to the lips. And his eyes – but Anne shuddered and looked away. There was nothing romantic about this. Must proposals be either grotesque or – horrible? Could she ever forget

Gilbert's face?' (188–9). The stark intensity of feeling is more potent than anything Anne has yet experienced.

Afterwards, Anne faces Phil's condemnation: 'You don't know love when you see it. You've tricked something out with your imagination that you think love, and you expect the real thing to look like that' (190). It is interesting that Montgomery chooses to have Phil rather than the narrator or Anne herself interpret Anne's dilemma. Within the story, Anne's self-delusions are apparent to a good friend who herself makes discoveries about romance and self-delusion. But since Anne cannot yet recognize her mistake, her initial reaction to rejecting Gilbert is a belief in her own unfitness for the kind of love her friends approve. Faced with this disapproval and her own unhappiness, Anne does the human thing – she searches for the kind of love she believes in, hoping a discovery of the Real Thing will justify having given Gilbert pain. Anne accepts the cultural inevitability of marriage without a murmur, especially now that she evidently feels she must justify refusal of one man by acceptance of another. Thus, Montgomery's novel reinforces its own focus.

One hundred pages later Anne prepares herself for a flat world. She has been going out with Royal Gardner for two years and everyone expects her to accept him. She herself expects it, since he is her dreamy, dark ideal, the Byronic-looking hero of her long-ago visions with Diana. Most appropriately, the proposal chapter is entitled 'False Dawn.' Anne tells herself she must be thrilled to be with Roy, since he is all that her imagination has ever conjured as the romantic lover – but she is bored by him and life seems insipid: 'She was deeply in love with Roy. True, it was not just what she had imagined love to be. But was anything in life, Anne asked herself wearily, like one's imagination of it? It was the old diamond disillusion of childhood repeated – the same disappointment she had felt when she had first seen the chill sparkle instead of the purple splendour she had anticipated' (298). Roy proposes to her in the park pavilion, where they had first met when Anne's umbrella had turned inside out. His choice is perfect, his speech is 'as beautifully worded as if he had copied it ... out of a Deportment of Courtship and Marriage' (299). Montgomery prepares the stage for Anne's refusal – the reader has seen what is coming, has been prepared for it by all the events and markers of the past hundred pages (if not by pure faith in the inevitability of the match between Anne and Gilbert). But for Anne the realization comes as a 'blinding flash,' and she is suddenly 'reeling back from a precipice' (300). As with the rejection of Gilbert, here, too, beautiful speeches and melting gestures have no place – the dialogue is realistically terse and strained. Roy leaves her swiftly, and again Anne encounters Phil who (again) scolds her for refusing a man everyone has expected her to accept. But the refusals are not identical; Anne has learned something from this experience, though she has not yet realized precisely what it is.

Montgomery uses a symbolic fog and its undercurrent of joy to suggest Anne's immediate confusion and eventual clarity: 'When Roy had gone she sat for a long time in the pavilion, watching a white mist creeping subtly and remorselessly landward up the harbour. It was her hour of humiliation and self-contempt and shame. Their waves went over her. And yet, underneath it all, was a queer sense of recovered freedom' (301). The fog works well here because we have seen it before – in fact Montgomery uses fog to describe Anne's dejection in a world without Gilbert in it. On the afternoon Anne meets Royal Gardner, she has gone to the park to clear her soul of fog: 'Anne roamed through the pineland alleys in the park and, as she said, let that great sweeping wind blow the fogs out of her soul. Anne was not wont to be troubled with soul fog. But, somehow, since her return to Redmond for this third year, life had not mirrored her spirit back to her with its old, perfect, sparkling clearness' (215). On the very next page Anne meets Roy. Roy is ushered in by fog and leaves with fog – and Montgomery shows us that though he may have kept the fog at bay briefly, he is not the one to dispel it.

It is no accident that Montgomery uses a storm to fill the hours of Anne's agonized vigil when she at last realizes she loves Gilbert and fears he is dying. At the end of the book, when morning comes and the air is clear again, Anne finds that Gilbert is alive and she knows they will love each other. Before Anne receives the joyous words from Pacifique about Gilbert's 'turn,' the narrator has already alerted the reader to the coming light and joy: 'The storm raged all night, but when the dawn came it was spent. Anne saw a fairy fringe of light on the skirts of darkness. Soon the eastern hill-tops had a fire-shot ruby rim. The clouds rolled themselves away into great, soft, white masses on the horizon; the sky gleamed blue and silvery. A hush fell over the world' (317). From the old Green Gables days we know the significance of sunrises and sunsets, and the images of fog and storm have prepared us here to recognize nature's reflection of the right order of things. Anne's and Gilbert's union, the whole story suggests, is part of life's elemental harmony. Prince Charming was a trick of the old imagination gone wrong – a will o' the wisp from the Haunted Wood – and the very sun itself rejoices in the restoration of balance between love and dream.

Fog, storm, and sunrise are but a few of the emblems Montgomery uses in the story to mark an important parallel, reversal, or repetition. In fact, when we look closely we find that the whole book is designed to use such emblems to turn the reader back to the past, to suggest a parallel reading of situations that differ in circumstance but not in emotion and impulse. We find several of these small markers toward the end of the book. When Anne casts aside Roy's graduation violets in favour of Gilbert's lilies of the valley, we are reminded of all the childhood and adolescent dreams Anne and Gilbert have shared – how they have shared ambitions and visions in school and community. The public celebration of a dream realized belongs, thus, to the past and Gilbert's lilies, not to Roy's violets (292). Gilbert gives Anne a tiny enamelled heart necklace in the Christmas of their final year, a year and a half after she has refused him. The enamelled heart is a comic replica of the candy heart Gilbert slipped under Anne's arm the day she was punished in Avonlea school by having to sit next to him. In childhood she had 'ground ... to powder beneath her heel' (*AGG* 122) Gilbert's peace offering. In adulthood she wrenches the chain and heart from her neck when Phil tells her Gilbert's engagement to Christine Stuart is to be announced as soon as Convocation is over (294).

Back in Avonlea there are even more poignant reminders of the past and of painful change. After leaving Kingsport for good, Anne returns to Green Gables only to find that the beloved old cherry tree, the Snow Queen, has blown down. The death of the tree marks the death of Anne's childhood dreams and life – the tree was one of the first things she named on arrival at Green Gables as a child, and into its branches she had gazed as she had dreamed and thought and planned the brightest of futures for herself. Now she grieves: 'The porch gable doesn't seem the same room without it. I'll never look from its window again without a sense of loss. And oh, I never came home to Green Gables before that Diana wasn't here to welcome me' (306). The old Snow Queen (herself cool, inaccessible?) belongs to another life – now Anne finds Diana having a baby, Jane marrying, Marilla getting old, the twins growing up, everything maturing and ripening except her apparently futile life.

Anne, out of the mainstream, possesses a BA and loneliness; all her friends are marrying and birthing. The loud, clear message about the necessity for and desirability of marriage is artfully reinforced with yet another heavily suggestive passage. Anne is already feeling that she belongs only in 'past years and had no business in the present at all' (310) when she goes to see Diana's new baby. While Anne is there, Mrs Allan (mother of several herself now since the old days when she first came to Avonlea as the new minister's bride) tells a story about her only recollection of her mother. What a poignant way for Montgomery to reflect (replicate?) the cultural pressure on Anne to get on with what is apparently meant to be the real work and only blessing of life – to be married and to be a mother. Radiant with new motherhood Diana says she cannot wait to hear her baby call her 'mother'; Mrs Allan chimes in with her sweet recollection of her mother's protective love (shortly before the mother died); and there is Anne, unmarried, an orphan, childless. She is outside the norm, already feeling that she has turned aside the best life has to offer. Montgomery plays up Anne's loneliness and isolation until they seem almost unbearable. Anne's only sensible choice, Montgomery's novel suggests, is to embrace her destiny, realize her love for Gilbert, and get married.

At the end of the chapter describing Diana's baby, Mrs Allan's story, and Anne's dejection, we find this rich description: 'Anne felt lonelier than ever as she walked home, going by way of the Birch Path and Willowmere. She had not walked that way for many moons. It was a darkly-purple bloomy night. The air was heavy with blossom fragrance – almost too heavy. The cloyed senses recoiled from it as from an overfull cup. The birches of the path had grown from the fairy saplings of old to big trees. Everything had changed' (312–13). The burden of her own ripeness, the 'overfull cup,' oppresses Anne, and we see that just as 'the fairy saplings' have become commonplace old trees so her tender dreams must give way to uncompromising realities. Such a description is perfectly suited to the mood of dejection and to the pattern of growth and maturity and change the whole book exploits. And here is where Montgomery shows herself the artist and works her material away from closure and fixity. Had Montgomery stopped with the 'overfull cup' and the older trees, we could feel that the patterns of the book were completed and the messages suitably if relentlessly expressed, but we would not feel that Anne herself had any freedom or choice or resilience or power. But Anne Shirley continues to live in the 1990s because she does not quite conform to reader expectation, to cultural stereotype, or to accepted convention. She does, overall, fit in and conform, but there is always that subtle twist to the good stories that shows Anne gently, discretely interpreting and responding to expectations and roles in an individual way. This saving something is found in the next words of this same description. Anne does not submit to the oppression of the 'overfull cup'; instead, she characteristically renounces romance and then is consoled by the very romance of renouncing romance: 'Anne felt that she would be glad when the summer was over and she was away at work again. Perhaps life would not seem so empty then. ''I've tried the world – it wears no more / The colouring of romance it wore,'' sighed Anne – and was straightway much comforted by the romance in the idea of the world being denuded of romance!' (313) This sighing over lost romance belongs to the childhood Anne and is, here, an ironically triumphant expression of her ability to turn the most oppressive cultural expectations into trials for her own (self-romanticized) melancholy individuality. This older Anne – so well educated, so apparently mature – is still, inside, the little indomitable soul who was much consoled by the romantic leave-taking of Diana, when Mrs Barry had forbidden them to play together. In other words, Montgomery's narrator assures us, Anne is not broken by her sorrows (as a romance heroine might be), but is still able to fictionalize her own suffering. Montgomery gets to have it both ways – Anne is herself, but we know that she will not have to subside into battered loneliness. Anne 'wins' because she does not relinquish her romantic, poetic, imaginative spirit, even though she must surrender false romance to embrace romance of another kind.

In fact, what we find here is that Montgomery has completed or repeated with the mature Anne, and in this novel, the patterns she began in *Anne of Green Gables* (but made no good use of in *Anne of Avonlea*). This story offers symmetry; its very narrative shape suggests fulfilment and completion. The language, images, and themes of the first chapter of the book are echoed and completed in the last chapter of the book. And while the cluster of markers or emblems at the end of the novel remind us of all former Avonlea life and the developments of Anne's and Gilbert's story, so the progress of events within the story repeats in miniature and sometimes comic form the larger lessons of the narrative. Montgomery uses irony and comedy to echo the implications of the attraction between Gilbert and Anne.

Notice, for example, the narrative pattern between the first refusal of Gilbert and the refusal of Royal Gardner. Immediately after giving up Gilbert, Anne discovers her parents and hears from a woman who knew them that her father was 'homely but awful nice. I mind hearing folks say when they was married that there never was two people more in love with each other – ' (194). The reader understands that Anne's father was no romantic ideal and that he and Anne's mother shared the most wonderful love and joy. Gilbert's offer to Anne is actually transcribed in her own past (even though Gilbert himself is handsome, he is not the dark hero of Anne's dreams). In the next two chapters Anne returns to Green Gables only to find things subtly different there – the child Davy has already picked out a wife, he says, and when Paul Irving visits, he can no longer find his beloved rock people. Clearly childhood is passing. And sweet, insightful Miss Lavendar / Mrs Irving puts her finger on the issue when she questions Anne about Gilbert and then says: 'you were made and meant for each other, Anne ... You needn't toss that young head of yours. It's a fact' (206). There is more here than just Miss Lavendar's recognition of their suitedness; her own story – a twenty-five-year misunderstanding and separation from the man she loved – is token that mistakes have a way of turning lives unhappily awry, dividing those who would be best together.

In the next three chapters we see Montgomery's deft use of repetition and irony. The three titles themselves – 'Enter Jonas,' 'Enter Prince Charming,' 'Enter Christine,' – suggest how she is reinforcing parallels to make a point. Phil's Jonas is the antithesis of her own ideal – she had always insisted she must marry a handsome rich man, and Jonas is ugly and poor. Phil's rapture is, of course, further reinforcement for the lesson that the apparently commonplace can mask the splendidly romantic. In keeping with the book's twist of convention that turns out to be conformity to convention, Phil's renunciation of riches and glamour and idleness for a life of poverty and cheerful usefulness is really the height of romance, after all. Then in the next chapter when Prince Charming comes, we see Anne stunned by Roy's dark good looks and mysterious air: 'dark, melancholy, inscrutable eyes – melting, musical, sympathetic voice – yes, the very hero of her dreams stood before her in the flesh. He could not have more closely resembled her ideal if he had been made to order' (218). The words 'made to order' give him away, of course. As subsequent events suggest, Roy is all trappings and no substance – a tailor-made, manufactured hero who, Anne later finds out, is even a little shop-worn, having twice before broken his heart and mended it. Gilbert is the genuine article. And then when Christine arrives and Anne suffers jealousy, we know exactly what Anne's interest in Roy is worth. In the three chapters together, we find the admirable model (Phil and Jonas), the hollow ideal, and then the instrument that punctures the hollow ideal.

Equally effective and thought-provoking is the comic sequence of events a short time later. Diana's wedding (where Gilbert and Anne as best man and bridesmaid make people exclaim over what a handsome couple they make) is immediately followed by one of the delights of the book, a five-page Dickensian miniature giving the story of 'Mrs Skinner's Romance.'[3] Twelve times in the five pages Mrs Skinner punctuates her narrative with 'Jog along, black mare' even when she is stopping the horse. This two-hundred pound, red-faced elderly woman in a tight, ten-year-old black cashmere dress proceeds to tell Anne all about her 'romance' with Thomas, to whom she has been married only a month. For the poor Thomas she declined the wealthy William Obadiah Seaman, since 'he didn't love me.' She repeats to Anne the dialogue she had with herself: 'you can marry your rich man if you like but you won't be happy. Folks can't get along together in this world without a little bit of love. You'd just better tie up to Thomas, for he loves you and you love him and nothing else ain't going to do you' (247). Even if Anne is not ready to make the connections between the Skinner romance and her own need for self-knowledge, the reader is – and the comic interlude offers yet another variation on that same theme, that love can come in the most unexpected guises and romance is merely an imaginative colouring for what the heart wants and accepts as worthy. After this comic brush with Mrs Skinner, Anne's failure in intervening to hasten John Douglas's courtship of Janet Sweet is not so surprising. There is obviously much about life and love that Anne does not know and will have to learn.

Anne of the Island has symmetry in itself, but it also makes the first three Anne novels work together to complete a picture of Anne's struggle with romanticism. Montgomery's insistent echoing of the past in *Anne of the Island* as a whole assures us of Anne's sameness while we are seeing her changes and need for change. Notice how opening and closing chapters of the novel fully complement each other and also fulfil patterns from *Anne of Green Gables* and the last pages of *Anne of Avonlea*. The motto that opens the book is from Tennyson – appropriately, from 'The Day Dream'; the title of the last chapter, 'Love Takes Up the Glass of Time,' is from Tennyson's 'Locksley Hall,' a line spoken by the man in recalling the days when he and Amy first declared their love for each other.[4] The first chapter opens with a description of an autumn afternoon, where the fields are bare and 'scarfed with golden rod' (1); the book ends with a September afternoon ramble in the woods and fields where the hills are 'scarfed with the shadows of autumnal clouds' (323). In the first chapter Anne and Gilbert stand on the bridge 'just at the spot where Anne had climbed from her sinking dory on the day Elaine floated down to Camelot' (6), the place where Anne's false idea of romance made her scorn the friendship Gilbert offered. At the end of the book, Anne and Gilbert walk back to Hester Gray's garden, that site of real romance in *Anne of Avonlea*, where a loving man and woman chose to live away from the trammel of the world. In the first chapter Anne revels in the love of place and home when Gilbert praises Kingsport: '"I wonder if it will be – can be – any more beautiful than this," murmured Anne, looking around her with the loving, enraptured eyes of those to whom "home" must always be the loveliest spot in the world, no matter what fairer lands may lie under alien stars' (6). At the book's end, Gilbert gives Anne a picture of his ideal home: 'I dream of a home with a hearth-fire in it, a cat and dog, the footsteps of friends, – and *you*!' (324).

In the 1990s we probably will not applaud the way Montgomery proscribes Anne's choices – or rather how Montgomery reflects her culture's popular proscription of women's choices – in making it seem that Anne must marry or be a failure. And yet, many of us may enjoy Anne's story because we discount the cultural pressures on Anne and pursue romantic fictions of our own, imagining Anne will be able to retain individuality and power within marriage and home. Others of us may question not only the inevitability but also the desirability of conventional romance – for Anne or ourselves – since it involves so many limitations and role expectations. However we choose to reinterpret romance, we can see that for Anne – for Montgomery – the rejection of chivalric romance or magazine-formula type romance and their stultifying proscriptions is indeed a triumph. Anne chooses, among others, two forms of romance to replace the chivalric ideal: (1) the romantic ideal of the freedom, power, and importance of the individual, (2) the belief in magical surprises within the everyday world. And, interestingly, the more we – in the 1990s – come to understand how our own cultures inhibit women's abilities to see ourselves clearly (Smith), the more warmly we can praise Montgomery's heroines and Montgomery's irony and humour and belief in beauty. We can relish with Anne and Montgomery the liberating dreams that rules may be bent and lives may just slip the groove and burst into splendour.

At the end of *Anne of the Island*, Anne no longer prefers Camelot to Avonlea, nor will she choose the romance of a broken heart over the comforts of companionship, shared values, and home. She has passed through her Book of Revelations, as Montgomery calls it, and she is affirmed in what she knew and purged of what she perversely imagined. The book insists on marriage, but it also insists on the crucial importance of self-knowledge. Montgomery's first three novels together show that happiness and maturity demand facing up to self-delusion as well as to different versions of romance. The switch from Camelot to Hester Gray's garden suggests that beauty is within reach for all of us if we determine to recognize/create it here, in ourselves, with our knowledge.

'This Enchanted Shore':

Anne's House of Dreams

Written from June to October of 1916, right in the bleak middle of the First World War, *Anne's House of Dreams* (1917) is a passionate celebration of home and love. Potentially the most sentimental of all the Anne books, since it presents the long-awaited marriage of Anne and Gilbert, Montgomery's fourth Anne novel is instead a tightly woven, wise story. This is not a novel about wedded bliss, but is instead about friendships, particularly Anne's with Leslie Moore. Facing grief and pain, each woman learns from the other something about the healing, active powers of love. Without referring to it, Montgomery is writing against the ravages of war – she conjures an 'enchanted coast' (175) where like-minded women and men reverence the beauty of the world and the drama of its rhythms and traditions. Change and evil threaten, even here, but home and trust can be built and rebuilt. *Anne's House of Dreams* is the most consciously poetic of Montgomery's novels, and the most unself-consciously philosophic.

This novel is full of poetry. The numerous descriptive passages, more even than in *Anne of Green Gables*, create atmosphere, reflect personality, and suggest the romantic, often symbolic, dimensions of Four Winds harmony. Montgomery had published a collection of poetry entitled *The*

Watchman and Other Poems in 1916, while she was working on *Anne's House of Dreams*, and the imagery and rhythms of the poems reappear in the novel. Injudiciously edited, the collection shows the songs of woods and field and hill and sea to poor advantage,[1] but in the novel Montgomery's favourite images and colours work well to show beauty through the loving eye (Epperly, 'Reworking' 40–6).

Montgomery chooses the sea as the subject of most of the poetic passages of *Anne's House of Dreams*. Abiding, yet ever-changeful, at times serene and at times savage, the sea suggests the quality of Four Winds life. The apparent power, beauty, mystery, melancholy, caprice, and joy of the harbour and gulf reflect as well as affect the moods and personalities of the novel's main characters. The sea is the novel's metaphor for tumultuous life, and the lighthouse beacon (tended by a male Hestia) is the promise of order and love and truth. While the sea is central to the atmosphere and the characters, it is, true to Montgomery's own experience, a landlubber's ocean – we gaze at it and walk along it, but we seldom venture onto it. Yet even though it is often at a distance, its power is pervasive.

Janice Kulyk Keefer notes that the sea of Canadian Maritime fiction is fairly tame, almost as cultivated as a field (15). In the first three Anne books the sea is often merely a strip of blue on the horizon, but in *Anne's House of Dreams* it is essential to life and scene. The old Avonlea version of the sea is offered on the opening page of this novel, where from the garret of Green Gables is 'glimpsed a distant, white-capped, blue sea' (1). The narrator remarks on Anne's new experience at Four Winds: 'There was a certain tang of romance and adventure in the atmosphere of their new home which Anne had never found in Avonlea. There, although she had lived in sight of the sea, it had not entered intimately into her life. In Four Winds it surrounded her and called to her constantly' (52–3). Moments after meeting Leslie Moore, Anne confides: 'The sea at Four Winds is to me what Lover's Lane was at home' (82). Every important character in the book is in some way involved with the rhythms or the beauties of the sea, but Anne's and Leslie's and Captain Jim's lives are most intimately implicated in the poetic passages.

As in *Anne of Green Gables*, we identify many of the descriptive passages in *Anne's House of Dreams* with Anne. This close identification explains why this novel can be filled with other people and their stories and yet make us feel that we are exploring Anne's thinking. The twenty-five-year-old Anne is the artistic fulfilment of the twelve-year-old beauty-loving Anne of the early Green Gables days. Perhaps Anne's recovered poetic dimension was what encouraged Montgomery herself to believe in 1917 that *Anne's House of Dreams* was the best book she had written thus far, including *Anne of Green Gables* and her own favourite, *The Story Girl*, written in 1911 (*Journals* 2: 222). Montgomery had not only recaptured something of the early flavour of *Anne of Green Gables*, but had seasoned it. At any rate, Anne's first view of her home is of the Four Winds Harbour. This description is typical of the novel's preoccupation with colour, precious stones and metals, and dreamy language. Elsewhere we also find sapphire, emerald, ruby, pearl, diamond, amber, gold, maize, crimson, scarlet, and the beloved purple. The fact that Montgomery had deliberately reworked this passage from one in a short story[2] suggests just how carefully she was setting the tone for the book's treatment of sea and home:

Her new home could not yet be seen; but before her lay Four Winds Harbour like a great, shining mirror of rose and silver. Far down, she saw its entrance between the bar of sand-dunes on one side and a steep, high, grim, red-sandstone cliff on the other. Beyond the bar the sea, calm and austere, dreamed in the afterlight. The little fishing village, nestled in the cove where the sand-dunes met the harbour shore, looked like a great opal in the haze. The sky over them was like a jewelled cup from which the dusk was pouring; the air was crisp with the compelling tang of the sea, and the whole landscape was infused with the subtleties of a sea evening. (29)

The riches of a 'rose and silver' mirror, the 'great opal,' the 'jewelled cup' work together with the homey 'dreamed,' 'nestled,' and 'infused,' and the bracing 'crisp' and 'tang' to suggest the welcoming beauty and changefulness of Anne's new spirit-home by the sea. Even her new little 'house of dreams' is part of the shore, resembling 'a big, creamy seashell stranded on the harbour shore' (32). Everywhere Anne looks she is greeted with the sea and shore and their multiple meanings.

At times the novel seems a kind of hymn to the shore, as though Montgomery, the homesick exile from Prince Edward Island, recaptures all her remembered and beloved past in rhapsodies about the sea. After her marriage in 1911 and subsequent move to Ontario, Montgomery made two vacation visits to P.E.I. before she wrote *Anne's House of Dreams*, one in 1913, and one in 1915. A letter to MacMillan about the 1913 visit sums up her rapture with the sea: 'I shall never forget my first glimpse of the sea again ... I was not prepared for the flood of emotion which swept over me when I saw it. I was stirred to the very deeps of my being – tears filled my eyes – I trembled! For a moment it seemed passionately to me that I could *never* leave it again' (*Letters* 68). Perhaps the sea became for Montgomery the essence of P.E.I. life itself, as she thought about her island and compared it with what she was much later to call 'smug opulent Ontario' (*Letters* 115). Montgomery could look to her own letters and journals for descriptions of the ocean's power – and separateness – which she celebrates in the fourth Anne novel. The narrator of Anne's story takes flight: 'The woods are never solitary – they are full of whispering, beckoning, friendly life. But the sea is a mighty soul, forever moaning of some great, unshareable sorrow, which shuts it up into itself for all eternity. We can never pierce its infinite mystery – we may only wander, awed and spell-bound, on the outer fringe of it ... The woods are human, but the sea is of the company of the archangels' (69–70). Since the sea is not predictable and cannot be tamed, human focus on it and identification with it involve power and mystery, too. Anne may turn to the shore as a replacement for Lover's Lane, but we never forget that she cannot be as intimate with the sea as with the woods. Something will always escape her – prod her to strange, sometimes even unwelcome fantasies.

For the most part in this novel, the sea is beautiful. Anne enjoys its 'sheeny shadows' and the 'curtain of violet gloom over the sand-dunes' (70); we enjoy the changing of the seasons by observing the change in lights and water. In spring, the beacon again 'begemmed the twilights' because the harbour is free of ice; the sea itself 'laughed and flashed and preened and allured, like a beautiful, coquettish woman' (137). Everywhere in the descriptions we find Montgomery's especial love – colour.

The sea and colour are essential to our appreciation of the novel's most complex character – Leslie Moore. Mary Rubio and Elizabeth Waterston have suggested that Leslie is the shadowed side of Montgomery's own mind (Afterword 282). Perhaps Anne and Leslie together are one personality, one psyche split into the ethereal and the passionate, the pink and the crimson. Certainly they operate as perfect complements; neither is complete without the softening or enriching of the other. Leslie's confessions to Anne and distrustful, even hostile responses to Anne's overtures sound very much like the self-distrust and self-loathing we all face when we examine minutely our own thoughts and prejudices. And Leslie's bitter experiences make her the life counterpart of Anne's as well – next to Leslie's, Anne's past sounds charmed, easy. Anne has never been made to suffer so hideously as Leslie has suffered.

Very like the innocent young going to war in Montgomery's own time, and like a survivor of abuse, Leslie is the victim of others' negligence, pain, or selfishness: at twelve she sees her younger brother crushed under the wheels of a tractor; at fourteen she discovers her father hanging from the parlour lamphook; at sixteen she marries a drunken, lascivious young man so that he will not foreclose the mortgage on her mother's farm (and her mother has urged her to make this self-sacrifice); at seventeen she becomes the caretaker of the look-alike cousin she believes to be her now imbecilic husband, who had gone to sea when he tired of Leslie and had (she thought) lost his memory and capacities in a drunken brawl. For years Leslie takes care of this supposed Dick Moore and is only released from imprisonment when an operation restores the man's memory. And here she meets Anne, newly, happily married to a man who seems in many ways to be her equal. Anne is immediately attracted to Leslie's sullen beauty, and the struggle between the bitter and the sweet begins. Perhaps the suggestion is that if Leslie can recover, the ravaged world, too, can recover. But it takes a special kind of love to restore life fully to Leslie, a love Montgomery would not have dreamed, in a domestic romance of 1917, of entrusting to another woman. Anne is only the initiator here – she is not herself the answer, and so her friendship with Leslie is not the final restorative. In keeping with the book's support of mating and pairing and conventional romantic love as parts of the homing instinct, the restored Leslie (or the reintegrated Montgomery?) must find an Other (male) in order to be fulfilled.

Whether we choose to see Leslie as counterpart to Anne or Montgomery or a separate individual or all of these, we can appreciate how Montgomery uses colour and the sea to make Leslie an intricate, passionate expression of Four Winds life. Romantic setting and colouring reflect romantic intensity.

Anne's first glimpse of Leslie establishes the colour pattern for the novel – Leslie's cold beauty is offset by red, the emblem of her restrained passion: 'her figure, in its plain print gown, was magnificent; and her lips were as crimson as the bunch of blood-red poppies she wore at her belt' (31). Anne does not know who the woman is, but shortly after, when she notices the gray house close to their own, whose 'windows peered, like shy, seeking eyes, into the dusk' (34), Anne is suddenly reminded of the mysterious beauty. Montgomery is using what was to be one of her favourite devices – having a house express the personality of its owner; we know that the beauty must live in the gray house, and we suspect that her coolness masks a shyness and eagerness Anne will touch. When Anne and Gilbert make their first visit to Captain Jim's lighthouse, the association between red and Leslie is reinforced in a lengthy description of sunset colour and its reflection on the windows of Leslie's house:

The day had begun sombrely in gray cloud and mist, but it had ended in a pomp of scarlet and gold. Over the western hills beyond the harbour were amber deeps and crystalline shallows, with the fire of sunset below. The north was a mackerel sky of little, fiery golden clouds. The red light flamed on the white sails of a vessel gliding down the channel, bound to a southern port in a land of palms. Beyond her, it smote upon and incarnadined the shining, white, grassless faces of the sand-dunes. To the right, it fell on the old house among the willows up the brook, and gave it for a fleeting space casements more splendid than those of an old cathedral. They glowed out of its quiet and grayness like the throbbing, blood-red thoughts of a vivid soul imprisoned in a dull husk of environment. (67–8)

The exotic association of a 'land of palms,' the use of the dramatic word 'incarnadined,' which may bring to mind Lady Macbeth's famous lines,[3] the association of the romantic word 'casement' with the lines from Keats's 'Ode to a Nightingale' ('Charm'd magic casements, opening on the foam / Of perilous seas in faery lands forlorn' 69–70) that Anne has already quoted (*AHD* 33), the comparison of the farmhouse windows with those of a cathedral – all these devices operate together with the fire imagery and the heightened colours – scarlet, gold, amber, red – to make us concentrate on the power of the 'soul imprisoned in a dull husk of environment.' The repetition of the reds and this second use of the house to suggest Leslie's passion prepare us to accept and be intrigued by the mysterious woman, who is so unlike, yet drawn to, the often ethereal Anne.

When Anne does finally meet Leslie, on the shore, she is struck by her 'splendid hair ... bound about her head with a crimson ribbon' and by her 'fine curves' encircled by 'a vivid girdle of red silk' (80). When a shaft of sunlight breaks through the clouds and falls on Leslie's hair, 'For a moment she seemed the spirit of the sea personified – all its mystery, all its passion, all its elusive charm' (80–1). Here Montgomery brings together unmistakably the associations of red and sea we continue to explore with Leslie in a number of ways. Much later in the novel, when Anne takes Owen Ford to meet Leslie, who rents him a room for the summer, Montgomery again uses the red and the sea together to suggest the powerful impression Leslie makes on Owen. This time Leslie wears a cheap cream-coloured dress, but around her waist is a 'girdle of crimson.' The narrator explains: 'Leslie was never without her touch of crimson. She had told Anne that she never felt satisfied without a gleam of red somewhere about her, if it were only a flower. To Anne, it always seemed to symbolise Leslie's glowing, pent-up personality, denied all expression save in that flaming glint' (177). The use of 'pent-up personality' here deliberately evokes the 'imprisoned soul' of the earlier description, and we are thus led to share in the analysis of Leslie and to understand her depth.

Owen does not know what we know and what Anne knows, but he sees Leslie's 'ivory-tinted' arms and her hair shining 'like a flame' against a 'purple sky, flowering with stars over the harbour' (177) and he is staggered into saying to Anne: 'I – I never saw anything like her ... I wasn't prepared – I didn't expect – good heavens, one *doesn't* expect a goddess for a landlady! Why, if she were clothed in a gown of sea-purple, with a rope of amethysts in her hair, she would be a veritable sea-queen' (177). Owen's appreciation of Leslie's beauty is one thing, but his transmutation of the purple sky and stars into 'a rope of amethysts' and his instinctive recognition of her goddess power and kinship with the sea recommend him as the appropriately sensitive romantic partner Leslie has never yet known. Thus it is that Montgomery uses colour and symbol in this novel to enrich our understanding of spiritual affinity and love of beauty.

Heartsick, much later, and confessing to Anne his love for Leslie, Owen believes he is saying farewell forever to Four Winds. Notice how Montgomery uses colour and image here to remind us of Leslie's potentially beneficent presence, promising through the description what the story cannot yet reveal: 'Silence and twilight fell over the garden. Far away the sea was lapping gently and monotonously on the bar. The wind of evening in the poplars sounded like some sad, weird, old rune – some broken dream of old memories. A slender shapely young aspen rose up before them against the fine maize and emerald and paling rose of the western sky, which brought out every leaf and twig in a dark, tremulous, elfin loveliness' (196). The young aspen, with its background of 'paling rose' suggests Leslie herself; as background sound, the sorrow of the wind is not so constant as the sea. We know love will be possible for the paired spirits, who seem to belong together as do the very colours and sounds of nature.

And when Owen comes back to a free Leslie, he declares his love for her in a chapter entitled 'Red Roses.' She explains her preference to Owen: 'I love the red roses ... Anne likes the pink ones best, and Gilbert likes the white. But I want the crimson ones. They satisfy some craving in me as no other flower does' (273). Montgomery uses the symbol of romantic passion to mark Leslie's search and release; with Owen Ford, the full weight of the novel's colours and scenes suggest, Leslie will explore the riches of her intensity. Purple and crimson, pink and white, like seeks like.

Montgomery uses the sea and sea fog to suggest bonds between Anne and Leslie. We associate Leslie with mysterious mist as well as with the tumult of the ocean and the energy of the colour red. The first time Leslie visits Anne and Gilbert, she comes when 'moonlit mists were hanging over the harbour and curling like silver ribbons along the seaward glens' (100). Two important scenes in the story of Anne's and Leslie's relationship use sea fog to suggest the blurred borders between fantasy and reality; between the psyches of the very different women; between hopelessness and faith. A few pages after Montgomery uses the sea mist to usher Leslie into the Blythe household, we find Anne alone in her house of dreams, almost afraid of an unearthly 'shrouding fog' (104) and its chilling fantasies. The ghostly quiet makes her think she can hear 'the footsteps of unseen guests' (105), and she decides to visit Leslie and leave her little house to its own vigil. Anne steals through the uncanny fog and slips unheard into Leslie's house, but there she finds Leslie 'weeping horribly – with low, fierce, choking sobs, as if some agony in her soul were trying to tear itself out' (106). Anne slips away unseen, instinctively realizing that Leslie would never forgive her witnessing such abandoned grief. Montgomery's use of the eerie fog is a truly masterly touch – it is as though the sea itself is in torment and veils its mourning; it is as though Anne is drawn to the centre of the chilling mist because she is somehow bound to Leslie's powerful emotions. But Anne has not yet experienced an adult grief that privileges her to claim kinship with Leslie's pain, and so she must leave Leslie without comforting her.

Anne is initiated into adult grief with the death of her day-old baby girl. Drawing on her own agonized experience of the death of her second child (*Journals* 2: 151–4), Montgomery writes with poignant economy and depicts the gladness and then the bitterness of the birth and death of little Joyce. Fog is the herald of death. Anne is at first oblivious to the condition of the 'wee, white lady' (149), but 'Then, as subtly, and coldly, and remorselessly as a sea-fog stealing landward, fear crept into her heart' (148) and she realizes that Joyce is not going to live. The use of the sea fog here reminds us of Leslie's own bitterness and pain, and we know that Anne has now endured one of the rites of passage that will rend the fog between her and Leslie.

And when another crisis comes to Leslie – her love for Owen Ford and her belief that she has shamed herself by loving him, since she is not free – we find another eerie fog. But this time, in keeping with the shift from isolation to kinship, Anne experiences the fog as a thing of charming fantasies, benign supernatural forces. In this enchanted mist Anne stumbles upon Leslie, who is walking restlessly on the shore to fight off her agony over Owen Ford's departure. Unlike the earlier eerie fog, which showed Leslie weeping and in company with chill and death, this fog suggests fairy-tale magic, unexpected reshapings. And the reader thus experiences through suggestion and association and direct reading the change in Leslie's soul. Anne is now the more knowledgeable of the two, having heard Owen's confession, and Leslie greets her as a spiritual comforter. Having passed through her own 'shrouding fog,' Anne can perceive and help to transform Leslie's morbid delusions into endurable sorrow.

When, earlier, we followed Anne through the ghostly fog and saw her barred from Leslie's confidence, Montgomery encouraged us to feel with Anne the chill of inadequacy – the recognition of pain and sorrow beyond our power to relieve or heal. Leslie must be left alone. After her own immersion in the fog Anne can discern new shapes in its shadows, and we recognize that in the spiritual integration of the two women – in the equal friendship they can now experience – Montgomery is showing us the strength of the mature, loving woman. Through faith and love they can endure grief and can share in the joys of life that are also a part of the Four Winds harmony and change.

When Anne arrives on the shore this time the scene is set for magic: 'It was warm for September, and the late afternoon had been very foggy; but a full moon had in part lessened the fog and transformed the harbour and the gulf and the surrounding shores into a strange, fantastic, unreal world of pale silver mist, through which everything loomed phantom-like' (198–9). The shapes Anne sees and the sounds she hears are bewitching, and we know something unusual is going to happen. She sees a real schooner as a 'spectral ship'; seagulls' cries are now the 'cries of the souls of doomed seamen'; foam from the waves is really 'elfin things stealing up from the sea-caves'; sand dunes are 'sleeping giants'; altogether 'It was delightful – romantic – mysterious to be roaming here alone on this enchanted shore' (199). What a perfect setting for Leslie's confession: romantic, mysterious, magical, perhaps a little dangerous. Leslie's pain in not something to be amused by, and Montgomery makes sure that we understand that though the outcome (as suggested) may eventually be positive, for the time being Leslie is in agony. Her language of confession is characteristically physical. She feels as though life has 'struck me a terrible blow.' 'When I turned back into the house this morning after he had gone the solitude struck me like a blow in the face' (201). To the sympathetic Anne, Leslie confides: 'Oh, when I think that I will never see him again I feel as if a great brutal hand had twisted itself among my heartstrings, and was wrenching them' (201–2). And, somewhat like the old Leslie, she wishes to cover herself with the fog and be invisible: 'Oh, I wish this mist would never lift – I wish I could just stay in it forever, hidden away from every living being' (202–3). The difference between this vigil in the fog and her earlier tearful one is that Leslie now has a friend who can understand, who shares her sorrows and her values and can take her back to safer ground while the fog lasts. When Leslie and Owen are finally together as free woman and man, we know that there will be other soul fogs, but they, too, will be of this latter kind, containing strange shapes only faith and love can make plain.

Without Leslie Moore, Anne on her own in this novel would be pale indeed. As I have said, Anne seems very much alive partly because of the power of the nature descriptions and partly because of the strength of the characters around her. Twinned with Leslie for much of the novel, Anne seems as necessary to Four Winds as the lovely lights and gentle ripples of the sea. At their very first meeting Leslie identifies herself with the thunder and riot of the sea: 'I don't like the sea so well when it's calm and quiet. I like the struggle – and the crash – and the noise' (82). Anne, on the other hand, characteristically enjoys the quieter beauties of the shore; true to her domestic bias in this home-celebrating novel, Anne delights in the sea she gazes on from her sewing room: 'The effects of light and shadow all along these shores are wonderful ... My little sewing room looks out on the harbour, and I sit at its window and feast my eyes. The colours and shadows are never the same two minutes together' (84). Montgomery is careful to make both the passion and the gentle love essential to a balanced Four Winds life – just as she carefully alternates tragedy (or perhaps melodrama) with comedy in the construction of the story itself.

Towards the end of the novel Montgomery reinforces the harmony between Anne's and Leslie's differences in a number of ways. They are now both Madonnas (247) in spirit as they share Anne's little Jem; even their laughter harmonizes: 'Anne's laughter was silver and Leslie's golden, and the combination of the two was as satisfactory as a perfect chord in music' (260). Captain Jim's farewell to the house of dreams involves a ritual blessing of these two women. Captain Jim has known all the brides and women of the little house and now reveres the home spirit he feels with Leslie and Anne guarding the hearth fire and the traditions he has honoured all his long life. Captain Jim's speech encapsulates the message of the novel – the praise to home and love that Montgomery depicts throughout. Read as her message to a war-torn world, and delivered as it is by one of her favourite character creations,[4] a rugged, golden-hearted figure right out of the best in Dickens's tradition of ragged heroes, Captain Jim's speech and blessing suggest the reason for Montgomery's twinning of Leslie and Anne:

'I see happiness for all of you – all of you – for Leslie and Mr. Ford – and the

Doctor here and Mistress Blythe – and Little Jem – and children that ain't born yet but will be. Happiness for you all – though, mind you, I reckon, you'll have your troubles and worries and sorrows, too. They're bound to come – and no house, whether it's a palace or a little house of dreams, can bar 'em out. But they won't get the better of you if you face 'em *together* with love and trust. You can weather any storm with them two for compass and pilot.'

The old man rose suddenly and placed one hand on Leslie's head and one on Anne's.

'Two good, sweet women,' he said. 'True and faithful and to be depended on. Your husbands will have honour in the gates because of you – your children will rise up and call you blessed in the years to come.' (274)

This sentimental scene works in the context of the novel because Captain Jim is such a dear old man, even if he does seem a little overdrawn at times. And the scene works because Anne and Leslie are clearly the heirs apparent to the tradition of home love that Captain Jim's own story epitomizes. As he passes on to them his accumulated wisdom and love, Anne and Leslie become the mothers of the human race who fulfil the words of 'The Song of the Pilgrims' from Rupert Brooke's poem that Montgomery used as a motto for this novel: 'Our kin / Have built them temples, and therein / Pray to the gods we know; and dwell / In little houses lovable.' Anne and Leslie are clearly emblematic of continuing traditions of love and home; they are one bright promise in a world whose changes can seem destructive.

In fact, Montgomery uses Captain Jim throughout the novel as a kind of living emblem of chivalry and kindness and truth. His love of the sea and his love of Lost Margaret, who disappeared on the sea, make him seem the incarnation of devotion and vigilance. Naturally he is the keeper of the light: as the 'beacon cuts swathes of light ... in a circle over the fields and the harbour, the sandbar and the gulf' (68) it is a constant reminder of hope and home. Since we identify the lighthouse with Captain Jim, we find that, even after he dies, the lighthouse continues to be a reminder of his beneficence. On the very last page of the novel, as Anne and Gilbert say goodbye to their house of dreams, 'The lighthouse star was gleaming northward' (291). Throughout the novel light plays an important part, and Montgomery ties the images together with the lighthouse (and, by both metaphor and metonymy, with Captain Jim); she uses the light itself, the lighthouse 'star,' stars, and firelight to suggest the various symbolic interpretations of illumination in darkness.

The lighthouse beacon is one of the charms Gilbert describes to Anne when he tells her about their new home (13); firelight greets the bride and bridegroom when they cross the threshold of their new home (32); when Anne meets Captain Jim, their souls commune as two lighthouses – 'Kindred spirit flashed recognition to kindred spirit' (34); even in the comfort of her bed Anne has time in the stormy November evenings to think of the 'great, faithful light, whirling through the darkness unafraid' (110); when Anne rapturously identifies their homelight, Gilbert calls it 'our beacon' (113); Owen Ford is enraptured with Four Winds even before he sees Leslie when he hears voices across 'a starlit sea' as 'The big light flashed and beaconed' (176); love illumines Leslie as a 'rosy lamp might shine through a flawless vase of alabaster' (190); Gilbert knows Captain Jim is dead when he spots the 'baleful star' of the lighthouse beacon burning after the sun has risen (281). Perhaps one of the most peculiar uses of language in the book is found in the passage describing Leslie's vigil the night she realizes Owen Ford loves her and has come to ask her to marry him. Montgomery uses rhyme to punctuate the image of Leslie and the light: 'But she watched the great revolving *light* bestarring the short hours of the summer *night*, and her eyes grew soft and *bright* and young once *more. Nor*, when Owen Ford came next *day*, to ask her to go with him to the *shore*, did she *say* him *nay*' (emphasis added 266). The first sentence sounds poetic; the second, like comic doggerel. Perhaps Montgomery was – even rhythmically – juxtaposing serious and comic. At any rate, we know that throughout the novel sea and symbol, character and rhythm reinforce the lessons about love and home and trust.

Everything in this novel is made to harmonize; all things, it is suggested, change in unexpected and (if we are patient and faithful) often delightful ways. In the middle of the book we experience such a harmonizing of images and attitude. New Year's Eve day has been 'one of those bright, cold dazzling winter days, which bombard us with their brilliancy, and command our admiration but never our love. The sky was sharp and blue; the snow diamonds sparkled insistently; the stark trees were bare and shameless, with a kind of brazen beauty; the hills shot assaulting lances of crystal' (123). But at the end of the day, 'a certain pensiveness fell over her beauty which dimmed yet intensified it; sharp angles, glittering points, melted away into curves and enticing gleams. The white harbour put on soft grays and pinks; the far-away hills turned amethyst' (123–4). The landscape here is a metaphor for life in general and Leslie in particular. Under the warming influence of Anne's friendship, she softens and becomes suffused with colour, not just marked by one red glint. Immediately after the description of the dusk, we find that, along with the lighthouse beacon, the sky is lit by the 'brilliant star of evening,' 'Venus, glorious and golden' (124). It is Leslie who recounts the myth about the shadow of Venus: that if you see it, within a year 'life's most wonderful gift will come to you' (124). It is Venus, of course, who triumphs in the love of Owen and Leslie, and Anne reminds Leslie of the shadow of Venus when Owen returns to woo her. On this New Year's Eve vigil, Anne watches Leslie transformed from cool restraint to a whirling Viking woman with 'crimson cheek and glowing eye and grace of motion' (127). Within the lighthouse itself, Captain Jim's valiant hearth fire warms acquaintance into friendship; loving friendship begins Venus's work. Montgomery brings shore, lighthouse, colour, and star together to suggest how all things illumine and modify each other if love (or the loving eye) is present.

Montgomery's poetic book is also wise. It is interesting that no single character in the novel is infallible or without a touch of forgivable perversity. Leslie is sullen in her unhappiness and is also incapable of seeing faults in her own family; Miss Cornelia is merciless in her faulting of men for all the ills in and out of Four Winds, and most particularly here she believes that Gilbert should not meddle with (the supposed) Dick Moore's old head injuries; Anne also opposes Gilbert's interference with Dick Moore (and thus both Anne and Miss Cornelia would have been condemning Leslie to an unbroken career of miserable servitude); Gilbert is too quick and smug early in the story in judging the unhappiness with her husband of a woman he does not know. He remarks to Anne about Leslie: 'A fine woman would have made the best of it. Mrs Moore has evidently let it make her bitter and resentful' (87). And even lovable old Captain Jim misjudges women. Much as he admires them, he believes them incapable of serious thinking or work. The fact that his story is created and told by a woman makes his own comment the more interesting: 'Captain Jim thought women were delightful creatures, who ought to have the vote, and everything else they wanted, bless their hearts; but he did not believe they could write ... "A writing woman never knows when to stop; that's the trouble. The p'int of good writing is to know when to stop"' (184). Even chivalry (especially chivalry?) has its blind spots.

The fact that no one is always right seems a deliberate part of Montgomery's philosophy in the novel. Just as Four Winds is an idealized version of the world – a place where all things harmonize, where even ugliness and violence are admitted, though they do not triumph – so it is also a miniature of the world Montgomery knew, and in it all people have lessons to learn or gaps in their understanding that others may discern but that they themselves may be incapable of discerning.

Unlike the pedantic narrator in *Anne of Avonlea*, the narrator in *Anne's House of Dreams* shares insights with an equal. From first to last the book assumes in the reader a sympathetic interest in what motivates people to thwart themselves or others and what makes people capable of giving and loving. The interactions of the characters of course explore these conflicting tendencies fully, but the narrator makes separate commentary occasionally (in addition to speaking through the numerous descriptions). For example, notice this brilliant little sketch used to suggest the persistent gloom of a Mrs Jasper Bell: 'She belonged to the type which always has a stringy black feather in its hat and straggling locks of hair on its neck' (12). In a more serious vein, when Leslie faces the decision about an operation on Dick Moore that may restore his faculties, she withdraws from everyone, and the narrator wisely observes: 'When one great passion seizes possession of the soul all other feelings are crowded aside' (228).

For the most part in the novel we experience the kindly knowledge of human nature through the created exchanges between characters – the characters come to realizations or the narrator presents a scene so that we come to the realization though the character cannot. Anne's agony over the death of her baby is wrenching to read, but we see that in saying all the bitter things death has made her feel, Anne is on the way to recovery. Montgomery had learned to confide in her journal the kinds of things that here are expressed by the narrator and then shared openly – after great effort – by the characters. The healing, the novel shows, comes with the expression. The narrator describes Anne's slow recovery: 'Anne's convalescence was long, and made bitter for her by many things. The bloom and sunshine of the Four Winds world grated harshly on her; and yet, when the rain fell heavily, she pictured it beating so mercilessly down on that little grave across the harbour; and when the wind blew around the eaves she heard sad voices in it she had never heard before' (150). This suffering and depression are exactly what Montgomery experienced over the death of her own baby. But when Anne expresses her bitterness to Marilla we know that she will begin to recover. This bitterness, too, is what grieved Montgomery and what as a minister's wife, she (probably) could confide only to her journal: 'Why should she be born at all – why should any one be born at all – if she's better off dead? I *don't* believe it is better for a child to die at birth than to live its life out – and love and be loved – and enjoy and suffer – and do its work – and develop a character that would give it a personality in eternity. And how do you know it was God's will? Perhaps it was just a thwarting of His purpose by the Power of Evil. We can't be expected to be resigned to *that*' (AHD 151; *Journals* 2: 153). Marilla is shocked; but, having said the worst of what she thinks, having literally expressed the venom from herself, Anne regains the will to live. Again, when we remember that this novel was written in war-time and think of the despair facing the people and nations who had to struggle daily to feed the will to live, we realize the context in which Montgomery offers Anne's grief (though the novel itself is set some twenty years before the war). In the Four Winds idealized miniature of the world, grief and suffering are expressed, not repressed, and healing is allowed time.

Exposing evil is what cures Leslie of her morbid, sullen anger. Anne hears Leslie's story from Miss Cornelia, but Leslie herself can speak of her brother's death, her father's suicide, her hideous marriage, and her resentment of Anne's happiness only after Anne has lost little Joyce. And when Leslie is able to speak of the old pain and the recent ones, we see in action the purging and healing Anne herself has undergone. Leslie says, 'Talking it all out seems to have done away with it, somehow. It's very strange – and I thought it so real and bitter. It's like opening the door of a dark room to show some hideous creature you've believed to be there – and when the light streams in your monster turns out to have been just a shadow, vanishing when the light comes. It will never come between us again' (162). In the thousands of books that have been published since 1917 about the facing and dispelling of fears is there anything plainer than this?

At the end of the chapter 'Barriers Swept Away,' Anne and Leslie make a spiritual pact – one that foreshadows the ritual blessing Captain Jim will confer near the end of the book. Here the two mature women make a vow that is the self-reflective complement of the romantic oath Anne and Diana made in the Barry garden in Green Gables days. Anne and Leslie are in Anne's own garden, and in response to Leslie's question about whether Anne, having heard all the truth of Leslie's hatreds and pains, still wants to be friends, Anne replies: 'I am your friend and you are mine, for always ... Such a friend as I never had before. I have had many dear and beloved friends – but there is something in you, Leslie that I never found in anyone else. You have more to offer me in that rich nature of yours, and I have more to give you than I had in my careless girlhood. We are both women – and friends forever' (165). Montgomery has suggested all along that they are complementary spirits, and now they have allied themselves permanently; after this point, their joint story is all healing and rebuilding, culminating in the blessing of Captain Jim.

Montgomery wisely steers clear of too many of these solemn vows and blessings. As in the best of all her writing, here we find, too, the solemn and the serious alternating with the comic. The harmony of Four Winds, in fact, depends on this alternation as surely as it relies on the rhythm of the sea. The most amusing character is Miss Cornelia. Just when Montgomery is establishing the sea as the heartbeat of Four Winds, Gilbert describes Miss Cornelia's arrival in a way that makes her seem elemental to the place: 'Do I or do I not see a full-rigged ship sailing up our lane?' (55). Throughout the narrative Miss Cornelia offers wonderfully pungent remarks: of their minister – 'I consider him a reverend jackass' (62); on the solidarity of women – 'We've got enough to endure at the hands of the men, the Lord knows, so I hold we hadn't ought to clapper-claw one another' (90); on the vote for women – 'I'm not hankering after the vote, believe *me* ... *I* know what it is to clean up after the men' (120); on the likelihood that Dick Moore did *not* get his head smashed in a drunken brawl – 'Pigs *may* whistle, but they've poor mouths for it' (227). Montgomery uses Miss Cornelia as an antidote to sentimentality and melancholy; her bustling energy makes her, the narrator tells us, personify 'the comedy that ever peeps around the corner at the tragedy of life' (197). Again and again in the novel her Dickensian self-contradictoriness (heart of gold / rough tongue) reminds us to enjoy the beauty and the perversity of human interactions.

Since poetry plays a large part in the descriptive passages and in the rhythms of *Anne's House of Dreams*, it is not surprising to find poetry quoted often, as it is in most of Montgomery's novels. But here we find a fascination with Tennyson in particular. Montgomery makes (at least) twenty-four allusions to the Bible (twelve serious and twelve jocular) and some nine playful references to Shakespeare; in addition we find Pope, Blake, Coleridge, Keats, Burns, Wordsworth, James Montgomery, Mrs Hemans, Longfellow, and Robert Browning (Wilmshurst 26–9). There are ten references to Tennyson: two to 'Ulysses,' one to *In Memoriam*, one to 'The Lotos-Eaters,' one to the 'The Miller's Daughter,' one to 'Oenone,' and four to 'Crossing the Bar.' Three of these works are preoccupied with the sea – Ulysses addresses his old mariners and urges them to follow him on new adventures rather than to stagnate at home; the shipwrecked mariners in 'The Lotos-Eaters' become incapable of action as they dwindle into passivity and memory on the enchanted beaches of the lotus land; in 'Crossing the Bar' Tennyson uses the ocean and the last voyage as images for death, and life beyond it, for a soul satisfied to have struggled with truth and right during this life. We recognize much of Captain Jim in the poems – and he himself identifies with them, choosing 'Crossing the Bar' as one of the wisest expressions of acceptance and faith he has heard. Ulysses' yearning is what the land-locked sailor must feel with old age, and the apparent passivity of 'The Lotos-Eaters' is what Anne uses to characterize the apparent passivity of Four Winds to the newcomer, Owen Ford (175).

The truth of the novel is reflected in the simple but profound imagery of 'Crossing the Bar,' with its faith in the divine pilot. We are perhaps reminded of its language when we hear Captain Jim confer his blessing on Leslie and Anne. In the last stanza of the poem we find: 'For though from out our bourne of Time and Place / The flood may bear me far, / I hope to see my Pilot face to face / When I have crost the bar' (13–16). Captain Jim advises the young people to use love and trust because 'You can weather any storm with them two for compass and pilot' (274). When Captain Jim moves beyond Four Winds, he hopes to meet 'face to face' the great Pilot whose gifts of love and trust he has himself used all his life. There is a yearning in Tennyson's poetry that is wholly appropriate to the self-searching and self-discovery of the novel's main characters. And each character ultimately finds something of the promised peace of 'Crossing the Bar.' Captain Jim's life associations with the sea and the lighthouse beacon are thus reinforced in the poetic (and thematic) echoes of the novel.

Anne's House of Dreams is a very carefully constructed novel; even the sensational look-alike-cousin mix-up that frees Leslie is welcome and believable in the context of Four Winds. The novel begins with a leave-taking from the Green Gables world of childhood, and it ends with the leave-taking of the early married joy and sorrow of the house of dreams. Montgomery drew from favourite writings – prose and poetry – of her own to construct the Four Winds 'enchanted shore' (199). It is a novel about self-discovery and self-integration; Leslie and Anne as individuals or as parts of the same spirit come to recognize their greater powers. What is distressing about the book, when we examine it closely, is the final disappearance of Anne as she was suggested to be in *Anne of Green Gables*. We do not find here just the loss of childhood or the acceptance of adult sorrows; try to reinterpret as we will, we are bound to see that this Anne is not as free as the earlier Anne. This Anne day-dreams while Captain Jim and Gilbert talk about Real Ideas; this Anne downplays her writing ability and says she has a little knack of putting together pretty thoughts but could not, oh my, write something really serious or important. Not like Owen Ford, for instance. Anne endures the death of her child and yet claims to herself that she does not know tragedy and therefore cannot write Captain Jim's story! While Captain Jim's own dismissal of women's writing seems funny in the story, since Montgomery is writing *his* story, Anne's admission of inadequacy seems like a betrayal of old dreams and faith. And this dreamy Anne dismisses politics as meaningless beside the cooing of her little Jem. When the men talk excitedly over the surprising Liberal majority, Anne's response suggests the (irritating) stereotype of the contented little homemaker. Anne 'was not much excited over the tidings. Little Jem had said "Wow-ga" that morning. What were principalities and powers, the rise and fall of dynasties, the overthrow of Grit or Tory, compared with that miraculous occurrence?' (251). Montgomery's tone is mocking, and Anne is the object of it, and readers of the 1990s may ask themselves if Montgomery's depiction of the harmony of Four Winds isn't just a little too predictably diminishing of the female.

But there is, as always with Montgomery, another side to the mockery.

After all, the whole book asks, where is the virtuous and admirable life? Captain Jim cannot write his own story, but he is the wise and beloved and honoured man. Anne is not a powerful writer but she has a powerful nurturing spirit and a genius for friendship and is the complement for Leslie. Gilbert's professional life would be hollow without the house of dreams to come home to. And after all, the capitulation into marriage of the supposed man-hater Miss Cornelia reminds us that the book is determinedly genial in its treatment of life's possibilities. Miss Cornelia's dismissal of the vote as a panacea must have galled suffragists of Montgomery's time[5] – but Miss Cornelia's scepticism about what the vote could *do* sounds very much like the most radical of feminist commentary today (Johnson). Even Anne's dismissal of politics as of no consequence in comparison with the development of her baby sounds more like an affirmation of an 'ethic of caring' (Noddings 79–103) than a deliberate diminution of Anne. And didn't war in Europe illustrate ably where (male) partisan politics can lead?

And so we continue to read Montgomery. In this last decade of the twentieth century we may not so readily endorse marriage and conventional romance as universally good (Kreps) – and we have Leslie's marriage to Dick Moore as a warning about inappropriate marriages even here – but we can appreciate that Montgomery's analysis of Leslie and Anne suggests a determination to explore what love and home can mean to the whole as well as to the tormented or to the grieving spirit. The magical backdrop and inspiration for this exploration is the sea and the shore of Montgomery's beloved and yearned-for Prince Edward Island. And perhaps that is part of the reason for the book's continuing appeal – it is written in the crisis of wartime by a woman separated from her roots and homeland. The poetic, loving descriptions make that romantic, wished-for, far-off home a reality – a place where the Four Winds light always flashes welcome and hope. Anne leaves at the end of the book, but she goes where she can still see the lighthouse 'star' – and readers are assured that Four Winds, with its harmonizing of harsh and sweet, is there any time they need it.

Heroism's Childhood:
Rainbow Valley

Anne's House of Dreams was written in the middle of the war as though there is no war in store for Anne. The novel is set some twenty years before the First World War, and Montgomery is careful not to include anachronistic, direct references to it. Yet the whole book is really a response to war – it demonstrates what the home fires mean, what the beacon of faith and trust can mean. In short, Montgomery's poetic novel suggests that love is an active force that can defeat evil. The Four Winds life is open to all who cherish the traditions of home and the interactions prompted by love and faith. The exploration of friendships focuses on (what Montgomery suggests to be) the yearnings closest to the human heart.

The next Anne book, *Rainbow Valley* (1919), makes a leap of thirteen years in the life of Four Winds, and it, too, is about traditions and love and home. But this fifth Anne novel is openly a war book. It is dedicated to three young men in Montgomery's parish who died in battle, and the book itself is constructed upon the values that Montgomery believed prompted Canada and Britain's other allies to fight against Germany. Even so, in the story the war itself is years away yet – this is a novel about the children who were to mature into the soldiers and the workers of the war.

For Montgomery, the Great War was a conflict between the powers of darkness and the powers of light, on a mythic scale (*Journals* 2: 150–270). Her novel about Anne's children and, more correctly, about the Meredith children, is a conscious rendering of the code of ethics that prepared Canada and the allies of Britain to fight against Germany. Like John Meredith and Anne Shirley Blythe in this novel supposedly about childhood, Montgomery believed that some fights must be fought. *Rainbow Valley* describes the moral childhood of the nations – and Montgomery hopes and suggests that, with such promising values and admirable souls winning adulthood through the battles against evil in Europe, the world could be, afterwards in peace, a better place than it had been.

Montgomery encourages us to believe that the sturdy children of Rainbow Valley hold within them the best of the past as well as their own fresh individuality. This patriotic novel shows how a romantic heritage of beauty, enchantment, love, and home is entrusted to the children who frequent the little valley below Ingleside. In this novel about values (most especially chivalry) and the childhood of free humanity, Anne is reduced to an echo, an image, a reminder of the past.

When the novel opens Anne (and Gilbert) have just returned from three months in the British Isles, and Miss Cornelia and Susan Baker are on hand to fill her in on all the local news.[1] Montgomery's immediate audience would no doubt have felt the intended jolt of the contrast between this depiction of a Europe before the war and the wartime Europe they had been reading of in the daily papers. The long-range suggestion is that Anne and Gilbert have seen Europe in peace and will remember vividly its beauty and goodness when the days of war come. Canada is thus allied with the best of Europe's traditions. But the most obvious function of the trip and the discussion of it is to give Anne a basis for her patriotic assertion about Canada: ' "The old world is very lovely and very wonderful. But we have come back very well satisfied with our own land. Canada is the finest country in the world, Miss Cornelia ... And old P.E.I. is the loveliest province in it and Four Winds the loveliest spot in P.E.I.," laughed Anne, looking adoringly out over the sunset splendour of glen and harbour and gulf' (17–18). The love of Canada and pride in the maple leaf are imprinted everywhere in the book.

Surrounding this idyllic Four Winds is the shadow of war to come; to

Montgomery's readers at the time the painful irony of many of the novel's references would have been plain. Anne remarks that thirteen-year-old Jem is 'passing through the stage where all boys hanker to be soldiers,' and Miss Cornelia refers to the Boer War as though it is the war to end all wars: 'Well, thank goodness, he'll never be a soldier ... I never approved of our boys going to that South African fracas. But it's over, and not likely anything of the kind will ever happen again. I think the world is getting more sensible' (74). But even if Miss Cornelia and Anne and even Mr Meredith all believe that the world is safe from war, there is the warning of a shrewd woman like Ellen West, who believes that the Kaiser of Germany is the most dangerous man alive. Montgomery creates in the novel both the false calm and the Cassandra-like warnings she evidently believed characterized the post-Boer War Canadian political environment.[2]

Jem Blythe wishes to be a soldier, dreamy Walter Blythe reads about battles and the Holy Grail, and the Meredith children are brought up with Tennyson's 'Sir Galahad.' We have only to remember the importance of Tennyson in Anne's stories to note the continuity of vision and ideal here with Anne's children and their dearest playmates. The young Anne Shirley delighted in the romance and chivalry of Tennyson's courtly love stories; the bride Anne Blythe discovered that Tennyson's noble, yearning lines perfectly captured the spirit of the sea and of Captain Jim's chivalry; Anne's children and their playmates are inspired by Tennyson's romantic battles and high quest. Tennyson, chivalry, and romance are parts of the Rainbow Valley code of ethics: love of honour, defence of women and the weak (alas, these two often seem synonymous), demand for truth, insistence on justice. The children of the new generation play with Tennyson's Camelot just as Anne Shirley did, but here fighting is central. Anne's early romantic visions included battle, but this generation embraces conflict in more immediate ways. Walter fights; Faith battles public opinion; Carl braves illness to reclaim his dignity; Mary Vance struggles for her very life.

The central dramatic event of this novel, and Montgomery's allegory for the First World War, is Walter Blythe's fist-fight with Dan Reese. A dastard belittles faith and womanhood (read here also beauty, truth, good, motherhood, kindness) and a young knight vanquishes him. The bully, Dan, calls Faith Meredith names, and Walter knows he must defend her.

But Walter hates ugliness and fighting and cannot bring himself to challenge Dan on the spot. He wrestles all night with his shame, and the next day, when Dan insults Faith and Walter's mother (Anne), Walter challenges him. They cannot fight that same day, but they agree to meet the next afternoon. Walter goes home to agonize over his fear of pain and dread of the blood he knows he will have to see. Walter cannot eat or go to the sand hills with Jem, and while Walter broods and steels himself to the coming battle, Jem (ignorant of the impending fight and unwilling to go to the sand hills without Walter) goes to his own attic chamber to 'picture himself a famous general, leading his troops to victory on some great battlefield' (188). Meanwhile, Faith goes home to confide in Una that in issuing the challenge to Dan, Walter looked 'just like Sir Galahad in that poem father read us on Saturday' (185).

This schoolhouse battle appears midway through the novel, when we are well acquainted with the quality of Walter's poetic visions and with his gallantry – he has already shielded Faith by pretending to his mother that it was his idea to race Faith through the village streets on pig-back (hence the epithet 'pig-girl' that Dan hurls at her). Walter knows from his reading and from the numerous kinds of discourse around him that chivalry demands the defence of Faith (and faith) and the sacrifice of his own feelings. The school battle would be meaningless in the context of the novel and in the larger context of the world war, if Walter, like Jem, had really relished fighting. It is Walter's hatred of fighting that makes his self-sacrifice so noble and his belief so inspiring. Walter, like the Sir Galahad to whom he is compared, is high-minded, using violence only because it is necessary. Montgomery's message is clear: the boy Walter Blythe, who detests blood, undertakes fighting in his clear-eyed recognition of right and honour, just as an adult Walter and other honourable men and women will also recognize the necessity to fight when faith is threatened and home values reviled by Germany.

The school battle itself is a swift victory for Walter because something almost murderous takes over his spirit. The schoolyard is not entirely jubilant in Walter's victory because the avenging energy that takes over him is itself terrifying. The little girls cry when they see Walter's expression, and Walter himself knows he could have killed Dan if something had not lifted the 'red mist' (190) from his eyes and made him look at Dan's spurting nose and realize where he was. Interestingly,

Montgomery does not openly pursue the murderous spirit battle obviously inspires in Walter. She suggests that vengeance – even in the name of honour – has a will of its own, but she then quickly turns the analysis away from it, and approves Walter's fight. Walter cannot stay for the other boys' approval, but runs to Rainbow Valley, where he 'felt none of the victor's joy, but he felt a certain calm satisfaction in duty done and honour avenged – mingled with a sickish qualm when he thought of Dan's gory nose' (191). But though Walter does not care to hear the boys' applause in the schoolyard, he is gratified by adult approval. The values of Montgomery's depicted culture are evident in the adult approbation of Walter's battle. Walter's chivalric code is endorsed by the Presbyterian minister (authority, tradition, religion, men) and by Anne (love, tradition, motherhood, women). Mr Meredith approves and then shares with Walter what is clearly the book's attitude to war. Walter asks if the minister thinks it is right to fight, and Mr Meredith says: 'Not always – and not often – but sometimes – yes, sometimes ... When womenkind are insulted for instance – as in your case. My motto, Walter, is, don't fight till you're sure you ought to, and *then* put every ounce of you into it' (191–2). Later Anne has much the same reaction and acts out in her ministrations to her young son the nurturing role traditionally assigned to women: 'she sympathized with him and told him she was glad he had stood up for her and Faith, and she anointed his sore spots and rubbed cologne on his aching head' (192). Walter tells her, 'You're *worth* standing up for' (192). However appalling (or, alas, welcome) we may now find these sentimentalized assumptions about males, females, and conflict, we can see the brutal truth of what Montgomery's story (perhaps partly unconsciously) suggests: chivalry and mothering shape the soldiers who will themselves fight wars to defend chivalry and mothering.

All the children of *Rainbow Valley* believe in chivalry and fight for what they perceive to be truth and goodness, each in a different way. While the code of ethics of the novel may seem to exclude an active expression of chivalry by the females, Montgomery shows that both chivalry and fighting come in many, surprising forms. The girls, too, are crusaders. The most obvious and vigorous champion of right is Faith. She mounts the pulpit to explain to a thunderstruck congregation that her father is not responsible for his children's bad behaviour; terrified but determined she goes to wealthy and notoriously cantankerous Norman

Douglas and asks that he return to church and contribute to her father's salary; she writes a lengthy explanatory letter to the local newspaper explaining to shocked parishioners and local gossips alike why she did not wear stockings to church one Sunday. Faith speaks out, and she is clearly the woman warrior of this novel, the perfect female counterpart in spirit and (limited) vision for Jem Blythe.

No goody-goody, Faith has spunk and fire and a keen sense of humour; her brand of valour is particularly appealing because it is not so strictly high-minded as Walter's. The episode about her pet rooster, Adam, and the unctuous Rev. Mr Perry is a good example of how Faith's sense of justice is tempered by mischief. Old Aunt Martha murders Adam so that she can serve the visiting minister a chicken dinner. Faith can barely sit through the meal as Mr Perry (admittedly ignorant that Adam had been a pet) shows off his plump white hands while he carves and lectures to the children about good behaviour and the models his own children are. We are reminded by Faith's boiling rebelliousness of the young Jane Eyre's response to the Rev. Mr Brocklehurst. But in this comic episode, Faith gets revenge. After dinner, standing before the fire, Mr Perry lectures Faith on her rudeness; Faith watches silently as Mr Perry's coat-tails get hot, smoke, and then burst into flame. How the young Jane Eyre would have enjoyed watching the black pillar Brocklehurst with his coat-tails on fire!

While Faith can be mischievous, she is almost invariably kind. When blue-legged, barefooted Lida Marsh of the harbour sits down on a tombstone to enjoy a chat with Faith and Una, Faith cannot bear what she imagines to be Lida's conscious misery and pained neglect. She strips off her own boots and stockings and gives them to Lida, never dreaming that not one of the harbour children has shoes in the spring or that Lida will take them off to save for special occasions as soon as she is out of sight of the manse children and will walk through freezing slush back to the harbour as unconcernedly as she had come. Faith is generous and impulsive, and she is meant to be seen as a crusader for goodness as valiant and gallant in her own way as Walter is in his.

But 'in her own way' is a very important distinction in the novel and in our understanding. Recognizing Faith's valour should not dull us to the fact that even in the story Faith is valiant in a different way from Walter or Jem because she is a girl. Chivalry imposes strict divisions between the sexes. Faith's treatment of Mr Perry is doubly daring because she is female – we enjoy her revenge, understanding the special insubordination and pluck it represents. But we should not forget the importance of sex roles in other episodes where to be female is to be helpless. If Walter is to be the champion, Faith must be a victim and powerless. When Faith flouts authority and goes to church bare-legged rather than wear hideous, scratchy, striped woollen stockings, she causes an uproar in the congregation and community. Ladies do not show bare legs (notice the largely unexplored contrast with working-class Lida Marsh). Similarly, Faith and Una are expected to show fear and be useless in their fright, while Jerry and Carl are expected to resist any behaviour considered weak (and therefore female).[3] Montgomery is not necessarily endorsing a diminution of the female, but we see in the story that chivalry demands certain limitations for the female, just as it demands certain rigidity from the males. Montgomery's story cannot have it both ways – rejecting a part of chivalry while supporting its values. Faith's energy may show Montgomery's efforts in the story to stretch the role of the female, but chivalry is exacting, and Faith can rebel or fight only as Anne Shirley rebelled – within limits. (It is only a matter of time before Faith, like Anne, is absorbed by the various roles and expectations designed for her. In *Rilla of Ingleside* she becomes a nurse and virtually disappears from the story.)

Jerry enforces the Good Conduct Club, a club the children form to punish themselves when they do anything that might hurt their father. Though he is a very sketchily drawn character, we are assured that Jerry struggles to uphold the justice he knows his father believes in but is too abstracted to enforce. The Good Conduct Club itself goes awry, interestingly enough, over chivalry. When Carl and Una and Faith run from what they believe is a ghost Mary Vance has told them about, their screams and running frighten an old woman into a fit, not to mention disgracing the manse yet again with their loudness. Jerry decrees that Carl should be punished most harshly because 'he was a boy, so he should have stood his ground to protect you girls, whatever the danger was' (306). As penance for this double cowardice, Carl has to sit in the graveyard alone until midnight. And Carl does sit there, even when it begins to rain. He nearly dies of the double pneumonia he develops as a result of his chill. What parallels, we wonder, did Montgomery's contemporaries draw between the misguided children and the young soldiers of the war acting under orders?

Perhaps it is only in the sceptical 1990s that the parallel would be so sickeningly obvious. Perhaps Montgomery intended only that we see how courageous Carl is; he is willing to suffer for the code he trusts, and his heart is in the right place, even if Jerry's judgment is not fair.

Shy, delicate Una is perhaps the bravest of all the children and the one who most closely fits a culturally endorsed sex-role stereotype – she is feminine, self-sacrificing, self-effacing, gentle, kind, and nurturing. Perhaps most in need of care herself, Una struggles valiantly to protect others. Her first act of real courage is to go to Miss Cornelia (Mrs Marshall Elliot), of whom she is afraid, and ask her to adopt Mary Vance. Braver still is her mission to Rosemary West, to ask her to marry her father, John Meredith. Mary Vance, that scrappy bearer of colourful misinformation, has told Una that stepmothers are all mean, no matter what they have been like before they marry, and that they invariably turn the father of the children against the children. Much as Una likes Rosemary West, she is terrified of losing her father's love. But when Una overhears her father talking to himself about Rosemary, she decides that her own happiness must be sacrificed for her father's. Montgomery pulls out all the sentimental stops here, and has Una make a secret visit to her mother's wedding dress, stored away in the spare-room closet. The language and image here belong to Victorian, sentimental (orphan) fiction. The old wedding dress itself 'was still full of a sweet, faint, haunting perfume, like lingering love.' Una kneels and puts her face against the dress: '"Mother," she whispered to the gray silk gown, "*I* will never forget you, mother, and I'll *always* love you best. But I have to do it, mother, because father is so very unhappy. I know you wouldn't want him to be unhappy. And I will be very good to her, mother, and try to love her, even if she is like Mary Vance said stepmothers always were"' (330). Una is willing to risk the only adult love she knows in order to fulfil her own code of honour – no one else's chivalry surpasses this. (We note that Una's love for her mother makes her sound like Walter, just as Faith's fiery energy makes her sound like the imaginary general, Jem. Montgomery uses the chivalry of struggle to prefigure conventional romance.)

Roughly treated, rough-tongued Mary Vance is also valiant. Mary is a reminder of the outside world – the brutal world familiar to Lida Marsh – far from the privileges of Rainbow Valley. The Meredith and Blythe children welcome Mary Vance and do what they can to defend her against adult bureaucracy and rules. Mary's background is a shock; for all the negligence of the manse, the Meredith children have never known cruelty or violence. When the children ask about her family, Mary's cool unconcern speaks eloquently: ' "I was two years in the asylum. I was put there when I was six. My ma had hung herself and my pa had cut his throat." "Holy cats! Why?" said Jerry. "Booze," said Mary laconically' (49–50). Mary has run away from her foster home not because of the regular beatings but because she believes she is going to be turned over to someone even worse than Mrs Wiley. She shows real courage in running away when we consider what she knew her punishment would be if Mrs Wiley caught her. Mary's slang and swearing and jealousy and anger and eventual smugness and self-righteousness make her a wonderfully realistic addition to the novel. The manse children can never forget the tongues and judgment outside their charmed valley so long as Mary is around to carry all information and misinformation to them. Within Rainbow Valley, Mary's eager adoption of the values of the Meredith and Blythe children speaks forcefully for the shaping powers of generosity and good example. Chivalry (not to mention Christian charity) demands protection for Mary, and the worthy children and adults do well by her. Also her need for protection is a potent reminder of evil in the world – there are Dan Reeses and Mrs Wileys and Kaisers of Germany bent on destroying through ignorance and/or malevolence.

This novel keeps a fairly sharp focus throughout on the Rainbow Valley children who will grow up to fight in and work for the Great War. Montgomery uses Walter's vision of the Pied Piper to suggest the inexorable movement of the world towards war and to give her novel shape. Just as Browning's piper was betrayed and so piped away the children of Hamelin in payment for his work, so Britain and Canada and much of Europe failed to heed warnings about the Kaiser of Germany, and hundreds of thousands of young men and women were forced to pay for their elders' mistake. Walter first sees the Pied Piper one day in Rainbow Valley when they are all discussing Browning's story. At first Walter speaks dreamily, but something else seems to speak through him when he says, 'You'll wait for us to come back. And we may not come – for we cannot come as long as the Piper plays.' Walter is proud of the sensation his story makes, but he also feels 'a queer little chill' because 'The Pied Piper had seemed very real to him – as if the fluttering veil that hid the future had for a moment been blown aside in the starlit dusk of Rainbow Valley and some dim glimpse of coming years granted to him' (84).

At the end of the book the Piper comes again just at sunset when, Walter says, the clouds are 'towers – and the crimson banners streaming from them. Perhaps a conqueror is riding home from battle – and they are hanging them out to do honour to him.' And Jem, inspired by Walter, wishes he could go to battle and be a soldier. Walter slips into reverie again and says, 'The Piper is coming nearer ... he is nearer than he was that evening I saw him before. His long, shadowy cloak is blowing around him'; the girls shiver in dread, but Jem leaps up on a hillock and proclaims the final words of the novel: '"Let the Piper come and welcome," he cried, waving his hand. "*I*'ll follow him gladly round and round the world"' (341). Near the beginning and at the end, we share Walter's vision of the irresistible, relentless Piper. And we know that it is these chivalry-loving children – whether frightened or jubilant – who will be the ones in a very few years to carry Canada through the Great War.

For all Jem's assurance at the end of the novel, Walter's vision and the girls' dread remind us that chivalry has another face. Perhaps because it is a children's story, the book only hints at the cruelty and terror of the war; perhaps because she wrote it in the final agonizing throes of the war, Montgomery was determined to applaud the bravery of the fighters and workers rather than to expose their naïvety. Nevertheless, the bleak side of chivalry is encoded in the book.

We remember that Montgomery quickly switches the focus away from Walter's murderous energy in his fight with Dan Reese and on to his grim satisfaction at a deed well done. But the murderous energy is there, and we have seen the little girls weeping in fear of it, even though the little boys cheer Walter's victory. At the very end of the novel when Walter sees the Piper again, the sunset city fades into grey, and Jem leaps up to wave his boyish comrades on to imagined thrills and splendours of battle, the resulting picture is surely as chilling as it is inspiring. Like the carefree knights often depicted in romance, Jem is eager to fight – any fight, anywhere. The war could not have been fought had thousands not responded with Jem's boyish, unthinking enthusiasm. In Montgomery's terms, evil would have won had the lads of the maple leaf and Britain's other allies not sprung to England's side with just this alacrity; but Montgomery herself was under no illusions about the quality of life in the trenches – nor about the senseless loss of promising lives. We remember that she used as the motto for *Anne's House of Dreams* lines from a poem by Rupert Brooke, one of the war's casualties. And her awareness makes the final scene of this novel both touching and subtly ambiguous. Jem's energy may be heartening because it is honest and warm and brave, but it is also heart-breaking because it is ignorant of the truth of war.

The various, perhaps conflicting, emotions evoked by the concluding pages of the novel are quietly encoded in the book itself. After all, when we look closely at situations involving adherence to a code of honour, the code itself seems seriously flawed: Ellen's and Rosemary's vow is unjust; the Good Conduct Club punishments are too harsh; the fight between Dan and Walter almost goes too far; Faith's repeated attempts to square herself with the community get her into more trouble. An allusion to Tennyson suggests a dual reading of the novel's chivalry and of the book's overall comment on the war. We remember that when Faith describes Walter's face to Una, she says he looked 'like Sir Galahad in that poem father read us on Saturday' (185). On the very next page she tells Una she is going to tie her colours on Walter's arm, since 'he's my knight' (186). Tennyson wrote two poems about Sir Galahad, a short piece in 1842 simply entitled 'Sir Galahad,' and a long section of the book 'The Holy Grail' in the lengthy *Idylls of the King*, published first in 1869. The difference between the tone of the two pieces is remarkable. The first depicts Galahad as a powerful and almost jaunty knight, proud of his prowess and his purity. The second shows Galahad as an unswervingly pious, no-nonsense knight who presses forward through darkness and decay, led by a vision. In the context of the full *Idylls of the King*, 'The Holy Grail' is the saddest book, for Arthur begs his knights not to go on the quest, knowing that only a tenth of them will return and that with their passing will pass the glory of the Round Table.

The difference between the two pictures of Galahad is really the difference between Jem's exuberant view of combat and Walter's grim determination. We cannot be sure which poem Faith's father read to them, but the shorter piece makes no mention of ladies' tying on of colours, and the long *Idylls* is full of such detail. Besides, it is quite possible Montgomery intended us to think of both poems, for both were familiar to readers of her time, especially readers hoping to find in Tennyson's descriptions of war some grand reason for the fighting present-day England had undertaken.

The rhythm of the first Galahad poem makes the words sound jolly even when they are not. The prancing music (of alternating rhyme and alternating iambic tetrameter and iambic trimeter) matches Galahad's surety:

> My good blade carves the casques of men,
>> My tough lance thrusteth sure,
> My strength is as the strength of ten,
>> Because my heart is pure. (1–4)

The whole of *The Idylls of the King* is written in the measured dignity of blank verse, and this noble Galahad is compelled forward by a holy 'blood-red' vision:

> And hither am I come; and never yet
> Hath what thy sister taught me first to see,
> This Holy Thing, failed from my side, nor come
> Covered, but moving with me night and day,
> Fainter by day, but always in the night
> Blood-red, and sliding down the blackened marsh
> Blood-red, and on the naked mountain top
> Blood-red, and in the sleeping mere below
> Blood-red. And in the strength of this I rode,
> Shattering all evil customs everywhere ... (468–77)

Only Galahad completes the quest, and some good knights tempted away from Camelot die on their fruitless journey. Montgomery's readers, and any now who read *Idylls of the King*, would recall Arthur's sorrow when the quest is over and so many good men have died needlessly.

Both attitudes to war (or quest) – that it is glorious and that it is desperate and bloody and something to be averted – are suggested in Montgomery's *Rainbow Valley*. At the end of the novel, the shades of mourning women and the chill of Walter's fearful vision are placed deliberately beside Jem's youthful gallantry and the red of the maple leaf. Montgomery's own belief in the necessity of the Great War no doubt made her downplay her own acknowledgment of the wisdom of *Idylls of the King*. She chose not to explore here the 'blood-red' murderous mist before Walter's eyes, nor to envision the slaughter on the battlefields of Europe. But true to her own clear perception of what war – any war – involves, she makes this child Walter grow in *Rilla of Ingleside*, a far more graphic book, into a Galahad of the *Idylls*. Though he is at first too horrified to enlist, the adult Walter is goaded by visions and, when he finally goes to war, he there pursues the grail relentlessly, charging through the charred quagmire of lost kingdoms until he, like Galahad, reaches the 'celestial city,' a conquering hero – dead.

Children are the life and centre of *Rainbow Valley*. Even the love story of the novel between John Meredith and Rosemary West supports the focus on the young – John wants a mother for his children as well as love for himself; Rosemary would like to mother the manse children as well as to find in John the soul mate she thought she had forfeited in her teens with the death of her young lover. It is interesting that, in this novel about values and chivalry, the obstacle to Rosemary's marriage to John is a sacred vow Rosemary made to her sister, Ellen. Ellen will not release Rosemary from her promise to live always with Ellen and never to marry, and so Rosemary – never unchivalrously breathing the truth about her sister's selfishness – refuses John's offer. Ellen feels no such scruples herself, and when Norman Douglas proposes to her, she tells him about the pact made with Rosemary, though she does not tell him Rosemary has refused John Meredith because of it. Selfish though she may be, Ellen in her turn refuses to marry Norman – even though Rosemary has released her from the vow – because she will not leave Rosemary to live by herself, and Rosemary refuses to live with Norman Douglas (it is a relief to see that the gentle Rosemary has enough gumption to resist sacrificing herself completely for Ellen). All in all, the sisters' double courtship is a romantic Gordian knot that only a child's innocence can cut. And of course, herself something of a heroine in her refusal to betray Ellen and also in her refusal to betray herself by living in the same house with Norman Douglas, Rosemary rightly characterizes Una: 'You're a darling – a heroine –' (334).

The adult heroine of this children's (chivalry) novel is not Anne Blythe, but Rosemary West. A distant cousin of Leslie West Moore Ford, Rosemary belongs to the Four Winds world of love and faith and home.

With her some of the romantic symbolism of *Anne's House of Dreams* is revived. As with Anne and Leslie and Captain Jim, we associate Rosemary with the firelight of home, the beacon of hope, and the star of love. In *Rainbow Valley* Montgomery is careful to revive the image of the Four Winds light early on. We remember that at the end of *Anne's House of Dreams* the lighthouse 'star was gleaming northward' (*AHD* 291) and that from the garret of the newly purchased Morgan house (later named Ingleside) you could see its light. In *Rainbow Valley* Una comforts Mary Vance in the garret of the manse, and she and Mary comment on the light. Una says, 'I love to watch it,' and Mary tells how it sustained her: 'Do you? So do I. I could see it from the Wiley loft and it was the only comfort I had. When I was all sore from being licked I'd watch it and forget about the places that hurt. I'd think of the ships sailing away and away from it and wish I was on one of them sailing far away too – away from everything. In winter nights when it didn't shine, I just felt real lonesome' (58).

The lighthouse in this novel, too, suggests the power of love. We are reminded of Captain Jim's lighthouse and of the windows of Leslie Moore's home in the image Montgomery uses to describe John Meredith's view of Rosemary West's windows. Mr Meredith has gone to visit the sympathetic Anne, but she is not home, and 'As he gazed rather hopelessly over the landscape the sunset light struck on a window of the old West homestead on the hill. It flared out rosily like a beacon of good hope' (153). Later, when John Meredith is on his way to propose to Rosemary West, he is aware of the home lights of Ingleside and compares them with the lights of the West home: 'On the right the lights of Ingleside gleamed through the maple grove with the genial lure and invitation which seems always to glow in the beacons of a home where we know there is love and good-cheer and welcome for all kin, whether of flesh or spirit ... but to-night he did not look that way. Far on the western hill gleamed a paler but more alluring star' (216). The identification of home light with the lighthouse and with the love star is Montgomery's deliberate repetition of the earlier novel's poetic pattern. To readers not knowing *Anne's House of Dreams*, the imagery is obvious enough; but to those who know it from the preceding novel, the repetition here of the images is a confirmation of faith – all that is good of the traditions of Four Winds is alive and well for the children of Anne and for Rosemary West, John Meredith, and the Meredith children. In the very last chapter of *Rainbow Valley* when Anne heaps up a driftwood hearth fire, we are reminded of Captain Jim's practice of bringing Anne driftwood for the fires of the house of dreams. Captain Jim's traditions live on, and the hearth fires warm the homeland. But Rosemary West is this novel's romantic Hestia.

Rosemary's romance with John Meredith is touching partly for its realism – it is easy to imagine its *not* working out for the hesitant lovers – and partly because it is fairy tale, and thus a perfect complement for the children's chivalry. John, the knight, comes to rescue Rosemary, the princess, and Ellen, the dragon, bars the way. The narrator prompts us to think in these terms, saying of Ellen's determination to keep John off, 'But not even the grimmest of amiable dragons can altogether prevent a certain change of eye and smile and eloquent silence, and so the minister's courtship progressed after a fashion' (222). As soon as John appears, Rosemary – long content with buried romance and old memories – begins to yearn for life. Montgomery describes Rosemary's abrupt change with a subtle, mournful echo of Tennyson's romantic 'Lady of Shalott'[4] and the familiar image of the passionate red rose. Rosemary has just faced Ellen's warning reminder of her vow: 'Upstairs, in her room, Rosemary sat for a long while looking out of the window across the moonlit garden to the distant, shining harbour. She felt vaguely upset and unsettled. She was suddenly tired of outworn dreams. And in the garden the petals of the last red rose were scattered by a sudden little wind. Summer was over – it was autumn' (141). Tennyson's poem ends in tragedy for the Lady of Shalott, and the dying red rose suggests that nature itself mourns with Rosemary and at the same time urges her to accept John Meredith before winter comes in earnest. Ultimately, Una brings springtime to the fairy tale when she acts out her own chivalry and rescues her father from despair. Chivalry, romance, and fairy tale are neatly tied together.

We spend more time thinking about Rosemary West than about Anne Blythe. After all, the Anne of this novel is really only a reminder of her earlier self. She is not a real person. She speaks to defend the manse children and to remind us of their similarities with her, but she is no longer an active individual. This Anne is a dreamy woman (maybe the Anne of *Anne of Avonlea* grown up?) in whom everyone wants to confide – Faith, Mr Meredith, her own sons and daughters, Miss Cornelia. We take everyone's word for it that Anne is alive and well, for she seems most often to have just left. The narrator and other characters assure us by frequent reference to her that she is alive somewhere, and the book is at great pains to show Rosemary West as a kind of Anne-in-training. Faith wants to tell Mrs Blythe all about Adam, but Mrs Blythe has just left, and Rosemary persuades Faith to confide in her. Later Faith says to Una, and their father overhears: 'She is just lovely, I think ... Just as nice as Mrs Blythe – but different' (214). For Mr Meredith, and presumably the initiated reader, this praise is the gold seal of approval. Anne is used throughout the book as a measure for others' claims to forgiveness or indulgence. When, for example, Jem Blythe wants to give the Meredith children advice about setting up the Good Conduct Club, he refers to his mother's assessment of them as proof to themselves that they are redeemable: 'Mother says you're all too impulsive, just as she used to be' (246). From the first mention of the manse children and all their scrapes, Anne has assumed the attitude she maintains throughout: ' "Every word you say convinces me more and more that the Merediths belong to the race that knows Joseph," said Mistress Anne decidedly' (17). Her recognition of them and her approval of them (apart from her slight shock over Faith's bare legs in church) is a repeated reminder that this new Rainbow Valley world is really the inheritor of the values of Avonlea and Four Winds.

In the romance of Rosemary West and John Meredith[5] we find the imagery of *Anne's House of Dreams* revived. In John Meredith's children we find kindred spirits for the young Blythes. In the adult and child values of the novel we find Montgomery explaining to us the inevitability of the Great War, given the collective chivalry of places such as Four Winds and the nature of the struggle in Europe. Unlike the shrewd, vocal pacifist Nellie McClung, Montgomery believed that fighting was necessary for Canada once Germany had begun its offensive. But Montgomery did not endorse fairy-tale versions of the bloodshed, and in writing a novel full of pride in Canada's soldiers and workers, she is careful *not* to suggest that blind chauvinism is a good thing. Jem may exult, but Walter is sickened by blood.

The last three pages of this novel are lyrical – Montgomery's narrator takes over the description of the red sunset, with its blood-red banners, and compresses into a few sentences a full commentary on the anguish of the war and on the childlike innocence of both the young men who signed up to fight in it and the young women left at home to carry on without them:

The shadow of the Great Conflict had not yet made felt any forerunner of its chill. The lads who were to fight, and perhaps fall, on the fields of France and Flanders, Gallipoli and Palestine, were still roguish schoolboys with a fair life in prospect before them: the girls whose hearts were to be wrung were yet fair little maidens a-star with hopes and dreams.

Slowly the banners of the sunset city gave up their crimson and gold; slowly the conqueror's pageant faded out. Twilight crept over the valley and the little group grew silent. (340)

The readers of the novel knew just how deadly would be the darkness and the cold when the sun had set; even within the context of the children's immediate story, the final chill is impressive. Walter's vision and Jem's exuberance are then together poignant reminders of the quality of talent and energy the darkness claimed.

Montgomery finished writing *Rainbow Valley* on 24 December 1918, fondly believing that war was over and hoping that the sacrifices made on 'the fields of France and Flanders, Gallipoli and Palestine' (340) would satisfy the Piper, perhaps even usher in a better world. She did not know that the war's cruellest blow for her was to fall in another month with the death of Frede Campbell or that she would live to see Europe again inflamed by war in twenty years' time. In the ending of the fifth Anne book, in which she celebrated and romanticized the childhood faith and chivalry of Canada's embryonic soldiers and wartime workers, Montgomery was assuring her readers that the symbolic home fires of Four Winds would continue to burn as ruddily as the maple leaf, as steadfastly as the lighthouse star.

Womanhood and War:
Rilla of Ingleside

More than any of her other novels, *Rilla of Ingleside* (1920) is Montgomery's celebration of the female. It is an authentic war novel, Canada's
only contemporary fictionalized woman's account of the First World War,
and Montgomery wrote it as a 'tribute to the girlhood of Canada' (Gillen
79). She dedicated it to Frede Campbell MacFarlane, her dearest friend,
who had become a war bride and had died in January 1919 of the Spanish
flu, the deadly plague the war brought in its wake. While *Anne's House of
Dreams* encapsulates home as an attitude and place beyond the desecration
of bayonet or trench, and *Rainbow Valley* recreates the childhood of the
nation's soldiers and workers, *Rilla of Ingleside* follows the battles of the
war and shows how the struggles of the women and men at home parallel
the deadly combat on the eastern and western fronts of Europe. This fine
novel offers a determinedly romantic view of heroism and the homeland
vigil; because the women 'keep faith' with the spirit of their men, Canada
is able to fight gallantly to preserve home from the 'ravager.'

As the third of the war books, *Rilla of Ingleside* repeats some of the
images and devices of the previous two novels. This novel begins, as
Rainbow Valley began, with local news, the comfortable gossip of Glen
St Mary. The same characters – Anne, Miss Cornelia (Mrs Marshall

Elliot), and Susan Baker – discuss current events and catch us up on the doings of all the Ingleside and manse children. Here the lighthouse is also an important emblem and presence; colourful descriptive passages illustrate moments of intense emotion; romance and chivalry play parts in the self-styled roles of the young people; small scenes portray in miniature the larger dramas of life; the Pied Piper is frequently invoked. But *Rilla of Ingleside* is a novel of sacrifice and nightmare. Evil and barbarism are believed to be the foes, and even the Presbyterian minister, John Meredith, preaches Montgomery's own belief about this war, using as a text Hebrews 9:22, 'Without shedding of blood there is no remission of sins' (51). Every symbol takes on new significance; every echo from earlier books has a sinister reverberation here. The chivalry of *Rainbow Valley* is concentrated in Walter, but Walter himself sees plainly the blood and cruelty of trench warfare. Jem's boyish enthusiasm for jolly swashbuckling is sobered by the reality of rats and mud and vermin and sodden rations and acres of stiffening bodies. The lighthouse is a symbol of the old world – during an innocent dance for young people, held at the lighthouse, comes the announcement of war. News comes to mean only war news – everything is measured by doings in Europe. Even the Pied Piper, Walter's childhood symbol of distant struggle, becomes the literal call to arms of war and the relentless, irresistible 'dance of death' for the young.

Montgomery used passages from her own diaries to recreate in *Rilla of Ingleside* the impact of European news on those who waited at home. Well over a hundred pages of the second published selection of Montgomery's journals chronicle her responses to the battles of the war. She uses her journal's very words throughout the novel – but gives them to different characters. Gertrude Oliver speaks much of Montgomery's gloom and dreams Montgomery's own dreams; Rilla learns to speak with the anguish and thrill of soul Montgomery felt; Anne occasionally slumps with Montgomery's fears but more often rallies with Montgomery's determination; Gilbert teases Susan with some of Montgomery's own doubts (though Gilbert probably sounds more like Ewan Macdonald than Maud Montgomery Macdonald); John Meredith finds strength in the words that inspire Montgomery; sensitive, poetic Walter speaks with Montgomery's voice; Susan Baker's red-hot patriotism was Montgomery's own. Authenticity breathes through the pages of the novel, and the reincarnation of Montgomery's words – summaries of news dispatches as well as summaries of emotional responses – sound appropriate in their concentrated, fictionalized context. The virtually unrelieved anguish of the real journals is leavened in fiction with humour, irony, and drama. Heroism takes many shapes.

Rilla of Ingleside is about heroism and womanhood.[1] The novel is invaluable as a social record, but it is also a wonderful study of psychology – of what the women left behind use to support themselves, what fictions they create to make the days and months and years bearable. At first it seems that the glory and the sacrifice will be all male, but while the men fight heroically in the trenches and later in the air, the women become heroines at home. When they first receive news that England has declared war on Germany, Rilla feels that her first grown-up party is spoiled and that her romantic evening is over. Moments before, she and Kenneth Ford have been sitting outside the lighthouse in the moonlight together, and now, she reflects bitterly (with obvious help from the narrator), 'His thoughts were full of this Great Game which was to be played out on blood-stained fields with empires for stakes – a Game in which womenkind could have no part. Women ... just had to sit and cry at home' (36). When Walter confesses to Rilla that he does not want to go to war because he is nauseated by the thoughts of pain and suffering, he expresses his self-contempt thus: ' "I – I should have been a girl," Walter concluded in a burst of passionate bitterness' (47). But soon enough, with the young men away and all the work of running the home and community and keeping up the spirits of those who did not go, the women find their own heroism. The humble, earnest words Rilla speaks to her mother are the focus for the novel: 'Mother, I want to do something. I'm only a girl – I can't do anything to win the war – but I must do something to help at home' (53). By the end of the novel we find that the apparently passive, apparently secondary role the women take is essential to the war effort and, equally importantly, to the continuation of a life of values and vision after the war.

We see very little of Anne in the book – she is there to mourn the going of Jem and Walter and Shirley, and the death of Walter, and we see her occasionally as she contemplates Rilla's growing steadiness or some special campaign or celebration. But this Anne, like the Anne of *Rainbow Valley*, is a mere place marker for her former self. The energy of the book is with the other characters, and Anne serves sometimes as a device within the narrative, an audience for Rilla's resolves or a recipient of Susan Baker's pungent remarks. Even the death of her son Walter, a centrally important event in the novel, is seen more through Rilla's eyes than through Anne's. When she hears that Jem will not be able to come home before he is shipped overseas, she speaks in a voice that in its paleness and attempted humour characterizes much of her presence in the entire novel: ' ' "Perhaps it is as well," said the disappointed mother. "I don't believe I could bear another parting from him – now that I know the war will not be over as soon as we hoped when he left first. Oh, if only – but no, I won't say it! Like Susan and Rilla," concluded Mrs Blythe, achieving a laugh, "I am determined to be a heroine" ' ' (80). She serves as a reminder in the novel as a whole of the millions of quiet, nameless women who watched their sons and brothers and lovers and husbands and friends go to the front. And Montgomery makes it clear that for this she is heroic, for this and for running the Red Cross and carrying on her daily life. Nevertheless, this Anne's heroism is suggested rather than explored. Anne has finally been absorbed completely by the roles conventionally prescribed for her – ones that Montgomery challenges only obliquely.

Rilla is active and at times reminds us a little of the young Anne Shirley. When she declares to her mother her determination to be a heroine, she is a vision the young Anne would have imagined for herself. She is a 'slim, white-robed thing, with a flower-like face and starry young eyes aglow with feeling' (59), and she says, 'I have been thinking it all over and I have decided that I must be as *brave* and *heroic* and *unselfish* as I can possibly be' (53). Anne Blythe listens to her daughter's italics, and she does not smile.

Rilla's heroism is impressive and inspiring because it grows with her. Like Walter, she is not brave and fearless to begin with, and she has to make painful leaps in soul development. She is a believable adolescent – more believable than Anne Shirley is at her age. Where Anne was simply impulsive or dreamy, Rilla is selfish and vain. She is even sarcastic to her mother in true teenager style and must learn to become generous and humble in order to keep faith with the women around her and with the men and women overseas. Because Rilla must develop as each new hardship comes to her, she is an inspiration for Walter as well as an uncritical admirer of him.

When the book opens, fifteen-year-old Bertha Marilla Blythe is content to laugh and sing and dance all day. She does not like school and has none of the ambition that drives Nan or Di or Faith Meredith; Gilbert calls her his one 'lily of the field,' and she is pleased with the epithet (15). Apart from looking pretty and having a good time she thinks she would like to be for poet Walter what Dorothy Wordsworth was for her brother, William (13). Such a sunny, thoughtless creature cannot realize the war, and when the grown-ups around her, including Walter, speak of it, she wishes it would go away and refuses to think about it. Montgomery does a wonderful job at the opening of the book in making Rilla seem believably adolescent and also likable. During preparations for Rilla's first dance, the fateful evening at the Four Winds lighthouse, Miss Oliver worries aloud about news from Europe and hopes war can be averted. Rilla's cheerful reply captures the unthinking insularity of the thousands who could not realize what was happening. Because Rilla is a mere child in awareness, and is looking forward to her first party, we forgive her unconsciousness. An unconscious adult – unless it is an eccentric like Susan Baker – could not be so charming. Rilla says of the possibility that war will not be averted: 'It will be dreadful if it isn't, I suppose. But it won't really matter much to us, will it? I think a war would be so exciting. The Boer war was, they say, but I don't remember anything about it, of course. Miss Oliver, shall I wear my white dress tonight or my new green one?' (17). And, shortly afterwards, when Miss Oliver tells Rilla her frightening (prophetic) dream about waves rolling all the way up the Glen to the steps of Ingleside and touching her hem with blood, the uninitiated Rilla is immediately anxious, though not about blood: 'I hope it doesn't mean there's a storm coming up from the east to spoil the party' (19). Miss Oliver's indulgent sarcasm is truly benign: '"Incorrigible fifteen!" said Miss Oliver dryly. "No, Rilla-my-Rilla, I don't [think] there is any danger that it foretells anything so awful as *that*"' (19).

But Rilla is intelligent and kind, and her unconsciousness is lost quickly with the events of that evening. She is soon making her vow to be a heroine, adopting a war baby, running the junior Reds, and – most difficult of all – trying to comfort her beloved Walter, who does not want to enlist. Rilla's deep love for Walter, paralleled deliberately in the text with the sentimental story of Dog Monday's instinctive worship of and vigil for Jem, makes her develop more rapidly than anything else. When Walter does finally enlist, and is for a moment exultant in his triumph over his own fears, Rilla, in listening to him, is transformed from adolescent into woman: 'Rilla did not sleep that night. Perhaps no one at Ingleside did except Jims. The body grows slowly and steadily but the soul grows by leaps and bounds. It may come to its full stature in an hour. From that night Rilla Blythe's soul was the soul of a woman in its capacity for suffering, for strength, for endurance' (125). Only a fully conscious, expansive-souled woman could realize the truth in what Rilla tells her mother the next morning. In Rilla's dictum we hear Montgomery's assessment of the quality of women's heroism – it is all love and sacrifice. Anne says that Rilla must bear up before Walter and 'not add to the bitterness of his sacrifice,' and Rilla's new womanhood makes her reply with hard truth: '*Our* sacrifice is greater than *his* ... Our boys give only *themselves. We* give them' (126). In depicting the weary years of waiting for the war to be over and for the men to return, Montgomery supports Rilla's new understanding.

Rilla's first real act of heroism, the rescuing of Jims from certain death, is typical of this book's mixture of realism and comedy. The genuine pathos of the baby's plight is undercut by Rilla's fastidious dismay. The father of the baby has gone off to England to enlist, the mother is lying dead in a squalid little shack, and the woman who is watching out for the infant until the mother's funeral is over is getting drunk and doesn't like children anyway: Mrs Conover 'put away her pipe and took an unblushing swig from a black bottle she produced from a shelf near her. "It's my opinion the kid won't live long. It's sickly. Min never had no gimp and I guess it hain't either. Likely it won't trouble any one long and good riddance, sez I"' (64). Rilla puts the ugly, naked baby in a soup tureen, gingerly balances it on her lap, and takes it home with her, fondly believing someone else will look after it, as though it is a stray and rather nasty puppy. But Dr Blythe says Susan and Anne are too busy to look after a baby and tells Rilla that, if she won't do it herself, it must be sent to Hopetown Asylum, where it is sure to die since it is so delicate. Rilla grits her teeth, accepts the challenge, and spends the next four years bringing up the baby with the aid of a book on infant care.

In finding that she can take care of the baby herself, and in finding too that she can manage her peers with the ease with which she changes the baby, Rilla comes into her own as an individual, a heroine. Out of the chaos of the war she finds reserves within herself. Caring for the baby teaches her to understand something beyond herself, to sacrifice for someone else. Montgomery is not suggesting through Rilla that all young girls should have to take care of babies – but she uses the baby to suggest Rilla's own self-centredness and self-containment before the war. Having learned that the nurturing of the baby must take precedence over her own cares or pleasures, having suffered through the war in daily dread of what the news would bring about her brothers and sweetheart and childhood comrades, Rilla Blythe becomes an emblem of tried and tested young Canadian womanhood. Precisely because she is emblematic she is also inspirational; Rilla did what Montgomery's readers had also done, or (so they could tell themselves) would have done.

Since to Montgomery the war against Germany was sacred, a holy cause, we should not be surprised to find the heroine, Rilla, and her war baby depicted as madonna and child (just as Leslie Moore and baby Jem are pictured in *Anne's House of Dreams* when Montgomery is endorsing home). When Ken Ford comes to say goodbye to Rilla, little Jims, the war baby, cries, and Rilla finally has to bring him down to the porch with her to share Ken's farewell. The idealized picture is characteristic of the novel's romantic view of womanhood and sacrifice: Jims 'cuddled down against her just where a gleam of light from the lamp in the living room struck across his hair and turned it into a halo of gold against her breast. Kenneth sat very still and silent, looking at Rilla – at the delicate, girlish silhouette of her, her long lashes, her dented lip, her adorable chin. In the dim moonlight, as she sat with her head bent a little over Jims, the lamplight glinting on her pearls until they glistened like a slender nimbus, he thought she looked exactly like the Madonna that hung over his mother's desk at home. He carried that picture of her in his heart to the horror of the battlefields of France' (139). Rilla may achieve individuality in her diary and may indeed develop 'gimp,' as the drunken Mrs Conover calls it, but she is certainly meant to be a cultural symbol worth dying for. The war against Germany becomes a crusade to restore what Montgomery's contemporaries understood as purity. (For wartime anger against icon, see Gilbert 293–7.)

In Rilla's and Ken's story, we find several kinds of romance. For Rilla, he is the white knight charging off to war; for Ken she is idealized woman – virgin mother and waiting sweetheart. In their love story Montgomery ties together all the most conventional roles and images of romance, worship, and war. Truly they are the new generation of chivalry. In this novel of authentic feeling, however, Montgomery does not freeze Rilla into the image of a young madonna and leave her there. Instead, we find Rilla's very worldly thoughts belying the picture she creates for Ken. He may romanticize her into icon, but we find her, in this farewell scene, confused and angry and eager to get rid of the baby. Rilla is furious that Jims will not stop crying and is spoiling her romantic last evening with Ken (just as she had been dismayed earlier when announcement of the war ruined her party at the lighthouse). But Rilla is no longer so selfish or self-absorbed as she was at the dance, and Jims makes her forget her anger here when he speaks for the very first time, and says her name. In her happiness over Jims' word she even forgets Ken, and this is when he sees her as a madonna. The scene is emblematic for both Ken and Rilla, but in complexly different ways. He is affirmed in his view of sanctified womanhood and in his role as protector and worshipper; ironically, she overcomes her role as adored object only when she forgets Ken and hugs Jims and is thus spontaneously nurturing, maternal, and unselfconscious (as stereotype would have her in the first place). The scene begins with conventional romance and ends with adolescent indignation (Susan returns and determines to help Rilla entertain Ken), and in its middle Montgomery both preserves and questions romantic stereotypes.

Throughout the novel Rilla is a flesh-and-blood girl who grows painfully and matures perceptibly as she assumes an increasing number of war-related responsibilities. The parallels between the war struggles and Rilla's home struggles are insistent throughout. Walter says of Rilla's spirit: 'It took more courage for you to tackle that five pounds of new infant, Rilla-my-Rilla, than it would take for Jem to face a mile of Germans' (70). Other campaigns include the organizing and running of the junior Red Cross and of a concert for the starving Belgians, bitter ordeals similar to the ones Montgomery herself experienced in Leaskdale amid querulous parishioners.

It takes considerable strategy to arrange a war wedding. Rilla persuades Miranda Pryor, daughter of the detested German sympathizer Whiskers-on-the-Moon Pryor, to defy her father and marry Joe Milgrave on his last leave before going overseas. The spiritless Miranda, the antics of her spoiled and overfed dog, who groans through the entire ceremony, and the incessant weeping of the groom make Rilla think that some battles are not worth fighting. Though she has defeated Mr Pryor, the victory seems flat and pointless – not worth the tremendous cost in energy and emotion. Rilla's questioning of the value of fighting is answered in Montgomery's final comments on the newlyweds. When Miranda says goodbye to Joe (after their brief honeymoon in the appropriately emblematic Four Winds lighthouse), Rilla sees in Miranda's eyes that which has transformed the colourless little bride into a woman who keeps the flame of homeland alive: 'All that mattered was that rapt, sacrificial look in her eyes – that ever-burning, sacred fire of devotion and loyalty and fine courage that she was mutely promising Joe she and thousands of other women would keep alive at home while their men held the western front' (168). Rilla has helped Miranda to belong to the sisterhood.

Even an episode in the novel that appears to be purely gratuitous, or simply an echo of Anne Shirley's experience with the ipecac bottle and the romantic rescue of Minnie May Barry from croup (in *Anne of Green Gables*), has its parallels with the war. Rilla and Susan have tried every remedy they can think of for Jims, who is strangling to death on a thickening membrane in his throat, when Mary Vance suddenly appears in the middle of the snowstorm. She coolly sizes up the situation and smokes out the membrane with sulphur. The episode comes in the novel just after Walter has died and Rilla has read his last letter. In this bleak space in Rilla's life, the rescue suggests that defeat is not inevitable, even with the threat of death. In the midst of the struggle to save the baby's life, Rilla, as she recorded later in her diary, thought: 'And I felt so utterly helpless. It was just as if we were fighting a relentless foe without any real weapons, – just like those poor Russian soldiers who had only their bare hands to oppose to German machine guns' (206). Since the tardy U.S. participation in the First World War follows so soon in the narrative upon the rescue of little Jims, one is almost tempted to see the bragging but undeniably efficient Mary as a soul twin for the American public. (Perhaps others made the connection, too, since Montgomery's American publishers were not pleased with the representation of the United States in the book [*Journals* 2: 404].) In any case, the surprise rescue of the war baby Jims reminds us of unexpected aid coming at the eleventh hour to those who have done their best.

Walter's death is at the heart of the novel, just as his fight with Dan Reese is at the centre of *Rainbow Valley*. In describing Rilla's view of the world after hearing of Walter's death, Montgomery draws on her diary entries following the death of her beloved cousin and best friend, Frede Campbell. In the diary, Montgomery says: 'When I returned to the apartment Wednesday night I found that my martyrdom was over. The fierce flame of torture had at last burned itself out – and gray ashes were over all my world. I was calm and despairing' (*Journals* 2: 301). In the novel, the narrator says of Rilla: 'The fierce flame of agony had burned itself out and the grey dust of its ashes was over all the world' (196). The war has taught Rilla that she can endure almost anything, and now she must learn that she can survive the death of her beloved Walter. And Walter's death is clearly emblematic of something else in the book – of the spirit of sacrifice itself. Walter, who so loved life and beauty, who wrote the most famous and inspirational poem of the war, 'The Piper,' who did not want to enlist and yet who felt no fear of the evils he could see, is emblematic of the sacrifice of youth and young dreams. His last letter, written the night before he is shot and arriving days after his death, inspires Rilla with its acknowledgment of truth and its determination for victory:

I'll never write the poems I once dreamed of writing – but I've helped to make Canada safe for the poets of the future – for the workers of the future – ay, and the dreamers, too – for if no man dreams, there will be nothing for the workers to fulfil, – the future, not of Canada only but of the world – when the 'red rain' of Langemarck and Verdun shall have brought forth a golden harvest – not in a year or two, as some foolishly think, but a generation later, when the seed sown now shall have had time to germinate and grow. Yes, I'm glad I came, Rilla. It isn't only the fate of the little sea-born island I love that is in the balance – nor of Canada – nor of England. It's the fate of mankind ... And you will tell your children of the *Idea* we fought and died for – teach them it must be lived for as well as died for, else the price paid for it will have been for nought. This will be part of *your* work, Rilla. And if you – all you girls back in the homeland – do it, then we who don't come back will know that you have not 'broken faith' with us. (199)

Rilla knows that she will always 'keep faith' with Walter and shape her world so that his sacrifice will not have been in vain, and she begins anew by making a supreme sacrifice of her own – she lets Una Meredith keep

Walter's letter, knowing that Una has nothing else of his and suspecting Una's wordless love for him. The letter itself is Montgomery's message about the war – all Walter's fierce determination and faith are echoes from Montgomery's journal entries. Perhaps in making Walter the hero, Sir Galahad, who is willing to be sacrificed for a noble idea, Montgomery was able to make some sense of her own immediate grief over Frede Campbell as well as to find a central figure whose worthiness makes him symbolic of the thousands like him who lay 'in Flanders fields.'

Montgomery is careful throughout the novel to emphasize the bond between Rilla and Walter. We identify Walter (as we did his mother, the young Anne Shirley) with beauty, and especially with the loveliness of the glen and Rainbow Valley. Most of the nature descriptions in the novel are of Rainbow Valley, and most of the passages are given as though through the eyes of Rilla. But Walter is always there, too. The first nature description of the novel is given through Walter's eyes just after Jem has been reminding Walter of his old vision of the Piper:

How beautiful the old Glen was, in its August ripeness, with its chain of bowery old homesteads, tilled meadows and quiet gardens. The western sky was like a great golden pearl. Far down the harbour was frosted with a dawning moonlight. The air was full of exquisite sounds – sleepy robin whistles, wonderful, mournful, soft murmurs of wind in the twilit trees, rustle of aspen poplars talking in silvery whispers and shaking their dainty, heart-shaped leaves, lilting young laughter from the windows of rooms where the girls were making ready for the dance. The world was steeped in maddening loveliness of sound and colour. He would think only of these things and of the deep, subtle joy they gave him. (20–1)

Already Walter is fighting with himself about the war and knowing that he will have to go away and leave all this familiar beauty behind. He does not have Jem's eagerness for battle, and that is why Montgomery uses him to speak the inspirational words about the war and the necessary sacrifice he – eventually, freely – makes. In the later descriptive passages we are reminded of Walter simply because everything around Ingleside is so precious to him and because Rilla thinks of him with every beautiful thing she sees. She has loved him so well, Montgomery suggests, that she is indeed as thoughtful of her brother as Dorothy Wordsworth was for 'William' (*Journals of*).

Poetry is important to *Rilla of Ingleside* in the nature descriptions – though there are only a little over half as many here as in the poetic *Anne's House of Dreams* – and in reminding us of a larger context for Walter's and Rilla's sacrifices. With Walter chivalry is mentioned directly only briefly, early in the book when he and Rilla and Miss Oliver talk (11), but it is there in everything Walter does. Interestingly, Montgomery has Walter, Rilla, and Miss Oliver quote from Sir Walter Scott when they want to make important statements about their ideas. Rilla quotes from Scott's romantic Highland poem *The Lady of the Lake* when she writes in her diary to declare that she wishes she, too, like Jem, could enlist and fight with the men (43). Walter quotes to Rilla from Scott's romantic battle poem *Marmion* when he explains to Rilla why he is proud of himself for having enlisted (124). And at the end of the book, when Miss Oliver has had another prophetic dream about the war, she persuades a reluctant Rilla to listen to it when she, too, quotes from *The Lady of the Lake* (254). These three good friends cherish the same values and obviously eventually see the sacrifices of war in the same way, and Montgomery's three uses of Scott are (to those familiar with Scott) subtle, almost subliminal, reminders of the quality of their shared vision and code of honour.

Montgomery uses Walter's *Rainbow Valley* vision of the Piper, as well as his poem about him,[2] to draw together the entire novel. First Walter and Jem discuss Walter's old dream (20); a chapter entitled 'The Piper Pipes' (29) announces the war, and in the same chapter Jem exults in the truth of Walter's old dream while Walter laments it (34); Walter confesses to Rilla that he cannot enlist, even though 'The Piper's music rings in my ears day and night' (96); on his last evening of leave Walter visits Rainbow Valley with Rilla, and there he sees the vision of the Piper again (130); Rilla watches Ken walk away after his last visit, and the narrator remarks that 'still the Piper piped and the dance of death went on' (144); Walter's poem 'The Piper' is published in England and becomes famous around the world (174); after the country battalion marches through the glen before going overseas, the final ceremony includes a reading of 'The Piper' (186); the night before Walter dies he sees the Piper clearly again and knows he is among his followers (198); at the Ingleside victory dinner when peace has been declared, Miss Oliver recites Walter's poem (275). The image of the Pied Piper piping away the boys of the homeland and piping them in death on to victory is both sentimental and poignant and gives continuity to the story of the lives of the children and adults of Canada's emblematic Rainbow Valley. Montgomery was careful to choose in the Piper an image that suggests simultaneously the helplessness of the listeners and the strength of their united numbers.

By the time Kenneth Ford returns from the war Rilla has changed from the schoolgirl who can look like a madonna to 'a woman with wonderful eyes and a dented lip, and rose-bloom cheek, – a woman altogether beautiful and desirable – the woman of his dreams' (284). The novel reads, on this level, like a formula romance. But this level is hardly ever exposed alone – instead, Rilla's budding love for Ken is kept well in the background of her love for Walter and Jims and the daily grind of junior Reds and sewing and home care. 'Keeping faith' is in the forefront of the novel, and some of the forms of heroism it takes give the novel a pathos and humour that are entirely separate from conventional romance.

Rilla is central to many levels of the narrative as the one who must mature to 'keep faith' and as one of the women who then endures with admirable strength. The heroism in the novel is often a solemn, even a poetic thing. Nevertheless, the most colourful heroine of *Rilla of Ingleside* belongs to comedy rather than to poetry. Susan Baker, not Rilla, most often serves in the book as the spirit of Canada. She makes her announcement about her determination to be heroic in characteristic dress and attitude. Standing at the foot of Anne's bed, 'arrayed in a grey flannel nightgown of strait simplicity ... [with] a strip of red woolen worsted tied around her grey hair as a charm against neuralgia,' she declares, 'Mrs. Dr. dear, I have made up my mind to be a heroine' (59). Susan, who in her comfortable sixty-four years before the war had known nothing of world geography, memorizes maps, rehearses war strategy, and argues with the newspapers about the military significance of villages and hillocks. Susan's indignation over the declaration of war, and especially over the necessity for the eldest Blythe boy to enlist, is expressed eloquently: 'She had her little store of homely philosophies to guide her through life, but she had nothing to buckler her against the thunderbolts of the week that had just passed. What had an honest, hard-working, Presbyterian old maid of Glen St. Mary to do with a war thousands of miles away? Susan felt that it was indecent that she should have to be disturbed by it' (50). But she never fails to give the appropriately patriotic response – even forgetting herself on the railway platform when the village has turned out to say farewell to its first batch of recruits. Rilla looks on in amazement to see staid Susan 'waving her bonnet and hurrahing like a man – *had* she gone crazy?' (58)

Susan bangs pots and pans when the Kaiser does anything particularly disgusting, knits drawers full of socks, bakes bags of cakes and sweets to mail to Jem and then Walter at the front, and through it all she lives by the philosophy the women of Canada have found to be most true: 'Whining and shirking and blaming Providence does not get us anywhere. We have just got to grapple with whatever we have to do whether it is weeding the onion patch, or running the Government. *I* shall grapple. Those blessed boys have gone to war; and *we women*, Mrs Dr. dear, must tarry by the stuff and keep a stiff upper lip' (60). Susan is a delightfully Dickensian eccentric; she mouths Montgomery's own observations about the war, but is able to give them a comfortable homeyness, or a sentimental poignancy, since we are meant to see her as the staunch woman warrior spirit of Canada – at once a reminder to the boys at the front of the homespun goodness behind them and a symbol to those who cannot go to Europe that the values and traditions of the country will be upheld as long as women like her stand guard. When her lugubrious Mrs Gummidge-like cousin moans that the Germans will probably be in Canada soon, Susan counters: 'The Huns shall never set foot in Prince Edward Island as long as I can handle a pitchfork' (248).

One of Susan's ways of 'keeping faith' is to help with the harvest. The farmer is at first dubious that a woman in her mid-sixties can keep up with the vigorous pace of the fields, but Susan triumphs in her ability to outwork any of the men there. The narrator's description of Susan makes her at once into a symbol of Canadian grit: 'Susan, standing on a load of grain, her grey hair whipping in the breeze and her skirt kilted up to her knees for safety and convenience – no overalls for Susan, if you please – was neither a beautiful nor a romantic figure; but the spirit that animated her gaunt arms was the self-same one that captured Vimy Ridge and held the German legions back from Verdun' (224). Susan gives a red-hot speech at a war-bond meeting and demands that all the men there pay up to support their country, and they do. And Susan routs her gloomy cousin Sophia at every bad turn of events, always believing that God is firmly on the side of the Allies. Perhaps the most endearing thing about Susan's passionate love of home is that she translates everything in the war into something local that she can understand (hence the destruction of 'Rangs Cathedral' is appalling to her because she can imagine how she would feel if it were the Glen church [79]). She believes that the Kaiser of Germany knows *and cares about* everything that happens in Glen St Mary, and she thus takes delight in every local event that suggests upset to Germany. The focus for this antipathy is Whiskers-on-the-Moon, the supposed pacifist, whom Susan and others believe to be a German sympathizer. Moreover, Susan believes he is a German spy who rushes immediately to Germany word of any anti-German goings-on in the Glen. Whiskers-on-the-Moon has the audacity to make an anti-war prayer at a church meeting held to support the morale of the families and friends of the soldiers, and Norman Douglas stops the prayer by grabbing the little man by the throat and shaking him like a rat, loudly denouncing him all the while. Afterwards Susan, who has never countenanced Norman Douglas before, says admiringly, 'You will never, no, never, Mrs Dr. dear, hear me call Norman Douglas a pagan again ... If Ellen Douglas is not a proud woman this night she should be' (183).

Montgomery thus carefully prepares the way for Susan's personal encounter with Whiskers-on-the-Moon. The scene in her kitchen is another of those instances where we see acted out domestically what is happening in Europe on the battlefields. Susan is admired by loyal citizens and also, unbeknownst to her, by Whiskers-on-the-Moon, whose daughter, Miranda, much to his disgust, has become a war bride. He knows that when the war is over he will lose his cheap live-in housekeeper, and he eyes the capable Susan Baker as a good and easy catch. Since we know that Susan has entertained herself through the war with imagined torment of Pryor, we expect fireworks when we see him in her kitchen. And we are not disappointed – the scene is delightfully recounted to satisfy expectation. When he proposes to Susan, she loses her head completely. The usually decorous Susan, careful always to apologize elaborately to the Blythes for any behaviour she fears is unladylike, stands stunned for a second by Pryor's smug proposal, and then, electrified, catches up from the stove a huge iron kettle of boiling dye and chases him out the back door and through the backyard. Fat Whiskers-on-the-Moon almost knocks Anne Blythe over as he lunges past her at the gate, and Susan then plumps down the kettle and confesses. The routing of the German sympathizer on

P.E.I. comes close to the end of the war, and Montgomery thus uses it as a comic miniature of the imminent German defeat.

When the miracle of the Marne is repeated, Anne Blythe knows that it is the beginning of the end. Montgomery turns our attention away from Anne or Rilla or Miss Oliver (who has had a dream about victory) and focuses as usual on Susan, whose words remind us of Canada's danger and of its loss, and yet whose gesture acknowledges the coming end of the death vigil:

'Thank God,' said Susan, folding her trembling old hands. Then she added, under her breath, 'but it won't bring our boys back.'

Nevertheless, she went out and ran up the flag, for the first time since the fall of Jerusalem. As it caught the breeze and swelled gallantly out above her, Susan lifted her hand and saluted it, as she had seen Shirley do. 'We've all given something to keep you flying,' she said. 'Four hundred thousand of our boys gone overseas – fifty thousand of them killed. But – you are worth it!' The wind whipped her grey hair about her face and the gingham apron that shrouded her from head to foot was cut on lines of economy, not of grace; yet, somehow, just then Susan made an imposing figure. She was one of the women – courageous, unquailing, patient, heroic – who had made victory possible. (255)

In *Anne of Green Gables* and *Anne's House of Dreams* love of home breathes in all the rapturous nature descriptions; in *Rilla of Ingleside*, the nature descriptions take second place to the colourful slides of Susan Baker's vigorous gestures.

Because of older women such as Susan, middle-aged women such as Anne, and young women such as Rilla, the homeland 'keeps faith' with its men and women overseas. Rilla herself gives credit and modestly takes some: 'It is mother and Susan who have been this family's backbone. But I have helped a little, I believe, and I am so glad and thankful' (267). Montgomery focuses on women throughout the novel, but in doing so she also emphasizes the connections between women and men. Notice, for example, how careful Montgomery is to align Miss Oliver's mysticism with Walter's prophetic visions and poetic responses. They are both, as mentioned before, readers of Scott, and it is Miss Oliver who reads Walter's poems and sees the promise in them. When Anne discusses her in the first chapter, she mentions Miss Oliver's dreams and says that she has a 'mystic streak in her' (9). Montgomery gives us three of these dreams, and all three come true – the first one, as mentioned above, predicts the beginning of war with the tide rushing up the Glen and bloodying Miss Oliver's skirt; the second involves the holding of the Germans back at Verdun ('They shall not pass' 170); the third is the reverse of the first, and heralds the allied victory as the tide quickly recedes from the Glen (254). Even the sceptical Gilbert (who has degenerated in this book to sound very much like the crusty old Doctor Dave whom he replaced in *Anne's House of Dreams*) learns not to sneer at Miss Oliver's dreams. The use of Miss Oliver's three dreams reinforces the frequent use of Walter's Piper; vision and dream are shared by the good friends and give the war itself an air of inevitability and high destiny.

Walter's quality of chivalry is evident in the way he views the war, just as Jem's and Shirley's views of the war also suggest their very different estimations of self and responsibility. In describing the differences among the three brothers' attitudes to war, Montgomery is also suggesting a range of attitudes shared by other young men – and the women who support them – and is also possibly suggesting a difference in the attitude to war that the passing of years brings – Jem is among the first enthusiastic recruits; Walter goes slightly later when the *Lusitania* atrocities make it clear that evil is the enemy; Shirley enlists late in the war when tenacity rather than high valour is called for: 'So Shirley went – not radiantly, as to a high adventure, like Jem, not in a white flame of sacrifice, like Walter, but in a cool, business-like mood, as of one doing something, rather dirty and disagreeable, that had just got to be done' (214). Walter's 'white flame of sacrifice' is related to Miss Oliver's mysterious dreams, to the shared literature of chivalry and romance and scripture, and particularly to the picture of Miss Oliver as she announces the allied victory she has just heard about over the telephone: 'Gertrude turned and faced the room dramatically, her dark eyes flashing, her dark face flushed with feeling. All at once the sun broke through the thick clouds and poured through the big crimson maple outside the window. Its reflected glow enveloped her in a weird, immaterial flame. She looked like a priestess performing some mystic, splendid rite' (274). It is no accident that Montgomery uses the maple leaf and the mystic flame to dramatize the news of victory – and we feel Walter's presence in the implications of the 'crimson ... glow.'

The sacrificial and the mystic flames belong to vigil, a unifying impulse in the book. Interestingly, the symbol for vigilance in the previous two books has been the lighthouse, and in this novel the lighthouse plays the parts, as already suggested, of the scene for announcing the war and for the honeymoon retreat of the German sympathizer's disobedient daughter and her soldier. But early in the book, with news of war, the lighthouse supports the flag, and the flag replaces the lighthouse star as the beacon for the homeland during war: 'Outside, the dawn came greyly in on wings of storm; Captain Josiah, true to his word, ran up the Union Jack at the Four Winds Light and it streamed on the fierce wind against the clouded sky like a gallant unquenchable beacon' (39). We remember that when the little war bride bids her husband farewell, after their short stay in the lighthouse, she sends him away with her eyes bright with 'sacred fire of devotion and loyalty and fine courage' (168). Every time the flag flies or spirits soar, flame is invoked, and sacred vigil is implied. Keeping the faith, tending the flame, legions of Hestias guard the homeland and its symbols.

Montgomery's war novel is an ingenious, impassioned reconstruction of her own journals. In building her story around Rilla's developing spirit, Montgomery comments implicitly and explicitly on the demands of sacrifice and love. Though the novel was written as a tribute to Canadian girlhood and womanhood, it was also meant to be a farewell to the Anne series. Montgomery made a 'dark and deadly vow' in her journal that this sixth book about Anne would be her last. Moreover, she said she had already been brooding up a new dark-haired, purple-eyed heroine named Emily, and she wanted to write about her (*Journals* 2: 390). *Rilla of Ingleside* is in many ways an appropriate conclusion for the Anne books – as Montgomery herself said, Anne 'belongs to the green, untroubled pastures and still waters of the world before the war' (*Journals* 2: 309), and Montgomery wanted to leave Anne's children with the promise, but not the working out, of a new world (a personal present Montgomery herself was finding ever more difficult in real life at the time). Anne's youngest (and auburn-haired) child fights her way to adulthood in the novel, ironically keeping a war baby from going to the very asylum in Hopetown that Anne gratefully left to come to Green Gables. And Rilla (named after Marilla) becomes engaged to Kenneth Ford of the House of Dreams lineage, the son Leslie Moore Ford named for her beloved younger brother who was killed before her eyes in childhood. The childhood and the adult friendships of Anne are thus involved in the unfolding of Rilla's story. Rilla is a living link between the old world and the new. Though she has spunk and eventually comes to be seen as a 'born manager,' she is certainly not one of the new women Montgomery's contemporaries were lauding (Prentice et al. 190–211), nor one, probably, that women of the 1990s can embrace without some qualifiers. Rilla wants no career outside the home; she is not violently moved by the prospect of the vote; she has no interest in high school or college. Anne Shirley had (at least in early life) far more ambitions than her youngest daughter. But Rilla is not a painted doll either, and while she may not be in her culture's terms a modern woman, she does not fit perfectly the stereotype of contented domesticity – she hates sewing, cooking, and working with a budget. Clearly Rilla is destined to be a wife and mother, but the episode with Mrs Mathilda Pitman (entirely unnecessary as it may appear) at least shows us that Rilla has a will of her own and can stand up for herself. In fact, one gets the feeling that Rilla will pack a lot of living and observing and organizing into her future life with husband and children. At least we are assured that she has the best of the Avonlea and Four Winds and Glen St Mary traditions and values involved in the shaping of her life.

By the end of *Rilla of Ingleside*, Rilla and Anne have become close friends (the motherless Montgomery was never really comfortable depicting mother-daughter relationships). As keepers of the faith and as kindred spirits they are both richly endowed with the gifts the world around them evidently needs so much (and gives romanticized endorsement for): courage, imagination, faith, (a measure of) independence, and love of home. Anne seems to have lost her voice with age, but Rilla develops a voice as she writes in her diary, and readers can *hope* that in her life with Ken she will continue to cultivate the speaking out and the speaking up that the war has released in its womenkind.

Recapturing the Anne World:
Anne of Windy Poplars and *Anne of Ingleside*

Despite Montgomery's solemn oath in 1920 that she was finished with Anne, *Rilla of Ingleside* was not to be the last of the Anne books. In 1936, to satisfy 'pleading publishers,' Montgomery published *Anne of Windy Poplars* (called *Anne of Windy Willows* in Britain); and then in 1939 she filled in more gaps in Anne's story with *Anne of Ingleside*, her last completed novel. *Windy Poplars* covers the three years, before Anne's marriage, that she was principal of Summerside High School, and *Ingleside* deals with the early days of Anne's children (before *Rainbow Valley*). Nor were these two the end of the Anne stories. Before her death Montgomery had prepared another manuscript she entitled *The Blythes Are Quoted*, dealing with the goings-on in Glen St Mary when Anne's children were young, and grown. The original book was divided into two parts, each headed by a description of an evening in the Blythe house, and then filled with stories and poems about past and present events and people. This manuscript was never published as such, but eventually appeared in 1974 as a collection of short stories under the title *The Road to Yesterday*. Though the stories have been rearranged and the introductions removed, we can still read the book as an incomplete addition to the Anne series (Foreword). So, although Maud Montgomery thought herself to be finished with Anne in 1920, she revived her in the late 1930s when the 1934 talkie film of *Anne of Green Gables* opened up more markets for Anne books (*Letters* 177).

Montgomery confessed to MacMillan that she had had difficulty at first thinking she could get back into the Anne series to write *Anne of Windy Poplars*: 'But after the plunge I began to find it possible – nay to enjoy it – as if I really had found my way back to those golden years before the world went mad' (*Letters* 177). And in many ways she is successful in transporting the reader back, too, to Anne's earlier, gingery days when she spoke up and got angry and meddled in other people's lives. Still, *Windy Poplars* has serious drawbacks as a novel. In 1939 the RKO Company purchased the film rights for both *Anne of Windy Poplars* and *Anne's House of Dreams*, and Montgomery commented to MacMillan with her usual honesty and shrewdness, pinpointing a central problem in the novel and, prophetically, describing what a 1980s film crew would later do with her work: 'I can't imagine how they'll make a picture out of Windy Willows (''Poplars'' in America) because it is just a series of disconnected stories strung together on the thread of Anne's personality but no doubt they will inject a good deal of their own invention' (*Letters* 195). How true! The novel is disjointed, eventually seeming more like a series of short stories or scenes than a coherent work. Perhaps even more interesting, however, is the second part of Montgomery's observation. We may never know what the RKO Company did with the novel, but we have *Anne of Green Gables, The Sequel*, the smash-hit, made-for-television movie, by Kevin Sullivan Productions, which draws liberally from the novel and certainly 'injects' freely. Montgomery herself would probably have laughed to see the Summerside, P.E.I., setting of the novel switched to a Kingsport that evokes the stately homes of England translated to Ontario. 'Grand' is perhaps the right word for the setting of the movie version of the novel. But, irony and carping apart, it is interesting to speculate on the Sullivan Productions' choice of material. Why, with the original Anne books available in their poetic and romantic narrative intensity, do we find the megabucks sequel to *Anne of Green Gables* drawing from one of the most disjointed of the Anne books – a work published sixteen years after the original series and clearly tailored to fill in the three-year gap in the original chronicles of Anne's life?

One could argue that the Sullivan writers made a shrewd choice, recognizing, as Montgomery did, that the book was a series of stories that cried out for dramatization. And, interestingly, the Anne in this novel sounds more like a grown-up Anne Shirley of Green Gables days than the entertaining but obviously thoughtful and poised young woman of *Anne of the Island*. In going back to add to the series, Montgomery gave her recreated Anne some of the fire and ginger Anne had lost as she grew up in the imagination of a pre-war Montgomery. It is regrettable that an Anne who is most welcome in being like her old tempery self comes to us in a book that just never gets off the ground.

The trouble with *Anne of Windy Poplars* and *Anne of Ingleside* is that they are neither quite children's books nor quite adult novels. *Anne of Windy Poplars* begins with a bold experiment: not only does Montgomery try to get back into the pre-war, pre-marriage days of Anne, but she uses first-person narration, something she had used only rarely before with Anne herself, though she had used it in *Rilla of Ingleside* with Rilla and extensively in the Emily series. The book opens with letters to Gilbert Blythe, a medical student at Redmond College, and for the first thirty pages or so we are reintroduced to Mrs Lynde (though she has very little to say) and introduced to the widows, Rebecca Dew, and the house Windy Poplars and its environs – all through Anne's chatty letters to Gilbert. Most of the love passages are coyly deleted by an imaginary editor.

At first the tone seems just right; Anne sounds bubbly and intelligent and loving, and she gives us some comical sketches of Rebecca Dew and her new house that are worth reading. But the method palls. Part of the joy of the other Anne books is in a narrator who appreciates Anne but who puts her into context for us. With Anne doing all the talking – even though her voice sounds authentic – we miss Montgomery's narrator's irony, explanations, descriptions, and occasional incisive turns of phrase. Evidently Montgomery, too, found the epistolary method taxing; when she broke away from it, she used little of it in the remainder of the book. In the 116 pages of 'Year One,' 54 pages are letters and 62 are narrative; in 'Year Two,' 10 are letters and 62 narrative; in 'Year Three,' 8 are letters and 50 narrative. Unfortunately, the quality of the narrative parts does not necessarily improve as they take over. The novel seems more and more episodic as it progresses, until at the very end we are jerked unceremoniously from one story to another with very little of the transition and continuity the letters provided. Such episodes may be wonderful trove for a dramatist, but they make difficult reading for either an adult or a child who is expecting to find a novel with a story line.

Yet Montgomery is always a professional, and even with the crazy-quilt pattern of one short story hastily stitched onto another, we find narrative threads and colours that almost unify the whole. Each year has its theme, and each theme is worked out in the narrative passages of the story. In the first year we are introduced to the book's three big concerns – the Pringles, Katherine Brooke, and Elizabeth Grayson – but we concentrate on only one, the Pringles. In the second year, Katherine is the focus, and in the third, Elizabeth. Montgomery fleshes out each of these main stories with anecdotes about the tower room where Anne lives or with Rebecca Dew's sayings or with wisps of Green Gables doings. In each of the three sections, even in the first with its a fairly even split between letters and narrative, Montgomery gives us the really interesting interactions in third-person narration, not in Anne's letters. And it is, even from this first year, the third-person portions of the story that the Sullivan Productions writers mined for their material.

The account of Anne's triumph over the Pringles in the matter of the play about the life of Mary Queen of Scots, where the Pringles pulled out their Mary at the last minute and Anne surprised them all by having Sophie Sinclair trained in the part and ready to take over, is covered in a few quick paragraphs of the narrator's summary of events (the Sullivan movie uses this as a key event). But the Pringle capitulation is given due space. The matriarch of the clan actually comes to Anne to surrender when she finds, in an old sea log Anne has discovered and loaned to them, that a Pringle patriarch and some of his crew survived shipwreck by eating one of their dead shipmates. The little scene is delightful drama in the style of the best of Montgomery's writing, showing Anne in her innocent surprise and the clanswomen in their cynicism, pride, and forced humility – and in the wings comical Rebecca Dew is bursting with curiosity to know why Maplehurst has thus descended upon Windy Poplars.

'Year Two' has the very sentimental and in some ways touching story of the 'little fellow,' but its surprise ending of the long-lost, look-alike cousin, so popular in short stories of the turn of the century (we see a good sampling in *Akin to Anne*), is really out of place in this modern-sounding *Anne*. In the first part of the novel, despite the presence of Elizabeth and the triumph of Anne over the Pringles, the story is preoccupied with the comic perversities of the human spirit. This second year seems a parody of itself; its anecdotes deal with sentimental surprises and comic self-delusions, but its central story – the conversion of Katherine Brooke – is serious and seems undercut by the sentimental or comic excesses of the flanking pieces. The year, introduced with the 'little fellow,' is rounded off with Cousin Ernestine's pointless grumbling and malapropisms and the long story of Hazel Marr's crush on Anne and Anne's well-meant but resented interference in immature Hazel's love affair. Little Elizabeth's magical visit to Green Gables actually ends the strangely assorted 'Year Two.'

The middle of the second year is occupied by the story of Katherine Brooke, and with it Montgomery achieves one of those flashes of really impressive and powerful writing that makes us turn to this uneven novel with interest. Katherine has been presented in 'Year One' as a forbidding and somewhat repellent character. Students are afraid of her; adults despise her pride and cold manner. An excellent teacher, she has nothing else to recommend her, and she pushes Anne away, obviously hoping Anne will fail to beat the Pringles. In 'Year Two' Anne decides to trust her own instincts (one of the truly wonderful lessons Montgomery's books continue to offer to girl readers), and she visits Katherine in her run-down boarding-house. Anne invites Katherine to Green Gables for Christmas, and the scene and its dialogue are realistic and moving. The bitter Katherine lashes out at Anne, and Anne's temper flares – and the honesty of the two eventually leads them to mutual respect and liking later on. Here Katherine is everything Anne is not – a perverse, unattractive woman – and it is the intensity of Katherine's bitterness and anger that makes her believable. It takes the Eden magic of Green Gables to effect Katherine's transformation, and the story is impressive and persuasive because we see how Katherine – without Anne – would have continued her career of sourness and loneliness. Montgomery's comic anecdotes may make us laugh at the foibles and perversities of the spirit, but Katherine's story makes us see how easily and how often tragedy results from neglect.

It is interesting that while Leslie Moore is the romantic, dark counter-part for Anne in Montgomery's visionary, romantic novel *Anne's House of Dreams*, here in a reconstructed early world, a world informed in its recreation by Montgomery's own sorrowful experiences of life, we find a counterpart for Anne of an entirely different kind from Leslie. Leslie's tragedies are believable, but they also, like Leslie herself, have colour, passion, even romance. But Katherine's life, devoid of romance, parallels Anne's own in its early experiences of neglect, and Katherine has become a pinched, starved, morbid, spiteful woman with a life of discontent and narrowness facing her like a road without a bend. The obvious passion and romance of the 1917 character and story are missing from the 1936 book, and yet Green Gables is still a magical place, so imbued with home love and beauty that Katherine is transformed while visiting there. A romantic heroine such as Leslie may have no place in the recreated Anne world, but fairy-tale changes are still possible at Green Gables, even for unbeautiful princesses. In the early and the late books, Anne embodies the home spirit of Green Gables, the House of Dreams, and Ingleside, and her loving 'eye' helps thwarted passion and bitterness to heal themselves. In such different ways Montgomery continues to give the message that genuine romance involves the conscious self and a sense of belonging. (Perhaps, late in her career, Montgomery recognized it was now safe to say that marriage is not for everyone – though she hedges her bets by making Katherine seem at odds with the world.)

When Anne comes to Katherine's room, Katherine is insulting. Anne begins with her accustomed exuberance, 'Oh, Miss Brooke, look at that sunset,' and Katherine responds, without moving to the window, 'I've seen a good many sunsets,' while thinking, 'Condescending to me with your sunsets!' (136). When Anne tells Katherine that she wants her to come home with her to Green Gables for Christmas, Katherine replies characteristically, 'Oh, I see. A seasonable outburst of charity. I'm hardly a candidate for that *yet*, Miss Shirley.' Anne loses her temper and crosses the room to look Katherine in the eye and say, '"Katherine Brooke, whether you know it or not, what *you* want is a good spanking." They gazed at each other for a moment. "It must have relieved you to say that," said Katherine. But somehow the insulting tone had gone out of her voice' (137). When they do get to Green Gables, where Montgomery lavishes half of the book's dozen nature descriptions, Katherine actually opens up. The crucial dialogue (again, one borrowed for the Sullivan production), is excellent drama. Katherine does not know about Anne's early orphan life and believes that Anne cannot understand how slights and neglect can twist the soul. Montgomery very shrewdly does not try to reproduce Anne's quick sketch of her early childhood misery; instead Montgomery leaves us to imagine what Anne says (a luxury television does not have) and provides Katherine's response. The two women together suggest what the spirit can do when encouraged by love. Anne is obviously the rarer spirit because she blossomed even in the desert of foster home and orphanage; but Katherine, perhaps more like the rest of humanity, needs only understanding and encouragement in order to blossom, even yet. The core of Katherine's story and the test of Montgomery's handling of tension and emotion is found as the two women, on a snow-shoe ramble one night, stop to rest. Katherine's tears surprise Anne, and Katherine lashes back,

'Oh ... you can't understand! [...] Things have always been made easy for *you*. You ... you seem to live in a little enchanted circle of beauty and romance. "I wonder what delightful discovery I'll make today," ... that seems to be your attitude to life, Anne ... [...] You seemed to have everything I hadn't ... charm ... friendship ... youth. Youth! I never had anything but starved youth. You know nothing about it. You don't know ... you haven't the least idea what it is like not to be wanted by anyone ... anyone!'

'Oh, haven't I?' cried Anne. In a few poignant sentences she sketched her childhood before coming to Green Gables.

'I wish I'd known that,' said Katherine. 'It would have made a difference. To me you seemed one of the favorites of fortune. I've been eating my heart out with envy of you. You got the position I wanted ... oh, I know you're better qualified than I am, but there it was. You're pretty ... at least you make people believe you're pretty. *My* earliest recollection is of someone saying, "What an ugly child!" ' (142–3: the ellipses in square brackets are mine; the rest are Montgomery's)

The scene and Katherine's whole story in the novel escape sentimentality or sticky sweetness. Even a regenerated Katherine is still somewhat aloof. Montgomery's loving descriptions of Green Gables scenery and her nostalgic reminders of Green Gables lore make Katherine's transformation seem as much a part of Green Gables loving magic as a result of Anne's tact and understanding. Katherine's conversion is a believable and welcome story in the context of Anne's love of home and home spirit.

But once Katherine is converted, we see very little of her – as is this novel's way. 'Year Three' lurches from one anecdote to another, and since its central story concerns the uninspiring little Elizabeth, this third portion of the book would be weak indeed if some of the filler anecdotes were not interesting. (I recommend the Tomgallon episode as a good spoof.) Since Montgomery recognized the whole book as a series of episodes, perhaps she realized, too, how soon the epistolary parts of her novel pall. At the end of the story, when Rebecca Dew is too moved to say farewell to Anne in person, she writes her a letter. The letter is obviously patterned on one Rebecca found in her copy of the *Book of Deportment and Etiquette*, and Anne laughs, though she is touched. Perhaps Montgomery's joke about Rebecca's letter contains a little self-mockery as well – Anne's letters to Gilbert have proved to be little more than convenient excuses for the narrator to interject with explanation and story. At least, however, the Anne depicted through the letters and the stitched-together short stories is an Anne we can recognize from Green Gables childhood.

Montgomery did not make the mistake of using first-person narration in *Anne of Ingleside* (1939). It, too, is episodic, but most of the episodes have to do with Anne's children. Like *Anne of Windy Poplars*, *Anne of Ingleside* suffers from mixing two modes of writing – here the writing aimed at children sits uncomfortably beside the writing aimed at adults. Neither kind is so well done that it can appeal to both audiences at once. The reader of the novel may sometimes feel like Walter within the novel, who wants to hear other parts of the story, but does not. Walter listens to the racy gossip of the women quilters (Anne is not among them) and, when he later asks his mother to tell him about Peter Kirk's funeral, which he has heard mentioned, she declines. Montgomery gives the story to us, however, and then has Anne say to herself at the end of what is meant to be Anne's reminiscence – 'But I think the story of what happened at Peter Kirk's funeral is one which Walter must never know. It was certainly no story for children' (195). If not, why is it here? To compliment her reader by saying that Walter may be too young to hear the story but the reader is not is not Montgomery's usual way, nor does it really explain the inclusion of the anecdote. The novel sometimes seems at odds with itself.

Like *Anne of Windy Poplars*, this novel, too, insists sporadically on a very different quality of realism from the obviously idealized realism of the early Anne books. Jem has a bad temper and is even exasperatingly sulky. Walter's persecution by the Parker children is convincing; Diana is deluded by two little girls, and Nan tricks herself into believing in a princess in the Gloomy House and then suffers disillusionment when a very prosaic woman appears. In part, the book is about the harshness of disillusionment. Yet, at the same time, this disillusionment seems always to be softened by the whole book's attitude of 'those were the good old days.' Nostalgia marks the book's opening and closing and suggests the rosy light Montgomery wanted to focus on the past as she entered again into a world as yet untouched by war. Realism and nostalgia compete throughout.

Montgomery's reconstruction of Anne's married pre-war days meant including 'old' characters from Avonlea and Four Winds. Writing about them may have made her long for many of the days themselves when she had originally created such people as Diana, Rachel Lynde, Marilla, and Leslie. Perhaps the writing of this late novel took Montgomery back to her own days on P.E.I. as well as to her sons' childhood and the days when Frede Campbell was alive. The book seems to yearn backwards (it begins with Anne and Diana going on a picnic and reminiscing about the days of their girlhood). At the same time, this is the only book in which Gilbert plays a conspicuous, adult part, and it is certainly the only book in which Montgomery hints at the possibility of real problems between wife and husband.

On the whole, *Anne of Ingleside* keeps Anne in view. Even when the episodes are about the children, they almost always end with some (romanticized) reference to the wonder of 'mother' or mothering, and it is usually Anne who listens to them and smooths out the troubles or takes out the sting. We may get a little tired of this 'mother dearwums' writing, but we also have the occasional sardonic flash, 'Mummy, is a widow really a woman whose dreams have come true?' (133).

What makes this late novel more realistic or at least less idealized than much in the earlier series is the closing look at Anne's brief unhappiness with her marriage. In the original series Anne and Gilbert, apart from the argument in *Anne's House of Dreams* over Leslie's being told about an operation for her 'husband,' never really quarrel or even talk at any length. By the time we read *Rilla of Ingleside* Anne is an echo or shadow and Gilbert is a disapproving grunt or a teasing question and little more. But in this book Anne and Gilbert do things together and are pictured as a couple. So much we could expect from a novel about family life. But at the end of the book Anne is distressed by Gilbert's silence and absentmindedness, and she turns angry and resentful in a startlingly realistic way. She even comes to that most adult of realizations – that children are no replacement for adult love. This insight could not have belonged to the earlier books, where children and home are harmony itself (with occasional discordant notes to forestall monotony). It is as though a tinge of the despair of Montgomery's own life and journals leaks into the otherwise nostalgic story. When Anne believes that Gilbert no longer loves her, she acknowledges privately that the children are not enough to live happily for: ' "There are the children, of course," she thought dully. "I must go on living for them. And nobody must know ... *nobody*. I will not be pitied" ' (242).

The dinner party with Anne and Gilbert and a widowed Christine Stuart is very good drama. Montgomery gives some of Anne's and Christine's thoughts in parentheses, and we recognize the scene as a duel for power between two privileged and successful women. (Power and success here mean attractiveness to males as well as status from enviable possessions.) Who takes precedence – a modestly dressed doctor's wife with six children or a childless but wealthy widow? We know Christine doesn't stand a chance, but Anne suffers keenly. Even if we are sorry to find in the book the unquestioning endorsement of sexual territorialism and competition inherent in the struggle between Anne and Christine, we will probably be intrigued to find the struggle so clearly and cleverly rendered. We sympathize with Anne and understand perfectly the culturally supported deception, the 'sly politics of the ego' as Bonnie Kreps calls it (80), that Anne later exercises when she and Gilbert have made up and he remarks on Christine's malice: ' "Christine was never very entertaining, but she's a worse bore than ever. And malicious! She never used to be malicious." "What did she say that was so malicious?" asked Anne innocently. "Didn't you notice? Oh, I suppose you wouldn't catch on ... you're so free from that sort of thing yourself" ' (244). Montgomery's 'innocently' is wonderfully revealing of the politics and role playing within institutionalized romance (marriage). Anne's pain and then her joy at finding out that Gilbert has been worried, not bored, are unlike anything we have been told before about their marriage. This later Montgomery acknowledges that a good marriage involves work and diplomacy and luck. This Anne has the gumption to resent mistreatment and the skill (alas, that she should need it) to hide her own self-preserving manoeuvrings. How far Anne has come since she smashed a slate over Gilbert's head!

In the years between *Rilla of Ingleside* (1920) and *Anne of Ingleside* (1939) Montgomery had written about other heroines, had experimented with adult novels, and had changed with the times themselves to include more realistic and less idealized detail. Her strength was still with humour and irony, and she still created romantic descriptions of nature (though there are only a dozen in this novel). Her fondness for repetition and for images or symbols is not evident in this, her last completed book. Similarly, the use of literary allusions is far less obvious in both *Anne of Windy Poplars* and *Anne of Ingleside* than in any of the other Anne books except, perhaps, *Anne of Green Gables* itself. The allusions are there, but sometimes woven in with deliberate reticence, as though Montgomery is joking now only with those of her readers who can sort the references out for themselves. For example, when Anne has persuaded Katherine Brooke to let Anne fix her hair and choose her dress, the narrator invokes Genesis to comment laughingly on the creation of the world and the recreation of Katherine: '"Clothes are *very* important," said Anne severely, as she braided and coiled. Then she looked at her work and saw that it was good' (*AWP* 151). Similarly, the narrator makes an allusion to Tennyson's *Idylls of the King* to characterize the girlish Nan's starry-eyed rapture over the most unworthy Dovie: 'Nan looked up to Dovie, who seemed to her to be almost grown up, with the adoration we needs must give the highest when we see it ... or think we see it' (*AIn* 157–8).[1] Montgomery's narrator always enjoys a good joke, but in the later books the reader may need to share background to catch the playfulness.

Nevertheless, even if the pace and tone in these later Anne books differ from those in the original series, we do find the familiar preoccupation with the individual's search for and celebration of (a much romanticized) home. Anne looks for a home away from home in Summerside and finds the cheery tower room and Rebecca Dew; frequent reminders of Green Gables assure us that its hearth can furnish many others. And when Anne has left her little 'house of dreams' and has six children of her own at Ingleside, each of them discovers how wonderful it is to belong somewhere, to have understanding and loving adults as guardians, to explore for themselves how 'good' and 'bad' behaviour feel afterwards. Ironically, Anne herself is more alive and conspicuous in these late Anne novels than in several of the original Anne books. But whether we read of a fiery and vocal and manipulating Anne, or a dreamy and forgiving and virtually silent Anne, we experience Montgomery's most enduring romance: love of place or beauty, together with the sense of a belonging and conscious self, can make heroines of us all.

PART II

Emily

When Montgomery had finished what she hoped would be the last of the Anne books in 1920 and badly wanted a new heroine, she conjured up Emily. But in the very same breath that she told her journal about Emily, she also said: 'And I want – oh, I want to write – something entirely different from anything I have written yet. I am becoming classed as a "writer for young people" and that only. I want to write a book dealing with grown-up creatures – a psychological study of one human being's life' (*Journals* 2: 390). She did not write an adult novel until *The Blue Castle* (1926) and later, more determinedly, *A Tangled Web* (1931). Perhaps she was finally free to try adult stories because she had truly explored, in a 'psychological study' of Emily Byrd Starr, the boundaries between child and adult. She had created with Emily her literary autobiography (*Emily of New Moon*, 1923; *Emily Climbs*, 1925; *Emily's Quest*, 1927).

To draw this portrait of the artist as a young girl and woman, Montgomery had to explore thoroughly her own thoughts about writing[1] and the female as artist. Montgomery had to come to terms – far more explicitly than she ever had with Anne – with forces that shape and thwart the female who aspires: tradition, established sex-roles, male and female gatekeepers for the establishment, and conventional romance. Emily's is a passionate struggle for voice as well as a (perhaps partially unconscious) record of Montgomery's own ambivalent battles with autonomy and conformity. As far as they are able, Montgomery and Emily transcribe themselves as literary heroines, offering us a fascinating double portrait, of the kind that Mary Jacobus and Jonathan Culler (43–64) describe, of reading women reading and writing themselves as women. Emily, like Montgomery, uses what she reads and what she writes to determine the limits and the context for her own voice.

Montgomery gives a chronicle of her childhood reading and its influence on her in the 'story of her career,' supposedly written expressly for *Everywoman's World* in 1917 and eventually published separately under the title of *The Alpine Path* (1975). Now that Montgomery's journals are available, we know that the autobiographical article was taken right out of her own diaries. When she was fifteen Montgomery had destroyed her childhood journals. In 1916 she had begun to think that she should jot down ideas about her childhood so that if she were asked to give an account of her life, she would have the material ready in her journal. The long pages of recollections were thus at hand when she needed them for the prominent Canadian magazine. But more important for our study of Emily is the fact that in 1919, just as Montgomery was trying to escape from Anne and come up with a new heroine, she decided to recopy all her journals – from 1898 to the present – into uniform-sized ledgers. So, in the early 1920s, when she was establishing Emily, Montgomery had recently published her autobiographical account of her very young career and was also copying out recollections of her own early adult life. Is it any wonder that we find whole sections of her journal transcribed into the Emily novels? Events in Montgomery's life and writing career are found in Emily's story, as are clan stories and accountings of Cavendish customs and doings. The Emily trilogy reproduces, in a way no 'great-man' or 'great-event' history can, the cultural rhythms and values of turn-of-the-century Prince Edward Island farm life.

But this is not all. Montgomery gives to Emily her own imaginative heritage as well – Emily reads what Montgomery read; Emily's ideas about art and life are fashioned by the same Romantic-Victorian-feminist views that inspired Montgomery the woman and writer. From the time Montgomery herself had been a small girl, she had devoured books and poetry and magazine fare – whatever came her way in the intelligent but somewhat limited range of materials found in the Macneill homestead and on the shelves of the Cavendish schoolhouse or of friends. By looking at what Emily read and loved, we gain insight into what Montgomery is doing with Emily. At the same time, as we see the deliberate intertwining of Emily's imagination with the imaginative lives she has read about, we appreciate a dimension of Montgomery's artistic struggle that it would otherwise be easy to undervalue. Passages in Montgomery's journals – especially where she talks about her passionate love for Herman Leard, her wedding, the birth of her first child, and the death of Fredericka Campbell MacFarlane – sound very much like the literary works that influenced her powerfully.[2] Both Emily and Montgomery are revealed most tellingly with *Jane Eyre*, Elizabeth Barrett Browning's *Aurora Leigh*, and Olive Schreiner's *The Story of an African Farm*.

The Emily novels' romances are enriched by literary allusion and exploitation of literary formulae. The rough outline of the Emily trilogy is purely conventional, conforming to the expected romance formula of denial-recognition-separation-reconciliation in Emily's love story with

Teddy Kent. But the story is far from simple, and Teddy Kent is not the most powerful romantic presence in the novels. Instead Emily's real threat and temptation as woman and artist come from the needy, sexually powerful,[3] consummate art critic, Dean Priest. In Montgomery's happy-ending series, the struggles with Dean eventually bring out Emily's powers as woman and writer and actually enable her to free herself from his stifling romanticism, but her escape is narrow and she turns from one man to another. Teddy may seem a pale rival for Dean, but at least with him Emily is free to pursue her own work. Teddy, who becomes a famous painter, accepts Emily as his equal without question – and that, Montgomery's story slyly encourages us to see, is fairy tale.

Montgomery is unwilling or unable to explore fully the tremendous energy she generates with Dean Priest, and it is no wonder many romance-endorsing readers lament that Emily could not somehow have worked out things with Dean. And yet what Montgomery is doing is having Emily face in Dean – at once – the most seductive and deadly forces of romance and, implicitly, culturally accepted roles for men and women. From his very introduction in the series, Dean is associated with the most romantic of novels, *Jane Eyre*, and we see that Emily's struggles against Dean are also the artist's struggle against the lies and silencing of conventional romance. It is ironic that Emily's enduring love for Teddy and eventual marriage to him make the trilogy look like a simple love story. In fact, Montgomery's apparently conventional fairy-tale plot is a peculiarly wry and complex commentary on the alternatives and possibilities available to a woman. Since Montgomery did believe, along with Jane Eyre and Aurora Leigh, that love was preferable to lovelessness, Emily is destined to be with *someone*. Montgomery had no wish, in Emily's final solution at least, to accept Olive Schreiner's radical, disturbing vision of how a woman's passion can destroy her in a culture where sex-roles and life scripts are rigidly prescribed. Probably neither the romance-loving nor the truth-seeking reader can be wholly satisfied with Teddy, but then Teddy *is* pictured as a liberating rather than a restraining force.

When Emily is able to deny Dean Priest, she declares her right to her own woman's voice. His very name suggests the potent patriarchy behind him and its excluding knowledge and powers. The manuscript of the novel shows that Montgomery considered the name carefully; she originally called him Dean Temple.[4] It is no accident that Dean Priest is a connoisseur of literature; for Emily's struggle to have meaning, Dean Priest must be sublime and authoritative as well as crushingly condescending. To join him means she is one of the privileged few, one of those chosen to share the glimpses into the tombs of the nineteenth Egyptian dynasty or the heart of Emerson's transcendentalism; her guide will be the cynical, mysterious, passionate self-exile who sees in her a worthy intellect and spirit. If Emily succumbs to Dean's authoritative, flattering entreaty, she will consign herself to silence or to mimicry of his male voice. In struggling against him, Emily Starr is fighting against the collective weight of male privilege and authority. She can join the voice of privilege and authority if she loses her own voice; Emily's apparent love struggle with Dean Priest is nothing less than the female writer's fight for survival. Just as Montgomery inverts the conventions of romance fiction with Anne Shirley, so with Emily, Montgomery makes the apparently conventional love story of Emily and Teddy actually a triumph of the female artist over the crippled and crippling constraints of male authority and domination. Emily wins, keeps her voice, and is true to the imaginative influences that have enriched her individuality.

Emily's reading is a key to her personality and to her conceptions of art; reading and writing are the first romances of her life. In her reading we find the love of beauty and the rebellion against authority that enable her to attract and eventually withstand the very literary Dean Priest. We can look at Emily's reading – the texts Montgomery chose from her own reading – to see how Montgomery prepares the reader for the dimension of profound struggle involved in Emily's later refusal of Dean. And we can trace in Emily's awareness of and responses to literature and language the growing self-awareness of the artist and the woman. Each of the three Emily novels is characterized by a special treatment of allusion and the power of language.

The Struggle for Voice:
Emily of New Moon

As we experience Emily's growing up, we feel how the books and poems she savours are shaping and reflecting her own sense of self. The narrator reinforces, by allusion or echo or ironic association, what Emily is actually going through. *Emily of New Moon* (1923) chronicles Emily's early development – the book opens when she is eleven years old and ends when she is thirteen. At the outset her father is about to die and leave her an orphan. The narrator tells us, in a few paragraphs, about Emily's rapture with language and her determined search for the right words in her diary to describe what she sees and how she feels. Her father, too, is a writer and has nurtured her love of language and encouraged her to read aloud to him her early pieces. All this we learn in a few pages, and Emily's closeness to her father is sustained through much of this first novel in the form of letters she writes to 'Mr. Douglas Starr, on the Road to Heaven.'

Living with her old aunts and old Cousin Jimmy, Emily develops in private her love for writing. She is only allowed to read select books from the Murray shelves, and her own father's books are locked away from her when stern Aunt Elizabeth finds her putting a pencil dot under the words she loves most. She is forbidden to read novels, though she reads some at Ilse's, where virtually nothing is forbidden, and she is permitted to read the Bible, Tennyson, Mrs Browning, Mrs Hemans, Thomson's *The Seasons*, Hans Andersen's fairy tales, Irving's *The Alhambra*, Scott's poetry (and stolen glimpses of *Rob Roy*), Arnold's *Sohrab and Rustum*, some Shakespeare (she loves *A Midsummer Night's Dream*), *Pilgrim's Progress*, *Alice's Adventures in Wonderland*, the *Memoirs of Anzonetta B. Peters*, the stories of Little Katy and Jolly Jim, and Reuben and Grace (which, she tells her father in a letter, are not novels because the hero and heroine are 'brother and sister and there is no getting married' 104), and *Nature's Mighty Wonders*. There is no restriction on her reading when she goes to Wyther Grange to visit Great-aunt Nancy Priest, and she borrows some books from Teddy and Ilse. In school she revels in the Royal Reader series, and she probably found a journal or two somewhere about, as Montgomery herself had with the popular monthly magazine *Godey's Lady's Book*, which her grandmother Macneill subscribed to in Cavendish. All the books Emily was allowed to read and reread and that she loved are ones we find mentioned in Montgomery's journals (and then in *The Alpine Path*).

Since most of *Emily of New Moon* is written from Emily's viewpoint, and often – through letters to her father – in her own words, we expect, and find, the references to literature to belong to a budding consciousness. When writing in 1917 of the importance of her own early reading to her, Montgomery says of poetry what her three novels prove also to be true for Emily: 'Poetry pored over in childhood becomes part of one's nature more thoroughly than that which if first read in mature years can ever do. Its music was woven into my growing soul and has echoed through it, consciously and subconsciously, ever since ... ' (*Alpine* 49). The magnificent cadences of the Bible, the electric power of Shakespeare, the sonorous music of Tennyson, the impassioned convolutions of Mrs Browning, the melancholy tread of Thomson, all, Montgomery's story suggests, worked their lasting magic on Emily the writer and the woman. Emily tells us the words she marked in her father's books – 'dingles, pearled, musk, dappled, intervales, glen, bosky, piping, shimmer, crisp, beechen, ivory' (190) – and in her choices we hear the Romantic and Victorian preferences that characterize Montgomery's own volume of verse, *The Watchman and Other Poems*. Throughout *Emily of New Moon*, Emily is tasting words and testing ideas; she is groping towards a sense of self and an understanding of her gift to see and her desire to tell.

Emily identifies her favourite authors and pieces in *Emily of New Moon*, and in *Emily Climbs* and *Emily's Quest* she debates the merits of works of literature. In *Emily of New Moon*, we perceive the impact of literature on Emily partly through her self-dramatizations. Like Anne Shirley, Emily imagines herself a heroine, but Emily's heroism is tied to her identity as a writer. When Emily does not characterize her own adventures in terms of or with the consciousness of literature, the narrator does it for her. Either way, we are always reading Emily as though Emily is reading herself writing. When she sits underneath the table in her old home, listening to the unflattering assessment of her by the relatives who are trying to decide who will have to bring her up, she consoles herself with finding the right words to describe each of her kinspeople. She first becomes conscious of herself as a writer when she faces jeering classmates at recess during her first day at school. They taunt the New Moon girl simply because she belongs to the proud Murray clan, and in resisting them, Emily, for the first time, proclaims herself. Asked about her accomplishments in a humiliatingly long list of questions she can only respond to with a 'no,' Emily is forced to answer a final question: ' "Then what *can* you do?" said the freckled-one in a contemptuous tone. "I can write poetry," said Emily, without in the least meaning to say it. But at that instant she knew she *could* write poetry. And with this queer unreasonable conviction came – the flash!' (83). Emily's 'flash', that tantalizing glimpse of a world beyond, where beauty lives, consecrates her to poetry. In standing up to her peers she has found a voice and has declared herself.

From that moment Emily begins to write poetry and even discovers the rapture of listening to a thrilling reading of Tennyson's 'Bugle Song.' Perhaps it is one of Tennyson's unfortunate maidens she imagines herself to be when she eats a large apple in Lofty John Sullivan's workshop, is told as a joke by him that it was full of rat poison, and goes home to die. She imagines out her death and the remorse of everyone around and laments to herself that, 'She had thought she was going to live for years and write great poems and be famous like Mrs Hemans' (141). Her farewell note to Ilse echoes the death scenes in the most melodramatic of Victorian and Romantic verse: 'Don't let anybody do anything to Lofty John because he did not mean to poison me and it was all my own fault for being so greedy. Perhaps people will think he did it on purpose because I am a Protestant but I feel sure he did not and please tell him not to be hawnted by remorse. I think I feel a pain in my stomach now so I guess that the end draws ni. Fare well and remember her who died so young. Your own devoted, Emily' (142–3). Later, Aunt Elizabeth's bitter words to Lofty John for teasing Emily with the story of rat poison cause the fiery Irishman to swear he will retaliate by cutting down the protective bush that means so much to New Moon farm, and to Cousin Jimmy's flower garden in particular. When Emily is sorrowing over the prospect of losing Lofty John's bush the narrator suggests Emily's despair with a Biblical echo: 'One day by the banks of Blair Water Emily sat down and wept' (196). The parody of Psalms 137:1 ('By the rivers of Babylon, there we sat down, yea, we wept, when we remembered Zion') captures the rhythm of Emily's self-dramatization.

Emily tests herself or is tested by three men in *Emily of New Moon*: Father Cassidy, Mr Carpenter, and Dean Priest. In each of these situations literature is directly or indirectly involved, and each man somehow challenges Emily's conception of herself as writer-heroine. It is interesting that Montgomery makes Emily's principal early mentors and critics male, having Emily, as T.D. MacLulich says, 'define her identity through her relationships with men' ('Literary' 13). Her first teacher is her father, whose imagined presence continues to influence her until she feels fully comfortable with New Moon. Cousin Jimmy provides constant support and the blessed blank books for writing. Father Cassidy appears to approve Emily's writing; Dean Priest feeds her reading and imagination; Mr Carpenter admonishes her to take pains but also encourages her to 'climb.' The females, on the other hand, are not supportive. Aunt Elizabeth, a female-clad patriarch (Rubio, 'Canada's' 4) of the old world, strongly disapproves of Emily's writing and, as a gatekeeper of the establishment, insists on duty to tradition and domesticity. Aunt Laura, Elizabeth's stereotypically female opposite, cannot understand why Emily doesn't give up writing, since it vexes Elizabeth. As we follow Emily's career, we find that males and females both thwart Emily. On the surface of it, the males, as Judith Miller says, '*seem* to encourage writing' (163), but the underlying and encoded messages about woman's place in the male literary establishment eventually make their quality of support suspect (not Cousin Jimmy's or her father's, but then Cousin Jimmy is 'simple,' and her father is dead). Emily clearly has to write her own drama if she is going to be a literary heroine.

Emily's decision to visit Father Cassidy is itself heroic – since she is a Protestant and he is a Catholic priest. When she is there, she is delighted to find that he knows all about fairies; she talks to him about writing an epic and the difficulty of working into her poem 'dispensation,' which is what, he dryly assures her, her heroine needs. Emily's earnestness is touching, since she little suspects what is really happening with him. The scene with Father Cassidy reminds the reader how imperfect Emily's understanding is, but it also alerts us to a familiar patronizing of children and females. Emily is pleased, though not completely at ease, with Father Cassidy, but we see that he is baiting her for his own fun. He is charmed by her pretty unconsciousness and does intercede with Lofty John, but he does not take her writing seriously, whatever he may say to her. To many readers this will be a chilling chapter – though Montgomery may not have meant it to be. As I read it, the Catholic priest is emblematic of knowing, tolerant, amused, male authority as it indulges the young female's vivacious ignorance. Emily herself at one point suspects he is laughing at her, but when she 'gravely' asks, 'Are you making fun of me?' she is disarmed by his reply (though the reader may not be): 'The saints forbid! It's only that I'm rather overcome. To be after entertaining a lady av New Moon – and an elf – and a poetess all in one is a bit too much for a humble praste like meself. Have another slice av cake and tell me all about it' (205–6). His subsequent muttering over her trite, sentimental, melodramatic poem does not seem entirely unfriendly since the reader, too, knows Emily has not found her own voice and is merely imitating – as Anne Shirley does – her own undigested reading. However we choose to interpret Father Cassidy's overall treatment of Emily, we will probably agree that his sarcastic (and to Emily baffling) aside – 'One av the seven original plots in the world,' (206) – is a reminder to readers that adults have hidden standards and make veiled criticisms that a frank and intense spirit will be too trusting to perceive. Emily leaves Father Cassidy feeling validated as a writer and is content to ignore what she cannot fathom in his behaviour. Readers may be nettled by his humour, but as we read the series, we see that his patronizing is but a gentle prelude to the caressing contempt Dean himself will later show for Emily's 'pretty cobwebs.' Here Emily's innocence helps her to feel heroic; later with Dean she must undergo a psychic experience to be able to free herself. Montgomery's novels suggest how radically life scripts must change if the female is to read herself as heroine.

The most important test over her writing that Emily faces in *Emily of New Moon* is her interview with Mr Carpenter, the gruff, irascible teacher who rants at Emily's mistakes in composition and is clearly one of the gatekeepers of the literary establishment. Montgomery ends this first volume of Emily's life with the chapter 'Emily's Great Moment,' describing how Mr Carpenter responds to Emily's work. He requests the interview: 'Probably you can't write a line of real poetry and never will. But let me see your stuff. If it's hopelessly bad I'll tell you so. I won't have you wasting years striving for the unattainable – at least I won't have it on my conscience if you do. If there's any promise in it, I'll tell you so just as honestly. And bring some of your stories, too – *they're* trash yet, that's certain, but I'll see if they show just and sufficient cause for going on' (342). Even if we are bothered by the gatekeeper's attitude to the presumptuous female, the chapter still makes delightful reading to anyone curious about Montgomery's ideas about poetry and criticism. Many of the comments made by Mr Carpenter to Emily are ones critics could have made about Montgomery's own verse or prose:[1] he questions her sincerity, tells her to describe only what she knows and can see on Prince Edward Island, insists that she avoid the trite topic of June, warns her away from imitations of Wordsworth, mocks her preference for the colour purple, and yet ends by telling her to 'go on – climb!' He takes her seriously if irritably; he sees ten good lines amid the trash and, when she mistakenly gives him an unflattering description of himself after a week-end bender, rather than the short story she meant to give him, he cries, 'Why, I wouldn't have missed this for all the poetry you've written or ever will write! By gad, it's literature – *literature* – and you're only thirteen' (349). From this interview, unlike the one with Father Cassidy, Emily leaves truly triumphant. She has asked for validation from the (male) world and has received it – her friendship with Dean Priest and her brush with death (in a psychic experience I will describe later) have hastened her maturity and consciousness. The novel ends with Emily back in her room, savouring Mr Carpenter's few drops of praise. She hears Ilse and Perry and Teddy playing and knows she will go to them, but she wants first to begin a new work, a diary. Into this, as did Montgomery, the maturing Emily will pour out her disappointments and dreams – the novel closes with Emily confident that she has a story of her own and a voice to tell it.

Though Mr Carpenter's interview with Emily ends the book and shows

Emily in relationship to her work, it is the encounter with Dean Priest that marks Emily most significantly as female and as writer. His instant sympathy with her is an invitation to a new dimension of thought and feeling. Teddy is always there as her (apparent) equal and beloved, but Dean offers her the allure and mystery her own dramatic interpretation of literature has encouraged her to believe is her true element. The narrator and Dean Priest together show us the literary influence that best suggests the quality of Emily's self-dramatization. Charlotte Brontë's *Jane Eyre* shapes much of *Emily of New Moon*.

Emily does not herself refer to *Jane Eyre* in the first Emily book – it is Dean and the interpreting narrator who call our attention to it. But readers familiar with Jane's story will inevitably make comparisons between the heroines, especially since Jane's autobiographical account of her early years, in particular, parallels what in her most depressed or angry moods Emily thinks of herself. They are both orphans; they both nurture their romanticism through early reading (Rowe 69–89); they both live with an unsympathetic relative; they are both consigned to punishment in a 'haunted' room by a stern aunt; they are both passionate, desperate for friendship and love, convinced of the importance of the affections over arbitrary rules, devoted to one special friend who is neglected by her father, hungry for experience and a larger scope than convention allows to females, eager to earn their own way in the world, and pleased to acknowledge as superior that which they feel to be larger or better than themselves. So much any reader of the two novels could point out without having to deal with the presence of Dean Priest. But it is Dean's use of *Jane Eyre* and his evident identification with its hero that suggests a stronger purpose in Montgomery's parallels and echoes of the famous, polemical novel. When we realize that Dean Priest identifies himself with the brooding, Byronic Edward Rochester, we know that Emily is going to have to confront in him an almost irresistible romantic pattern (Radway 119–56, Kreps 14–38). He is the dark, passionate, self-destructive exile who can be redeemed only by the love of a woman powerful enough to fling her soul into the void between them. The pattern Brontë exploits with Rochester is one that has held women in thrall for centuries – the self-immolation on the altar of this wounded god who chooses her and her alone as his redemptress. In Emily's case the wounded god seems to offer her the knowledge she craves about the exotic world far beyond the ken of New Moon. For the child Emily, Dean's friendship seems a harmless gift – but the reader remembers the Rochester connection and the fetters Emily feels and knows that Emily the woman will have to struggle with her very life to escape the supposed ideal her culture has told her is the reward for passionate difference. The woman will have to choose between her own understanding of herself and what the traditions she has honoured tell her she should feel and choose. No wonder Montgomery conferred psychic powers on Emily – only a vision can break the spell literature and imaginative traditions have cast over her. (Ironically, we remember that a supernatural voice frees Jane from slavery to St John Rivers so that she can return to Rochester.)

But this story of the weaving of the spell and the breaking of it belong to the second and third books, where Emily herself refers to Haworth Parsonage and the Brontë sisters and where Dean begins to disparage Emily's ambitions. In *Emily of New Moon* we are alerted to the imaginative stage upon which Emily's later drama will have to be enacted. Let us look at some similarities between the novels *Emily of New Moon* and *Jane Eyre*.

The opening pages of *Jane Eyre* offer an unforgettable picture of the ten-year-old orphan sitting in a window recess reading about the savage, icy splendours of Norway, Lapland, and the Hebrides, while she is trying to escape the notice of her cruel cousin, John Reed. When he finds her and then knocks her down and cuts her head, she flies at him like a wildcat, driven at last to turn on her long-time tormentor. No one who has read the famous opening can forget how the cold aunt refuses to listen to Jane, and chapter one ends with these words of aunt and narrator: ' "Take her away to the red-room, and lock her in there." Four hands were immediately laid upon me, and I was borne upstairs' (9). Without even knowing what the 'red-room' is we shiver with the horror of it. The inexplicable cruelty of adult to child is nowhere better painted than here, where all the weight of privilege and class and age bear Jane down; Brontë captures perfectly the spirit of the passionate, intelligent child unjustly punished by a baffling adult code.

Emily would have loved the savage power of this scene and the almost Gothic terror of the next chapter, where Jane is imprisoned in the red-room, which she remembers suddenly to be where her uncle died. She terrifies herself by looking into the gloom and seeing her own haunting face in the mirror. The description of Jane's view is enough to conjure up all the fear of childhood: 'A bed supported on massive pillars of mahogany, hung with curtains of deep red damask, stood out like a tabernacle in the centre; the two large windows, with their blinds always drawn down, were half shrouded in festoons and falls of similar drapery; ... the bed rose before me; to my right hand there was the high, dark wardrobe, with subdued, broken reflections varying the gloss of its panels; to my left were the muffled windows; a great looking-glass between them repeated the vacant majesty of the bed and room' (Brontë 10–11). Soon Jane remembers her dead uncle and thinks his ghost may decide to relieve her here in her distress. The thought almost paralyses her, and then she sees a gleam of light gliding up the wall to the ceiling, and her screams bring her aunt, who thrusts her back into the room and turns the key. Jane falls unconscious and is roused from stupor much later to find herself in her own bed being tended by an apothecary.

Whether or not Emily herself had read *Jane Eyre* early in the pages of *Emily of New Moon* is doubtful. But Montgomery had read it, and Montgomery's readers would probably have read it, and Emily's imagination has been fed – even in the early pages – by reading from her father's books. Besides, Brontë is capturing the quality of terror the sensitive orphan feels; Montgomery's description of Emily's similar adventure echoes Brontë's and suggests the quality of Emily's imagination and spirit.

Shortly after Emily comes to New Moon, she defies Aunt Elizabeth in a way that makes that headstrong woman eager to have revenge. For punishment, she locks Emily in the spare room where so many Murrays have died. Montgomery's style is very different from Brontë's – third person rather than first, explanatory rather than minutely evocative – and yet we hear in Montgomery's lines echoes of Brontë's famous passages. In Brontë we find windows 'with their blinds always drawn down' and 'shrouded' in drapery; the bed 'rose before me' and a 'great looking-glass' repeats the 'vacant majesty of the bed and room.' In Montgomery we see: 'The window was hung with heavy, dark-green material, reinforced by drawn slat-blinds. The big canopied bed, jutting out from the wall into the middle of the floor, was high and rigid and curtained also with dark draperies. *Anything* might jump at her out of such a bed. What if some great black hand should suddenly reach out of it – reach right across the floor – and pluck at her? The walls, like those of the parlour, were adorned with pictures of departed relatives. There *was* such a large connection of dead Murrays. The glasses of their frames gave out weird reflections of the spectral threads of light struggling through the slat blinds' (114). When Jane remembers her dead uncle, suddenly 'a light gleamed on the wall ... gliding up to the ceiling and quivered over my head' (Brontë 14). When Emily has stared at all the portraits of the dead Murrays and terrified herself with imagining the stuffed owl leaping at her from the wardrobe, suddenly: 'A beam of sunlight struck through a small break in one of the slats of the blind and fell directly athwart the picture of Grandfather Murray hanging over the mantel-piece ... In that gleam of light his face seemed veritably to leap out of the gloom at Emily with its grim frown strangely exaggerated. Emily's nerve gave way completely' (115). The feelings of injustice and terror of the two children are similar; the settings for their torture, the unused room with the bed and windows with full, gloomy drapery, are similar; both children remember dead relatives. The glass on the pictures of the dead Murrays acts like the huge mirror in the red-room; the beam of light drives each child to action. Afterwards, Jane wakes up in the nursery seeing this emblematically appropriate combination: 'a terrible red glare, crossed with thick black bars' (Brontë 15); her unconscious acknowledges hell and prison and shadows of the red-room before her consciousness translates them into the fire's glow beyond her crib rails. So much of Jane's story is a story of flight from imprisonment – the red-room scene is suggestive of the plight of a female of her condition in the England of her time. Jane leaves the Reed home, she leaves Lowood, she flees Thornfield Hall, she turns from Moor House – each place threatens her identity and values in a peculiar way. Thornfield Hall, suggestive of all the opulence and privilege that have oppressed a determined individualist such as Jane, must become a charred ruin before Jane is free to join Edward Rochester in marriage.

The aftermath of Emily's terror, though radically different from Jane's, is appropriate to Emily's individualism within the culture surrounding her. While Jane falls unconscious, Emily leaps to the window and tears open the blinds. In floods the light, and terror is banished. And not only is there sunshine, but there is a ladder to take her out to meet up with the vibrant Ilse, who is to become her best friend and is truly her complement in every way. As in all Montgomery's novels, so here: freedom is literally in your own backyard. The destined mate, in such a world, is again almost literally the boy next door, whether he is Teddy or Gilbert or Jingle. Joy and salvation would seem to be more accessible to a female in Emily's world than in Jane's, but the apparent simplicity of Emily's difficulties is deceptive. Terror and taboo are complexly intertwined for Emily with creativity and self-assertion. When Teddy and the sunny Tansy Patch are inaccessible to Emily she mistakes Dean Priest's shadowy world of art for the rightful home of the artist spirit. To burst into sunlight – so simple in this early (disrupted) echo of Brontë's red-room episode – becomes the most difficult of Emily's challenges.

A playful reminder[2] of Brontë's red-room appears later in one of Emily's adventures at Wyther Grange, the home of Great-aunt Nancy Priest. Here Emily experiences terror in the Pink Room. The name 'Wyther Grange' is itself reminiscent of Thrushcross Grange and Wuthering Heights in Emily Brontë's *Wuthering Heights*, and it is Gothic horrors Emily thinks of when she first enters the old house. The Pink Room episode is Montgomery's miniature parody of Gothic terror and Gothic novels. Emily's over-fed imagination brings to mind not only Jane Eyre but also Catherine Morland, Jane Austen's heroine of *Northanger Abbey*, that novel-length joke about Gothic thrillers, especially Mrs Radcliffe's. Montgomery seems at pains to show Emily in a comic light, as though to emphasize that Montgomery's narrative distinguishes clearly between what is genuinely terrifying and what is merely the product of imagination nurtured inappropriately. Emily has been indulging in too much Gothic-horror reading, and the narrator interprets her responses to the rooms of Wyther Grange: 'They went through the spacious hall, catching glimpses on either side of large, dim, splendid rooms, then through the kitchen end out of it into an odd little back hall. It was long and narrow and dark. On one side was a row of four, square, small-paned windows, on the other were cupboards, reaching from floor to ceiling, with doors of black shining wood. Emily felt like one of the heroines in Gothic romance, wandering at midnight through a subterranean dungeon, with some unholy guide. She had read "The Mysteries of Udolpho" and "The Romance of the Forest" before the taboo had fallen on Dr. Burnley's bookcase. She shivered. It was awful but interesting' (247). Great-aunt Nancy and her cousin Caroline are like crones, and Emily feels only pleasantly spooked when she is told she will sleep alone in the Pink

Room. But in the night, when she hears an incessant rustling and fluttering and crying in the wall behind her bed, her Gothic-fed imagination betrays her: 'Every ghost and groan, every tortured spirit and bleeding nun of the books she had read came into her mind' (255). Emily's very real terror in the spare-room experience is not reproduced here; Montgomery instead is having fun with the Wyther Grange chapters and their references to Mrs Radcliffe's popular Gothics and allusion to Brontë's red-room. The reader is intrigued to know the source of the noise, not indignant or frightened on Emily's behalf.

The Gothic play would seem a gratuitous departure in the book if it were not so soon followed by two very real and chilling episodes. Comparing Emily's fright in the Pink Room with what later happens at Priest Pond is, as Montgomery no doubt intended, like comparing melodrama with drama. The Gothic allusions remind us of artifice, and then Montgomery's narrator introduces us first to the shatteringly and then to the agonizingly real.

Since coming to New Moon and first hearing about Ilse's mother, Emily has wondered what happened to her. No one will speak about her, and no one is allowed to mention her to Ilse's father. Ilse indifferently assumes she is dead. She suffers herself from her father's hatred, and she does not trouble herself with a mother she cannot remember. Emily is innocently reading the popular romance *The Scottish Chiefs* one day when Great-aunt Nancy and Caroline revive the sordid story about Ilse's mother. Young Beatrice Burnley is supposed to have left her little baby in order to stow away on board the ship of a dashing cousin. Her husband had waited patiently at home for her return from her farewell visit to the cousin. People had seen Beatrice enter the cousin's ship, but none had seen her leave. The ship later sank, taking all lives. Emily's horror over what she hears has none of the comforting picturesqueness of melodrama or Gothic romance. The old women think she is going to faint, but Emily turns on Caroline: '"Don't touch me!" she cried passionately. "Don't touch me! You – you – you *liked* hearing that story!"' (268) Emily cannot believe Ilse's mother would desert her; the hideousness of such betrayal poisons her days and nights. The very depths of her beauty-loving soul are stirred and she broods over the story – she cannot believe it and despairs that she cannot solve what she knows must be a mystery.

It is as though the springtime of Emily's young life is blighted by the story. The narrator quotes from Browning to suggest this loss: 'There was a drop of poison in every cup. Even the filmy shadows on the great bay, the charm of its fir-hung cliffs and its little purple islets that looked like outposts of fairyland, could not bring to her the old "fine, careless rapture"' (270). The phrase from Browning's famous, yearning poem, 'Home Thoughts from Abroad,' written in Italy about the beauties of spring in England, tells us that the 'wise thrush' repeats his song 'Lest you should think he never could recapture / The first fine careless rapture!' (15–16). The poetical phrase underlines the yearning of the normally beauty-loving Emily for her own spiritual innocence – a time she can never now recapture – before she had heard the hideous story of Ilse's mother's suspected betrayal. Emily is all but numb to the transporting charm of her surroundings.

Suffering about Ilse's mother, Emily then faces her own death. She goes on an evening ramble, thinking 'I wonder ... how much longer I have to live' (270), ventures too close to a cliff's edge in order to pick a spectacular aster, and when the ground gives way finds herself clinging to the crumbling bank. As she pictures herself smashed on the stones below, the will to live returns, but still mixed with thoughts of Ilse's mother: 'She had faced death once before, or thought she had, on the night when Lofty John had told her she had eaten a poisoned apple – but this was even harder. To die here, all alone, far away from home! They might never know what had become of her – never find her. The crows or the gulls would pick her eyes out. She dramatized the thing so vividly that she almost screamed with the horror of it. She would just disappear from the world as Ilse's mother had disappeared' (272). In Emily's earlier brush with death (or imagined brush) she had borrowed from her reading to think of herself as part of a Victorian death scene complete with woeful mourners; now she faces her death and tries to read beyond the simple story of Ilse's mother's disappearance. Intuition prompts the developing artist to move beyond the familiar, to review Ilse's mother's death as though it is a misunderstood text.

Suddenly, Dean Priest appears and rescues her. He, like Emily, has been lured to the cliff's edge by the beautiful aster and then sees her below him. The dramatic and psychological moment is perfect – she has already abandoned despair and is working out alternatives for Ilse's mother. It is as though she thinks, if I am here and no one knows it, she could have disappeared in a way no one guessed. The artist in her identifies with the wronged woman, and her knowledge is profound. Her later vision of Ilse's mother is beginning here, where Emily, too, hovers close to death. She will have to go back to the borderland between worlds again before the clear vision of Ilse's mother can come to her. Montgomery may be suggesting that the artist is gifted to see truth because she will not settle for easy answers and because she dares to cross into the shadow lands where her spirit may face its own death. Just at this moment, when Emily is intuiting the truth about Beatrice Burnley, Dean Priest, pursuing the same love of beauty that has lured Emily on, arrives. As the *deus ex machina* of this drama, he seems at first an odd hero. Sitting on the bank beside him, she remembers what she has been told about him – that he is thirty-six, college educated, aloof, cynical, has a malformed shoulder (hence his hateful nickname 'Jarback'), travels the world, and is feared by his clan for his 'ironic tongue.' We listen to their dialogue and enjoy his dawning appreciation of Emily's worth. When we understand their meeting and ensuing friendship in relationship to *Jane Eyre*, we appreciate even more the position of rescued and rescuer.

Within half an hour of their meeting he says, only half ironically, 'I perceive you are an artist in words.' And seconds later he adds, 'I think I'll wait for you' (278). Emily thinks he is talking about their immediate situation, but the reader knows better. Already Dean Priest has focused his lonely soul on Emily. But when he, half laughing, lays claim to her a few pages later, Emily's spirit rebels even though she does not understand the vehemence of her own reaction. He tells her the old myth that the one who saves a life then owns that life, and Emily experiences 'an odd sensation of rebellion. She didn't fancy the idea of her life belonging to anybody but herself – not even to anybody she liked as much as she liked Dean Priest.' Dean sees what she is feeling and presses the point: ' "That doesn't quite suit you? Ah, you see one pays a penalty when one reaches out for something beyond the ordinary. One pays for it in bondage of some kind or other. Take your wonderful aster home and keep it as long as you can. It has cost you your freedom." He was laughing – he was only joking, of course – yet Emily felt as if a cobweb fetter had been flung round her. Yielding to a sudden impulse she flung the big aster on the ground and set her foot on it' (281). This is the most important gesture in all three of the Emily books – instinctively Emily fights against the power that wants to dominate her. And yet she leans towards Dean Priest, bends to him in the subsequent episodes, and does not understand that she, here, has rejected only part of his domination in refusing to acknowledge his right to own her. She will have to learn that, whenever she has accepted his judgment in place of hers, she has added to the cobweb fetters he flings round her. We notice that the narrator does not say that Emily broke through the fetters when she crushed the aster. Instead the fetters get tighter the closer she comes to accepting his standards of taste and value. The beginnings of a vision have brought them together and eventually, in the third Emily book, a vision will separate them – Dean Priest is deliberately associated with the most powerful forces in Emily's being.

Dean's use of *Jane Eyre* at the end of this rescue chapter throws the whole episode into a richly ambiguous context. As Dean watches Emily walk away, the narrator explains his actions for us:

He stooped and picked up the broken aster. Emily's heel had met it squarely and it was badly crushed. But he put it away that night between the leaves of an old volume of *Jane Eyre*, where he had marked a verse –
> All glorious rose upon my sight
> That child of shower and gleam. (282)

Dean's choice (Montgomery's choice for him) is fascinating. Dean's choice seems high-minded – it sounds as though he is putting the emblematic aster next to a Wordsworthian stanza that praises the fresh innocence of childhood. A closer look at *Jane Eyre* shows how false is this impression. You would have to know *Jane Eyre* very well indeed to know these two lines, buried as they are in the middle of a song Rochester sings to Jane. The song is not about childhood at all, but about a passionate, romantic love that is willing to brave all kinds of disasters, vengeance, and hatred. The lover says 'For Might and Right, and Woe and Wrath, / Between our spirits stood,' and yet 'I dangers dared; I hind'rance scorned; / I omens did defy': for finally, as the last stanza declares, he is rewarded because 'My love has sworn, with sealing kiss, / With me to live – to die; / I have at last my nameless bliss: / As I love – loved am I!' (Brontë 239–40). Rochester sings this to Jane when she has accepted him and they are spending together one of the evenings of the month before their planned wedding day. The song seems to be about Jane and Rochester, although we later see how differently they would interpret it: for her the barriers to their marriage are those of convention – money, age, rank; for him, the barriers are far greater, since he intends to defy the marriage vow itself in taking Jane as his wife while Bertha Rochester still lives. Within the context of the novel, the song thus gains poignant significance – Rochester's bold claims and ardour cannot hold Jane when she knows it is wrong to marry him.

Dean's choice of this passage is truly ironic and, on Montgomery's part, surely ingenious. On the surface he is praising the image of vivid freshness Emily has given him, but the deeper suggestion is that he already identifies himself as the middle-aged Rochester, craggy, misanthropic, and Byronic, who yearns towards the purity and revitalizing youthful love of Jane Eyre. In declaring that he will wait for her, Dean has cast himself in the role of future lover. The immediate context of Rochester's song is also revealing of the exchange Emily and Dean have just had. In the novel Jane has been trying to think of ways to fend off Rochester's too-ardent wooing. She refuses to see him, as he would wish, at all hours of the day, and eventually confines him to the evening, where she devises all kinds of distractions (such as having him sing to her) to keep him at arm's length. Rochester has greeted her injunction about evening meetings with loving threats about the future: ‘"it is your time now, little tyrant, but it will be mine presently: and when once I have fairly seized you, to have and to hold, I'll just – figuratively speaking – attach you to a chain like this" (touching his watch-guard)' (Brontë 238). Possession is what Dean wants and what Emily has already resisted. The working out of Emily's story is, in fact, a lengthy response to the kind of love that Rochester seems to propose and that Jane eventually gives to him. The violent, passionate, desperate love of Jane and Rochester is a tortured yet joyous duet of dominating and yielding strains. Such love – where the younger, purer woman redeems the darkened soul of a passionate equal – is translated for Emily into the realm of art. Dean believes that in order to possess her love he must master her love of writing and, in struggling to dominate her sensibility and eventually her voice, he forfeits any real tension for equality. He tries to tame Emily and he loses her. The dastardly thing is that Dean does, like Rochester with Jane, understand so much of Emily's soul. But while Rochester wants Jane as Jane, Dean Priest wants to change Emily (which makes Dean resemble St John Rivers rather than Rochester).

Montgomery alters Jane's story in significant ways. The meeting of Emily and Dean is an inversion of the meeting of Jane and Rochester, and since Brontë had deliberately made the meeting of Jane and Rochester an inversion of the pattern of the beautiful, helpless heroine / handsome, valiant hero, we see that the roles of Emily and Dean have been designed to suggest fairy-tale and damsel-in-distress motifs; Dean even refers to himself as her 'knightly rescuer' (276). In *Jane Eyre*, Jane is out walking to relieve the tedium of her predictable round at Thornfield Hall when Rochester appears on horseback and, having ridden past her, clatters to the ground when his horse slips on ice. The diminutive Jane rushes to assist the burly Rochester and endures his oaths and surliness as she lends him her shoulder. He later says he had thought she was a fairy that had stepped from the greenwood to bewitch his horse. When Brontë's novel appeared, this first encounter between hero and heroine was startlingly original – the reading audience had already come to expect a more conventional fairy-tale model (like the one Montgomery uses). Just as Jane's life is a series of imprisonments and flights from imprisonment, so her story with Rochester is one of demanding and expecting recognition of equality. The first meeting, then, rightly reverses the old order – the apparently weak Jane is the strong, essential staff for the apparently self-sufficient Rochester. Their story continues the balancing between forces; they find equilibrium in shared values and mutual acceptance. (It is a continuing and delightful irony in the history of literature that this most romantic of novels is also one of the most radically feminist.)

Now in Montgomery's story, Emily does not have the liberating surprise of physically rescuing Dean Priest. Instead the old order prevails, and the knight rescues the maiden (whom he also calls a fairy). And though Dean can identify himself as Rochester on one level, he does not learn Rochester's wisdom on a profounder level. He tries to curb Emily, not 'just' own her. Eventually his love for Emily resembles Rochester's for Jane only in that he, too, is an older man in need of a younger woman's respect and love. One wonders if the hump-shouldered Dean Priest identified himself with Rochester after he is blinded and maimed; in such identification his jealousy of everything she loves would be easier to understand, but no easier to forgive. For it is Emily's writing self, her very essence, that he eventually tries to destroy. Rochester lies to Jane in not telling her that his first wife is alive, but Dean lies to Emily by telling her that her writing is no good. Rochester seeks to alter circumstances; Dean tries to quench Emily's fire.

Dean's love for Emily, despite his intelligence and literariness, is really a very conventional thing, and the fairy-tale rescue is perfectly representative of his unconscious as well as conscious expectations for Emily. In the very next chapter after he rescues her, they are having one of their wide-ranging talks about history and literature when they disagree about the necessity for pain in the world. True to her own willingness to suffer to see the truth, Emily avers that some causes are worth blood. Dean dismisses her arguments with ' "And, like all female creatures, you form your opinions by your feelings ... remember that if there is to be drama in your life *somebody* must pay the piper in the coin of suffering. If not you – then some one else." "Oh, no, I wouldn't like *that*." "Then be content with fewer thrills" ' (284–5). Sensitive as he is to art and literature, to the stars and natural beauties around, Dean Priest does not want to suffer for knowledge. And he does not want Emily, either, to pay any price that may take a part of her away from him.

Yet Dean is no monster, and he has charm for Emily and for many readers because he is capable of Rochester's passion and perception of worth. A large part of him, too, belongs to the exotic world Emily's own love of beauty prompts her to admire. Unlike Jane and Rochester, Emily and Dean do not stand as true equals until each has caused the other great suffering and each has had to face the fact that neither loves the other as she or he thought.

In addition to the literary allusions and explorations, we find in each of the Emily books a central psychic experience. In each instance Emily rescues someone – as though her unconscious mind asserts itself to counteract the obligation Dean's rescue has placed on her. Her artistic powers make her an active, restorative force, equal to and surpassing the male (silencing) power she must resist if she is to develop as a writer. In *Emily of New Moon* Emily rescues Beatrice Burnley's reputation; in *Emily Climbs*, she saves a little boy; in *Emily's Quest*, she saves Teddy. Like the literary dimension of Emily's conscious (and unconscious) mind, the psychic experiences, too, belong to Emily the artist. They suggest that Emily is indeed attuned to another, deeper, richer dimension than most people can touch, and they give her legitimacy as an artist. The psychic experiences are to her intuition what the flash is to her visions of beauty:

Emily touches the artistic realm within and beyond the world of appearances. Each of the psychic experiences calls out from the deepest places in Emily's spirit. Emily's first vision stirs when she broods over Ilse's mother and clings to the earth above Malvern Bay – in the blankness she feels as her soul stretches over the borderlands, she meets Dean Priest. Later in the novel Emily comes down with measles and, when she is again on the borderland between life and death, she has a vision of Ilse's mother, actually sees her walking alone across the Lee pasture, singing as she returns home to her child and husband from the shipboard farewell to her cousin. Emily 'sees' her fall into the uncovered well and makes Aunt Elizabeth promise to have the well searched. When the now-unused well is uncovered and investigated, they find what is left of Beatrice Burnley. On the fateful day that Emily had herself clung to a cliff above Malvern Bay, she had identified with Beatrice Burnley's lonely death, though she had not yet recognized what she felt. Just as the whole first book shows Emily groping her way to recognition of herself as a writer, so this psychic experience suggests the struggle to consciousness of Emily's intuition and values.

Emily's psychic vision of Ilse's mother brings together a host of forces in Emily's life. Emily restores Ilse's mother to her, just as she feels her own mother has been restored to her, since she now occupies her mother's room. Aunt Elizabeth's promise to search the well strengthens the bond between Emily and the traditions of New Moon. The vision itself suggests the fertile, (re)creative powers of Emily's conscious and unconscious and gives her credibility within her clan and community as an old-world seer. Emily as daughter, friend, clanswoman, niece, mother-of-dreams, artist, and creator is validated in her value-affirming vision of a happy mother anticipating the return home to her child. Emily as artist lays claim to the past and the future and demonstrates her ability to see behind the veil that separates this world from 'the flash.' Emily, like Jane Eyre, knows herself to be the heroine of a rich and surprising story – her own.

Testing the Voice:
Emily Climbs

Emily's childhood is neatly partitioned off from her adolescence by the psychic experience of death and renewal (Ilse's mother's 'legitimate' death restores Dr Burnley's faith in women and life). *Emily of New Moon* ends on an upbeat note, with Emily's triumph with Mr Carpenter and her decision to write her own story as a diary. Emily has won a place and the liberty to explore it. In *Emily Climbs* (1925), which covers Emily's three years at Shrewsbury High School, we find her grappling with others' conceptions of art and with her own voice. Now she says what she thinks about some of what she reads, and her journal entries are as entertaining as many of Montgomery's own.

The psychic experience in *Emily of New Moon* comes near the end of the novel as a culmination of powerful forces in Emily's development; in *Emily Climbs*, the major psychic experience comes just over half-way through the book. The experience itself makes exciting reading, but is important in our understanding of Emily for the literary gift it brings for her. This time Emily's vision saves a little boy's life – she 'dreams' where the lost boy is to be found, and then, still in sleep or trance, draws a picture of the house she and Ilse had passed the day before, a house that had called strangely to Emily. The child is found, all but dead, on the floor of the little room Emily's trance-drawing marks with a cross. When she and Ilse wake, before Emily has seen her own drawing, they are honoured with a visit from old Mrs MacIntyre and with the telling of her story, which eventually becomes Emily's 'The Woman Who Spanked the King.' They later learn that Mrs MacIntyre does not tell her story to everyone, but has discerned Emily's specialness even before her drawing of Allan Bradshaw's whereabouts is discovered. She tells Emily, 'you haf the way and it is to you I will be telling my story' (193). As with the beginning of the vision of Ilse's mother and its accompaniment of the friendship of Dean Priest, so here it is as though the psychic experience prepares the way for some larger creative possibility. Emily's eventual publication of Mrs MacIntyre's story attracts the notice of a New York editor, and the meeting with her confronts Emily with one of her biggest career decisions – whether to go to New York as she has been invited to do or stay at New Moon, where she can develop a truly Canadian voice. In this second book, the psychic experience helps to precipitate a crisis of identity for the writer that then separates the apprentice from the skilled worker.

As its title suggests, *Emily Climbs* is about literary apprenticeship. Emily tests herself against others – Ilse, Teddy, Perry, Dean, Aunt Ruth, Cousin Andrew – and also tries her own literary judgments. The book has many wonderfully told adventures and scenes that I am not going to write about here but that I recommend for their scrupulous truth to adolescent ego, restlessness, and zest for life. Emily writes in her journal, sends poems out for publication, studies what is and what is not on the school curriculum, and even writes for the local paper. She is learning to know herself and is constantly exercising her new voice. She must frequently defy Aunt Ruth, another gatekeeper for the establishment; she is sensitive to criticism from others and is still shaping herself, in some ways, according to what others think of her abilities. The essay and then the story of 'The Woman Who Spanked the King' offer a touchstone for others' reactions to Emily and for her own to herself. This early in her career – the second Emily book takes her from fourteen to seventeen – Emily is independent enough to try to ignore Dean's growing condescension.

Mr Carpenter is still the literary mentor of most importance in *Emily Climbs*. He admonishes Emily to curb her departures from realism, to stick to what she knows, and to eschew the clever, caustic satire she is capable of writing, but that hurts others and will, he warns her, twist her own spirit. When Aunt Elizabeth makes Emily promise that she will not write any fiction while she is at Shrewsbury High School, Mr Carpenter is pleased – he believes sticking to truth and details will make Emily give up some of her more fatuous fancies. When Emily shows him the essay (Aunt Elizabeth's injunction keeps her from making it into a story) about Mrs MacIntyre's spanking of Prince Bertie, Mr Carpenter is frankly delighted. After the ban on fiction is lifted, Emily turns the essay into a story, and when a large New York magazine accepts it, she shows it to Mr Carpenter. He thinks it is 'absolutely good' (263) and praises her for not trying to improve on Mrs MacIntyre's way of telling the story: ' "But you didn't try to [improve it] – *that* makes it yours," said Mr. Carpenter – and left her to puzzle his meaning out for herself' (263). A good teacher, he frequently leaves Emily to figure out what he means, and she grows by searching. (One could argue that he doesn't bother to help her understand what he says.) He refuses to advise Emily about her career and says he will not tell her how to answer Miss Royal's offer to go to New York (though his opinion of it is perfectly clear).

Miss Royal, an Island woman who has made it big in publishing in New York, decides to visit her aunt on P.E.I. partly because she wants to meet the young woman who wrote the short story 'The Woman Who Spanked the King.' After a very funny interview with Miss Royal (the chapter 'Love Me, Love My Dog' is delightful reading) – a chapter of farce – Miss Royal invites Emily to come and live with her in New York, to live and work in the heady, sophisticated centre of talent and opportunity. Miss Royal has been attracted by the gifted pen of the writer, but she is charmed by Emily herself, and the invitation marks the turning point in Emily's career as a writer and a young woman. The double validation of herself as author and independent woman strengthens a voice rejections and Dean are doing much to quiet. Interestingly, Emily must learn to reject female and male mentors.

Montgomery does not tell us directly what Teddy Kent (or Ilse) thinks of the short story, but she does not have to. We believe without being told that Teddy is as thrilled for her as she is for him when a Montreal man buys two of his pictures for a price that allows Teddy to spend another year at Shrewsbury. To Teddy, Emily is evidently as powerful as she in her best moments believes herself to be. Shortly after Aunt Elizabeth has told Emily she cannot write fiction at Shrewsbury, Emily meets Teddy and together they dream about their futures. Emily predicts that he will be a 'great artist,' and then she sits with rapt expression, vowing silently that she will climb her Alpine path, no matter what the obstacles. Teddy rejoins most appropriately, 'When I am I'll paint you just as you're looking now ... and call it Joan of Arc – with a face all spirit – listening to her voices' (79). It is the 'random word,' the 'airy voices' that Emily hears that make her, in her own imaginings, as strong as the Soldier of Amiens. Teddy's choice of an androgynous image is particularly apt when we recognize the perdurable stereotype of femininity Dean tries to impose on Emily. Teddy's instinctive recognition of and reverence for the spiritual warrior is what makes him support Emily the artist – his admiration for Emily is, apparently, not merely a product of (male) romantic longing and fantasy, though it is pictorial and idealized. He sees Emily as Emily sees herself.

Dean Priest's response to the essay 'The Woman Who Spanked the King' exposes his jealousy and narrowness – fully to the reader, partly to Emily. In the very same breath that she records Mr Carpenter's verdict of the essay – 'excellent' – she describes in her diary Dean's dismissal of the piece and her own subsequent doubts: 'I think in a way Dean doesn't like to think of my growing up – I *think* he has a little of the Priest jealousy of sharing *anything*, especially friendship, with any one else – or with the world ... For instance, Mr Carpenter was delighted with my *Woman Who Spanked the King*, and told me it was excellent; but when Dean read it he smiled and said, ''It will do very well for a school essay, but – '' and then he smiled again. It was not the smile I liked, either ... It seemed to say, ''You can scribble amusingly, my dear, and have a pretty knack of phrase-turning; but I should be doing you an unkindness if I let you think that such a knack meant a very great deal.'' If this is true – and it very likely is, for Dean is so clever and knows so much – then I can never accomplish anything worth while. I won't *try* to accomplish anything – I *won't* be just a ''pretty scribbler'' ' (211). In this we hear all the dangerous susceptibility of the young woman writer – she thinks she understands Dean Priest's jealousy, and yet, insecure and admiring, she is willing to believe he does know best about her limitations. But in this second book Emily is still weighing and testing, and Dean's possessiveness does not destroy her hopes. She has a saving resilience here that enables her to turn the essay into a story and send it off to a big New York magazine despite Dean's condescension.

What is it that Dean is trying to make of Emily? After their meeting in *Emily of New Moon*, Dean Priest seems to feed Emily's love of language and hunger for knowledge about the world and the mysterious and faraway things Dean has seen and studied. Even in the opening pages of *Emily Climbs* he seems supportive. It is no accident that within two pages of each other Montgomery has both Dean and Mr Carpenter quote Emerson to Emily in order to encourage and strengthen her. But the lines of Emerson's poetry that Dean quotes to Emily give us a curiously ambivalent message:

> *The gods talk in the breath of the wold,*
> *They talk in the shaken pine,*
> *And they fill the reach of the old seashore*
> *With dialogue divine;*
> *And the poet who overhears*
> *One random word they say*
> *Is the fated man of men*
> *Whom the ages must obey.* (*EC* 10)

Can he be suggesting that Emily is that 'fated man of men' or is he showing her that even the blessed and inspired hear only a 'random word,' a piece of the truth, and cannot achieve whole knowledge? Even if Dean is encouraging Emily here, shortly after their ramble he first exposes his jealousy and possessiveness – his true feelings. Dean and Emily are rereading the magical *Alhambra* together, when Teddy whistles and Emily tells Dean she must go: '"He only calls like that when he wants me *especially* and I have promised I will always go if I possibly can." "*I* want you *especially*!" said Dean. "I came up this evening on purpose to read *The Alhambra* with you"' (29). Though he does eventually shut up the book and tell her to go, Emily feels that 'things seemed spoiled, somehow' (29). True to her thorough indoctrination in female accommodation of male ego, she does not blame Dean for being selfish.

Less than a week after Emily has answered Teddy's call, Dean and Emily are again talking, and this time the jealousy takes a new and, as the reader sees, unmistakably dangerous form. Dean is careful to laugh when he says it, but his sincerity is obvious. He tells Emily that Teddy puts a part of her in every picture he paints and he wants him to stop. Dean's words and Emily's response establish early in this book what should be the clear lines of Dean's desires and Emily's. Dean says, '"But let him keep his pencil and brush off *my* property." Dean laughed as he said it. But I held my head high. I am not anybody's "property," not even in fun. And I *never* will be' (31). The young Emily intuits the demands that are being made, and she has the ready answer. But the world around Emily so frequently echoes Dean's perception of the female, and of her in particular, that by the time she writes the essay about Prince Bertie, she is not sure anymore that Dean's objections about her writing are really what they so obviously are. Emily's inner voice saves her many times through this second volume, as in the first, but we can see how the culture around conspires to silence the woman writer and encourages her to marry and get on with her proper roles of wife, mother, and inspirer to men. Even the successful Miss Royal, we remember, is nothing in the eyes of Aunt Ruth and Shrewsbury because she is not married. Certainly no one knew better than Montgomery herself how the unmarried woman is regarded by neighbours and family – even the woman who writes a best-seller or is invited to meet the governor general of Canada because her writing has touched him.[1]

Dean does not want Emily to be just like everyone else, of course, because he sees himself as different and wants a soul mate. Her writing is getting to be too powerful, and we know he fears he may lose her. He steadily works to transform her into a priestess of some mystical (but inevitably domestic) rite, some besieged heroine who will exchange everything (even writing, of course, if she did any) for love.

Scarcely a month after Dean has tried to deflate her over the writing of her important essay, he is talking to her about romance and love – disguisedly, of course. Emily tells him that she sympathizes with the unfortunate heroine of Mrs Browning's poem 'The Lay of the Brown Rosary.' In the poem Onora trades her soul to the bewitched ghost of a nun, in exchange for life with her beloved. The nun has told her that she will not live to be the bride of her hero, and Onora sells her soul so that she can live and marry her love. On her wedding day, Onora's lover falls dead, slain evidently by the very evil to which Onora has mistakenly sold herself. In the poem, Barrett Browning makes it clear that Onora chose foolishly the life on this earth over the eternal life in heaven. Not surprisingly, Dean applauds Emily's sympathy with Onora. She says, ' "My favourite poem is *The Lay of the Brown Rosary* – and I am much more in sympathy with *Onora* than Mrs Browning was." "You would be," said Dean. "That is because you are a creature of emotion yourself. *You* would barter heaven for love, just as *Onora* did" ' (216). As with most of Dean's knowledge of Emily, he is partly right, or right for the wrong reasons. She may be willing to give up reward or even the promise of reward, for love, but she is not willing to give up her writing until she can no longer believe in it. What Dean would clearly like to see as the romantic renunciation of all for love, Emily sees as a possibility only when she no longer has an ambition to strive for. But that despair comes in *Emily's Quest*, and only after many defeats and Dean's own huge lie about her novel.

In this book, Dean is beginning to act as a lover, even though Emily chooses not to understand. She is sixteen (he is forty), and he calls her a woman, flattering her, she believes, but keeping her firmly in her place as inspirer to others, not creator in her own right. Even Mr Carpenter tells her cynically that being able to dress well will be of more advantage to her than all her understanding of poetry or prose (Miller 163–4), and Dean, as the aspiring lover, goes further in his bid to transfix Emily as beloved: ' "You looked like a seeress gazing into the future as I came down the walk," said Dean, "standing here in the moonlight, white and rapt. Your skin is like a narcissus petal. You could dare to hold a white rose against your face – very few women can dare that. You aren't really very pretty, you know, Star, but your face makes people think of beautiful things – and that is a far rarer gift than mere beauty" ' (215). Alive to his compliments, Emily does not know how she pays for them. His insistence here on her physical beauty and its power to inspire comes a very short time after his dismissal of her essay and her power to inspire through her writing. To listen to Dean Priest, intoxicating as his visions and stories and comments are, is to conspire in her own silence. Her inner voice becomes strong through success, but it is correspondingly weakened by rejection slips and by the subtle, insistent vision of herself as seer that Dean promotes. Her own failures and her own perception of her second sight serve to reinforce his silencing image. Dean's 'seeress' has only to embody her visions, not speak or act upon them. Teddy's picture of Joan of Arc listening to her voices is obviously empowering by contrast – for Teddy, Emily is inspired action. It will take all Emily's psychic power and spiritual introspection to enable her to throw off the image Dean has constructed for her and that her own culture – through its advocacy of marriage and domesticity and romantic myth – reinforces.

But Emily is able to throw off much of Dean's condescension in this novel because she is young and eager and resilient. Montgomery begins and ends the book with Emily's writing, and the whole novel, really, shows Emily experimenting with success and vision. She learns to trust much about her own judgment. A younger Emily or an older one might not have been able to disregard Dean's damning faint praise of her essay; but the adolescent Emily is full of grit and heart and wants to succeed. The very first chapter entitled 'Writing Herself Out,' shows Emily wrestling with Mr Carpenter's criticism, vowing to succeed, and even pulling from her mattress a secreted candle so that she can disobey the bedtime hour in order to write out a story that has just occurred to her. She is sure of her calling and in tune with her inner voice. Despite Aunt Elizabeth, Aunt Ruth, and the dampening condescension of an infuriating student, Evelyn Blake, Emily writes and sends out her poems for publication. Even the injunction against writing fiction does not keep her from revelling in her diary and in the writing of poems. She exercises her own literary standards – while she enjoys *The Alhambra* with Dean and discussions of the poetic, sentimental story of *At the Back of the North Wind* with Ilse, she is reading and thinking about books she formerly thought perfect. She learns to be her own best critic. Writing in her journal one night she describes a scene as she wants to describe it, and then finds just fault with it. As we read the sentence for ourselves, we can appreciate Montgomery's sly humour here. The description sounds very much like ones her detractors accused her of writing all her career (and which she may have been guilty of in many short stories but came dangerously close to in only one novel, *The Golden Road*): 'And every night we have murky red sunsets flaming in smoky crimson across the harbour, with a star above them like a saved soul gazing with compassionate eyes into pits of torment where sinful spirits are being purged from the stains of earthly pilgrimage.' But Emily (like Montgomery) pulled herself up short: 'Would I dare to show the above sentence to Mr. Carpenter? I would *not* ... It's "fine writing"' (259).

She recognizes that Mrs Hemans is not great, even though she defends her from Mr Carpenter's utter contempt by citing her own favourite, highly romantic lines (253). She also turns her criticism to Tennyson and Keats. Whereas a younger Emily found Tennyson wholly delightful (as did Anne Shirley throughout her life), a more self-reliant Emily judges with revealing coolness: 'I like Tennyson but sometimes he enrages me. He is beautiful – not *too* beautiful, as Keats is – the Perfect Artist. But he never lets us forget the artist – we are always conscious of it – he is never swept away by some splendid mountain torrent of feeling. Not he – he flows on serenely between well-ordered banks and carefully laid-out gardens. And no matter how much one loves a garden one doesn't want to be cooped up in it *all* the time – one likes an excursion now and then into the wilderness. At least Emily Byrd Starr does – to the sorrow of her relations. Keats *is* too full of beauty. When I read his poetry I feel stifled in roses and long for a breath of frosty air or the austerity of a chill mountain peak. But, oh, he has *some* lines – ' (256–7). This love of an occasional wildness, this passion, is what would attract Emily to the Brontës and ally her partly with Dean. Perhaps even more revealing of Emily's sense of herself is her outrage over Tennyson's men and women in *Idylls of the King*, a point of view unshared by anyone in the Anne books. 'I detest Tennyson's *Arthur*. If I had been *Guinevere* I'd have boxed his ears – but I wouldn't have been unfaithful to him for *Lancelot*, who was just as odious in a different way. As for *Geraint*, if I had been *Enid* I'd have *bitten* him. These "patient Griseldas" deserve all they get. Lady Enid, if you had been a Murray of New Moon you would have kept your husband in better order and he would have liked you all the better for it' (222). It is revealing that Emily did not fault Guinevere for adultery, as Tennyson clearly did, and it is appropriate that Emily would reject the pale, virtuous, long-suffering Arthur, as well as the distracted and self-loathing Lancelot. Clearly Emily believes Geraint's uncourteous treatment of women could be remedied by spunk. The emerging portrait of the strong woman is perfectly in keeping with the heroine Jane Eyre and also with the characters in two other novel-length stories we later find in the third Emily volume to have been influential in Emily's construction of her self-concept: Aurora Leigh in Barrett Browning's novel-poem *Aurora Leigh,* and the combined characters of Waldo and Lyndall in Olive Schreiner's *The Story of an African Farm.* Through her literary apprenticeship Emily gains a strong sense of self-worth, but, as we have also suggested with Dean, this self-image is dependent on her faithfulness to her own voice, and the ability to hear that voice clearly is dependent on her success as a writer.

Emily is strong in this novel, but we can see where her vulnerability lies. She pledges herself to her Alpine Path and to the 'airy voices' from Keats's poem, and she dares to write her pivotally important essay and then to defy Dean's judgment and rewrite it as a story. But before she hears of the story's acceptance, her inner voice has been sorely tried. She has received rejection after rejection and has vowed to keep trying: 'Still, her inner voice had grown rather faint under so many discouragements. The acceptance of *The Woman Who Spanked the King* suddenly raised it into a joyous paean of certainty again. The check meant much, but the storming of that magazine much more' (263). Flushed from this victory, Emily becomes conscious for the first time of loving Teddy Kent. Teddy and Perry and Ilse and Emily are storm staid in an abandoned farmhouse. As they sit together, Emily and Teddy both know the other loves: 'For just a moment their eyes met and locked – only a moment – yet Emily was never really to belong to herself again' (269). This belonging to someone else is very different, we see, from Dean's notion of ownership. Montgomery underscores the difference by making Emily, minutes later, inspired with the idea for a story. It is as though Teddy fits into Emily's artistic world, can even call out the best creative impulses in her. Dean wants to kill what he cannot touch. Here Teddy says, 'I've a pocket full of dreams to sell ... What d'ye lack?' and 'Emily turned around – stared at him for a moment – then forgot thrills and spells and everything else in a wild longing for a Jimmy-book. As if his question, "What will you give me for a dream?" had been a magic formula opening some sealed chamber in her brain, she saw unrolling before her a dazzling idea for a story – complete even to the title – *A Seller of Dreams* ... it unrolled itself before her in the darkness. Her characters lived and laughed and talked and did and enjoyed and suffered – she saw them on the background of the storm ... Ilse had got drunk on Malcolm Shaw's forgotten Scotch whiskey, but Emily was intoxicated with immortal wine' (270–1).[2] This wonderful story, inspired by Teddy, is only an outline for the apprentice Emily, but in *Emily's Quest*, she writes the novel and it is as rich and rare and vital as she dreamed it could be – and she kills it for Dean.

Throughout *Emily Climbs* the questions about identity and love and art are bound up with each other. Dean belongs to the enchanted world of the *Alhambra*; it is appropriate that the real Alhambra is only a ghost of its former grandeur, a legend of mystery and passion. Readers of Irving's work would find it significant, too, that there is always something sinister about the Moorish ruins, with their blood-stained marble courts and their legendary key and lions. Dean's charm for Emily is always tinged with danger – she does not yet know how intimately he can undermine and manipulate her as a woman and as an artist. Teddy, on the other hand, is always associated with Emily's deepest emotions – with what she feels and thinks, not with what he wants and tries to impose on her. The coolness readers feel about Teddy shows how difficult Montgomery's problem with romance is: jealousy and possessiveness are violent and all-consuming; friendship and equality are tepid in terms of conventional romance (Kreps 145–54).

Montgomery intensifies the difference between Dean and Teddy and their power with Emily in an early episode in this novel. She ironically reveals Teddy as Rochester and Emily as Jane Eyre, but with the actions, again, reversed from Brontë and conforming to traditional rescue of the damsel in distress. While the discovery of the little lost boy may be the central psychic experience of the novel, this early echo of Jane's rescue from St John Rivers sets the tone for the romantic events and questions of the novel. Emily is accidentally locked in the church at night with mad Mr Morrison, an old crazed man who wanders everywhere looking for his lost child bride, Annie. Emily is terrified that he will touch her, mistaking her for Annie, and in her agony she calls out to Teddy. The church is tightly closed and Teddy lives more than a mile away, but Emily's call wakes him and he rushes to her and rescues her. When they are sitting safely outside in the graveyard together, Emily asks Teddy how he knew where she was. His answer reveals the psychic quality of the experience: '"Why – I don't know," said Teddy confusedly. "I didn't stop to think – I just seemed to *know* you were in the church when I heard you calling me, and I must get here as quick as I could. It's – it's all – funny," he concluded lamely' (53). Readers familiar with *Jane Eyre* will have no trouble accounting for the power of the voice. After Jane has been estranged from Rochester for more than a year, she is being hard pressed by the bloodless minister St John Rivers to marry him so that she can serve with him as his missionary wife in India. He does not love her, and he uses the arguments of duty and love of God and declares that she should spend her life in servitude not in earthly pleasures. Jane is stirred to the depths of her strong being and, when she cries out for a sign from God, she hears Rochester's voice calling her name clearly, over the miles of heath and mountain. It is Rochester's call that gives her the courage to leave St John Rivers – in rushing to rescue Rochester, she rescues herself. In the novel, Jane Eyre explains the phenomenon modestly, saying that in the long-distance message nature did 'no miracle – but her best' (Brontë 370). When she is back with Rochester he tells her, in his inimitably passionate way, how her voice came to soothe him as it replied to his call. Emily's call to Teddy is modelled on this famous, romantic experience of Jane and Rochester. As with the rescue of Emily by Dean, Montgomery again chooses the more conventional form of having the knight rescue the lady – Brontë's heroine, on the other hand, is always, it seems, rescuing the hero. But, roles apart, the message is unmistakable: Teddy is the one spiritually joined with Emily. Since Teddy has complete faith in Emily and her voices, the love-link with him is a reinforcement of her artistic independence. Thus, when the novel ends and Montgomery is neatly tying up threads about love and career, she can show that Emily's love for Teddy is a source of happiness, not a fetter. The relationship with Dean causes her a literal nightmare in which she chooses Teddy over Dean and leaves Dean lamenting in despair that 'My star has set' (322). Psychic experience, dream vision, and artistic inspiration link Emily with Teddy.

Guilt and sorrow threaten Emily as shadows of the future, but for now, Emily is happy to be on her own and to taste the successes of her pen. Emily's thoughts about Teddy and his possible indifference to her (after all) suggest the optimism and honesty of this book: 'I am conscious of three sensations. On top I am sternly composed and traditional. Underneath that, something that would hurt horribly if I let it is being kept down. And underneath that again is a queer feeling of relief that I still have my freedom' (320). This 'queer feeling of relief' will buoy Emily through more years of her struggle as a writer, but will fail her when she truly thinks Teddy and his love are gone. Montgomery's story pictures the inseparability of the dancer from the dance, Emily the writer from Emily the woman. Whether sincerely or wishfully or falsely, Montgomery suggests that romance and art are somehow fundamentally connected.

It is Emily's determined listening to her inner voice – her determination to be whole – that enables her to refuse Miss Royal's offer to live with her in New York. The offer and the refusals of those she consults to give advice about it show how far Emily has come in being recognized within her family and by Mr Carpenter as an independent woman. Something about Miss Royal's offer does not strike Emily right – she keeps thinking that Miss Royal won her own way to New York and that she should somehow win her own way, too. And perhaps Emily detects in Miss Royal's slight patronizing a female version of the male ownership/dismissal power she feels from Dean. As a proposal, Miss Royal's should be the fairy tale come true, and Emily's refusal may suggest several levels of suspicion and rebellion operating at once. With Miss Royal, Emily also rejects the bachelor-girl life and/or the lesbian love relationship (Tausky 12) and/or the economically dependent artist's position. But more potent than any of these subliminal reasons for rejecting Miss Royal, we find that Emily's identity is bound up with New Moon farm and with Prince Edward Island. Her aunts leave the decision up to her; she does not want to ask Teddy what he thinks, Dean is away (mercifully), and even the old peddlar, Jock Kelly, refuses to advise her. Mr Carpenter, predictably, comes closest to giving her the best reasons to refuse the offer – claims for Canadian literature: 'Janet Royal *is* Yankeefied – her outlook and atmosphere and style are all U.S. And I'm not condemning them – they're all right. But – she isn't a Canadian any longer – and that's what I wanted you to be – pure Canadian through and through, doing something as far as in you lay for the literature of your own country, keeping your Canadian tang and flavour. But of course there's not many dollars in that sort of thing yet' (305–6). It is interesting that Mr Carpenter uses Haworth Parsonage in his argument. When Emily says she is 'not a Charlotte Brontë' he does not argue the point, but he does not agree with her, either. He clearly believes that talent should stand out no matter where it is found. Emily, taking the part of most Canadian writers of the time, says she needs more than talent to get anywhere. But at the end of the interview Mr Carpenter throws her back on her own wishes – he leaves her to consider her own voice and its demands. She eventually accepts the lesson: she must decide for herself, know her own mind. Then the decision is effortless. She tells a very sceptical and disappointed Miss Royal that 'Some fountain of living water would dry up in my soul if I left the land I love' (311). And then Miss Royal gives her what is better than sympathy

– she gives Emily a challenge. She says that if she ever thinks she is wrong and Emily is right about staying, she will write and tell her so. With this challenge in the back of her mind, the young woman Emily is ready to leave apprenticeship and move into the difficult world of career. She has recognized her own voice; now she must, in the third book, *Emily's Quest*, find out what she wants to say in that voice.

Love and Career:
Emily's Quest

The first eleven chapters of the total twenty-seven of *Emily's Quest* (1927) focus on the relationship of Dean and Emily and on Emily's consequent mistrust of her inner voice. The central psychic experience of this novel occurs in these chapters as a response to the deepest needs of the woman and the writer. Because she believes so implicitly in Dean – despite her intuition of his jealousy – Emily does not credit herself with understanding when her writing is good. Instead she lets Dean decide and, when he lies to her, she is almost destroyed – as woman and as writer. This last Emily volume, like the earlier two, insists on the inseparability of the woman from the writer; to doubt and betray one is to silence and revoke the power of the other.

In *Emily Climbs*, Emily listens to many people in order to decide about her own abilities – Mr Carpenter and Dean are rivals for her ear, but in apprenticeship Emily favours Mr Carpenter. Mr Carpenter dies early in *Emily's Quest* and, though Emily continues to live by his teaching, she does not have the benefit of his critical judgment to offset the condescension of Dean. Besides, by the age of seventeen, persuading Dean that she can write has become crucial, as she confesses to her diary: it is 'a sort of obsession with me to *make* Dean admit I *can* write something worthwhile in its line. *That* would be triumph. But unless and until he does, everything will be dust and ashes. Because – he *knows*' (15–16). Emily is right about Dean's knowing, but she is wrong about his having to admit what he knows; Emily's own moral standards make her believe that knowledge is power, but she does not understand that Dean's knowledge is useful to him only when he withholds it from her. Emily's eventual triumph shows that power *over* is not the most potent form of power. Emily regains her personal and artistic powers when she refuses to be dominated and controlled by Dean. Perhaps Montgomery was ahead of her time in (remembering?) suggesting that a partnership model (with Teddy) rather than a dominator model is truly supportive of men and women and art (Eisler).

The narrator is careful to alert the reader to Dean's methods of control. The scene where Dean suggests to Emily (rather than directly telling her) that her writing is frivolous and ephemeral is ingenious. For the scene to work, Emily's quick intelligence must not be able to detect what the reader must not avoid seeing; Montgomery's use of dramatic irony is admirable. Emily is telling Dean how lonely she will feel that winter since he and Teddy and Ilse will all be away: '"But I'll have my work." "Oh, yes, your work," agreed Dean with a little, tolerant, half-amused inflection in his voice that always came now when he spoke of her "work," as if it tickled him hugely that she should call her pretty scribblings "work." Well, one must humour the charming child. He could not have said so more plainly in words. His implications cut across Emily's sensitive soul like a whiplash. And all at once her work and her ambitions became – momentarily at least – as childish and unimportant as he considered them. She could not hold her own conviction against him. He must know. He was so clever – so well-educated. He *must* know' (30). The fact that the narrator qualifies with 'momentarily at least' suggests that Emily still has her own thoughts, that she can spring back from Dean's crushing patronage. But the threat is there – one day, it says clearly, she will not be able to resist and she will accept what he thinks. In the next few lines of the scene Dean speaks and, having lashed Emily with his partially disguised sneer, he compliments her beauty and at the same time reinforces his contempt for her writing: 'I shall see you sitting in your room by that old lookout window, spinning your pretty cobwebs – pacing up and down in this old garden – wandering in the Yesterday Road –

looking out to sea. Whenever I shall recall a bit of Blair Water loveliness I shall see you in it. After all, all other beauty is only a background for a beautiful woman' (30). And Emily and the reader, prompted by the narrator, isolate the sting within the honey: ' "Her pretty cobwebs – " ah, there it was. That was all Emily heard. She did not even realise that he was telling her he thought *her* a beautiful woman' (30–1). True to herself, Emily pushes the crucial question. Notice how the narrator carefully describes Dean's gesture of surprise. Emily can be forgiven for being taken in by this worldly, skilled actor: ' "Do you think what I write is nothing but cobwebs, Dean?" she asked chokingly. Dean looked surprised, doing it very well. "Star, what else is it? What do you think it is yourself? I'm glad you can amuse yourself by writing. It's a splendid thing to have a little hobby of the kind. And if you can pick up a few shekels by it – well, that's all very well too in this kind of a world. But I'd hate to have you dream of being a Brontë or an Austen – and wake to find you'd wasted your youth on a dream" ' (31). What a diabolical put-down. His pretended reluctance and surprise, his damning words 'amuse,' 'little hobby,' and 'shekels' are perfectly offset by the use of the names of Brontë and Austen, especially when we remember that Emily had claimed to Mr Carpenter (*EC* 306) that she did not regard herself as a Brontë. How clever of him to debase her work with so much apparent gentleness and then to hold up her mutilated scribblings next to the solid accomplishments of acknowledged genius. He lies easily to her, 'doing it very well.' As the narrator paints it, the wonder is that Emily holds out so long, not that she capitulates eventually.

For she does hold out a while yet – until she no longer feels, that is, that Teddy Kent is in love with her. Emily's belief in herself is firmly attached to her love for Teddy – her moments of greatest creativity (at least early in her career) and keenest pleasure are usually influenced by him, either directly or indirectly. Montgomery's point here is the same as Barrett Browning's point in *Aurora Leigh*: the two greatest creative forces – art and love – come from the same well-spring. Where Teddy (or hopeful thought of Teddy) is, there also will be inspiration. In *Emily Climbs* Emily looks at Teddy and imagines out a whole novel; in *Emily's Quest*, she writes the novel and gives to it the joy, love, life, and youth she shares – at least spiritually – with Teddy.

And, of course, it is this novel, *A Seller of Dreams*, that finally gives

Dean control over her. The fact that she has written it, has been rapt and remote from him during the six weeks that she wrote it, attests to the strength of her own voice. As with the essay 'The Woman Who Spanked the King' in *Emily Climbs*, so here Emily defies Dean's judgment in writing the story at all. She is true to herself. It is anguish over a cool visit and parting from Teddy that makes Emily dig out the old outline of the novel. It is as though in writing the story she recaptures the essence of her relationship with Teddy – their mutual acknowledgment of love in the old farmhouse where Emily was inspired with the 'immortal wine' of creation. Dean must take a second place to this story, though he does not know that she is writing it. He has witnessed the recent coolness with Teddy and rejoiced at it. Doubting her own voice, Emily gives Dean the manuscript to judge, and the narrator leaves the reader in no doubt about what that judgment will be: 'Dean looked inscrutably at the little packet she held out to him. So *this* was what had wrapped her away from him all summer – absorbed her – possessed her. The one black drop in his veins – that Priest jealousy of being first – suddenly made its poison felt. He looked into her cold, sweet face and starry eyes, grey-purple as a lake at dawn, and hated whatever was in the packet ... ' (51). When he comes to give his verdict, the narrator says, 'Dean looked at her, guilty' (51), and we know what he will say. His lie sounds very much like his other lies and is close enough to what Emily expects from the larger world to make her believe his opinion is honest: 'It's a pretty little story, Emily. Pretty and flimsy and ephemeral as a rose-tinted cloud. Cobwebs – only cobwebs. The whole conception is too far-fetched. Fairy tales are out of the fashion. And this one of yours makes overmuch of a demand on the credulity of the reader. And your characters are only puppets. How could you write a real story? You've never *lived*' (51–2).

Emily burns the manuscript. Crushed by Dean's words she contemplates the burning, and then she sees Vega of the Lyre, the star she and Teddy had gazed at long ago and promised always to think of each other when they saw. Urged by this despairing reminder of Teddy, she believes Dean at last, and in the death of the novel comes the symbolic death of her youth: 'Where had gone all the wit and laughter and charm that had seemed to glimmer in its pages – all the dear folks who had lived in them – all the secret delight she had woven into them as moonlight is woven among pines? Nothing left but ashes' (53). Emily flees the room, falls downstairs, and hovers for weeks between life and death. No saving truth comes to her, no vision of life over the borderlands, such as she experienced in *Emily of New Moon*; here she lives as a restless shadow of her former self.

This wraith, who forswears writing as a frivolous amusement, belongs to Dean Priest. So long as her inner voice, the voice of vocation, as Jane Urquhart calls it (332), is silent, Emily is willing and able to sacrifice herself to Dean. Montgomery is careful to show her readers just what this sacrifice means – Emily has moments when she feels the fetters too strongly and takes off Dean's emerald engagement ring, just to feel, guiltily, free. When she pictures out her future in their home to be and accidentally imagines Teddy there instead of Dean, she denies what her reviving voice is trying to whisper to her. Once she admits that the house they are furnishing together means more to her than Dean does, and then she quickly denies it. To the undiscerning or wishful, Emily looks the same, but the eyes of disinterested love know that this Emily is not what she was: 'For she was changed. Cousin Jimmy and Aunt Laura knew that, though no one else seemed to notice it. Often there was an odd restlessness in her eyes. And something was missing from her laughter' (84). Secure in his possession of her, Dean tells her where they will put her writing desk. Emily responds listlessly, 'I thought you didn't want me to write any more stories,' to which he replies with more candour than she is able to understand: 'That was when I was afraid it would take you away from me. Now, it doesn't matter. I want you to do just as pleases you' (78). But with her belief in herself shattered and without her buoying love for Teddy, Emily has no will or power to write. In response to Aunt Laura's gentle questions, she thinks 'She could not write – she would never try to write again' (85).

If Emily had not been psychic, she would have married Dean Priest, she would probably never have written again, and she would have frozen and buried her love for Teddy. Montgomery's cautionary tale is indeed powerful: it is only Emily's gift of second sight that saves her from the control and the silence that characterize the lives of many women, even (perhaps especially?) women of great talent. Perhaps she would not have needed psychic forces to liberate her if she had been able to listen more faithfully to her own voice, but Emily fights more than just Dean Priest in Dean's efforts to silence her. The cynical outcast is a wonderfully disguised representative of several binding traditions: he is part of the romantic-hero tradition (Radway; Kreps), a misunderstood misanthropic genius who can be humanized by perceptive love (the fairy tale 'Beauty and the Beast' is the prototype for the wished-for conclusion of the Byronic hero's story); he is the scholar who has, like the sculptor Pygmalion, helped to create in Emily the woman he loves and so believes he deserves to enjoy his own creation; he is the older man of authority and wisdom, one who knew Emily's own father and takes over from him in nurturing Emily's affections and her independence from the 'stifling' femaleness of New Moon; he is a man who demands that his woman be submissive to him and trust his weighty word over her own intuition; he is the wealthy, worldly man of a family as aristocratic as her own who asks to shelter and protect her feminine weakness from the ravages of a pitiless world; he is the man who has desired her and persisted in his suit despite the disapproval of clan and household and on whom she can confer happiness merely in offering herself. In short, Dean's offer to Emily carries with it centuries of endorsement for (romanticized) gender roles; by accepting Dean – outcast though he chooses to be – Emily is acting out the self-sacrifice and subservience her culture approves for her. And since family and clan do not approve of Dean, he has the added attractiveness of appearing to be different from them – and Emily can pride herself on seeming to make her own choice in their very teeth. But we have only to remember how much Emily prizes all the New Moon traditions to see that her form of rebellion is really a capitulation to the most potent and least acknowledged of their beliefs: the man rules and the woman obeys. For all his cosmopolitan cynicism about small-minded rural Blair Water, Dean would be a domestic despot. The boy next door, Teddy, would not. When we stop to analyse some of the forces that give Dean power over Emily, we may find it amazing that she is able to escape at all – hence the necessity and believability of the psychic force that liberates her from Dean and eventually enables her to regain her voice.

Looking into the gazing ball Great-aunt Nancy had willed to her, Emily sits in the living-room of the house she and Dean have been making into a home. As she stares, she is suddenly in a train station, and she knows Teddy is in danger. He sees her, responds to her command to 'Come,' and pursues her retreating figure down the platform. He misses his train and thus misses the ship *Flavian*, which subsequently strikes an iceberg and sinks. Emily finds herself sitting again in the living-room, and she knows that she cannot marry Dean Priest if she is still so intimately connected with Teddy that she can reach across the Atlantic to save him. But this knowledge and even the breaking of the engagement are not what restore Emily to herself. Even with the revived connection with Teddy, Emily is not whole. She is not herself until Dean acknowledges to her his lie about the novel. Only then does Emily have a chance of recovering her voice and regaining her will to love and create. The fact that Dean does acknowledge his lie keeps him from being a villain in the novels – he even achieves some of the nobility he formerly possessed before a jealous love warped him. The narrator says, 'If he had gone then she would never have been quite free – always fettered by those piteous eyes and the thought of the wrong she had done him. Perhaps Dean realised this, for there was a hint of some malign triumph in his parting smile as he turned away' (96). But he does turn back and, in his non-Priest generosity, he restores her faith in her writing: 'You remember that book of yours? You asked me to tell you the truth about what I thought of it? I didn't. I lied. It is a good piece of work – very good' (97). He is truly astonished that she burned it, and we know through his surprise that even he had no idea how powerful his judgment had been with her – he had not manipulated events neatly as a dastard would have done, but had, jealously and then wishfully, attributed Emily's change towards her writing to some love-leaning towards him. Even he had not realized what the artist's silence had cost her. He says, genuinely, 'It seems very idle to say I'm bitterly sorry for all this. Idle to ask your forgiveness.' But Emily is 'Her own woman once more,' and she can forgive him in knowing that 'The balance hung level between them' (97).

In recognizing that the loss of her romantic, youthful, witty novel is equal to the loss of Dean's future happiness, Emily for the first time in her relationship with him accords herself equality with Dean. At last she values herself and her creativity equally with (perhaps more than) her woman's role as healer and giver. It is interesting that although the psychic experience liberates Emily the woman from Dean the man, it takes Dean's word to liberate Emily the writer. Thus it is that Montgomery, in all her works, reinforces her belief in the interconnectedness of human beings. No character of hers is ever the richer for isolation. And it is further interesting that the psychic force itself is something that comes from Emily but does not belong to her. Dean wishes that the 'old Highland Scotch grand-mother who passed that dangerous chromosome down to you had taken her second sight to the grave with her' (95), but we can see that Emily's lack of control over the force is an endorsement of its sanctity. It belongs to the realm of mystical creative energies she must strive to be open to use – her Alpine Path and airy voices urge her to enter and grow into this realm. But the sanctity of the psychic force also suggests that her love for Teddy is incontestably allied to her creative energy. Dean silences Emily's best nature; Teddy releases it.

A less thought-provoking writer than Montgomery would have made Emily's subsequent writing somehow dependent on Teddy. Instead, in the remaining sixteen chapters of the novel we see Emily developing her voice independently. Her recovery is painful, and misunderstandings with Teddy persist. She even writes her second novel almost in defiance of him. His picture entitled *The Smiling Girl*, which Ilse writes to describe to Emily, is an international success, and it is nothing more nor less than a portrait of Emily, just as he had promised her in childhood he would make it one day. Rather than recognizing in the portrait his own medium's *A Seller of Dreams*, she is irritated to think Teddy does not love her but will still use her face. Half in defiance and wholly out of love, she writes a series of chapters to amuse Aunt Elizabeth who is convalescing from a broken leg. There is no flashing inspiration this time, as with the earlier book, but she becomes absorbed in the writing of it and eventually loves it. Bereft of the passionate intensity of her first creative effort, largely inspired by Teddy, she writes what proves to be a good, popular novel. Dean writes to tell her how good it is, and Miss Royal writes from New York to say that Emily had been right to stay on Prince Edward Island – she could never have written *The Moral of the Rose* in New York: 'Wild roses won't grow in city streets. And your story is like a wild rose, dear, all sweetness and unexpectedness with sly little thorns of wit and satire. It has power, delicacy, understanding. It's not just story-telling. There's some magicry in it. Emily Byrd Starr, where do you get your uncanny understanding of human nature – you infant?' (178). Emily goes on to write other books before the last chapter, where Teddy finally comes to her and braves her open rejection. They meet as adults in their thirties, having spent years yearning for one another while remaining determined to express them-selves on canvas and page.

They meet as equals and friends and lovers and satisfy Montgomery's own preference for a happy ending.[1] Their 'late' joining is not merely a sop to romantic convention, however, nor a denial of feminist principles, nor a pandering to audience taste. Montgomery does not let Teddy and Emily wed in their first youth perhaps because both still have so much to learn about their respective gifts. Through their separation Montgomery shows how a strong woman can live without conventional (or unconventional) romance if she once recognizes the power of her inner voice. Emily's psychic experience with Teddy shows her the foundation of her spirit, and she is true after that to both its dictates: the critical standards of the writer and those of the lover who knows only one choice. To have joined Emily and Teddy quickly would have made their union simply a matter of fairy-tale convention; but to let her young, talented heroine endure and grow for years suggests Montgomery's larger vision. I know few readers who have not been distressed by the lapse of years at the end of the book, the 'wasted time' while Emily and Teddy are kept (they think) perversely apart by misunderstanding and by the fear of Teddy's mother. Montgomery was too astute a writer not to know how she was challenging her reader. With so many years of sorrow and loneliness behind her, Emily's eventual marriage to Teddy is a relief rather than a positive joy. A more conventional book and story would not have risked so much. Montgomery has her way with the story and thus makes her points about the writer and the woman. This passage near the end of the book's penultimate chapter shows Montgomery steering away from convention (yet using it in showing Emily's sadness):

Alone? Ay, that was it. Always alone. Love – friendship gone forever. Nothing left but ambition. Emily settled herself resolutely down to work. Life ran again in its old accustomed grooves. Year after year the seasons walked by her door. Violet-sprinkled valleys of spring – blossom-script of summer – minstrel-firs of autumn – pale fires of the Milky Way on winter nights – soft, new-mooned skies of April – gnomish beauty of dark Lombardies against a moonrise – deep of sea calling to deep of wind – lonely yellow leaves falling in October dusks – woven moonlight in the orchard. Oh, there was beauty in life still – always would be. Immortal, indestructible beauty beyond all the stain and blur of mortal passion. She had some very glorious hours of inspiration and achievement. But mere beauty which had once satisfied her soul could not wholly satisfy it now. (221)

Is there any sense to the 'year after year' here? Montgomery is winding up the story, why didn't she just kill off Mrs Kent and make a few months pass after Ilse's jilting of Teddy?[2] The answer may be found in the nature of Emily's suffering and in her (partial) reconciliation of life and art. An immediate solution or resolution would be at variance with the other lessons of the novel.

Just as Emily's psychic bond to Teddy may find its prototype in the story of Jane Eyre, so Emily's determination to value and pursue her art is registered in another of Emily's favourite works, *Aurora Leigh*. The narrator reinforces the parallels between Emily's story and *Jane Eyre*, but it is Emily who tells us, in *Emily Climbs*, that she loves studying Mrs Browning and who quotes from *Aurora Leigh* to characterize her own feelings in *Emily's Quest*. There are some fascinating similarities between the lives and choices of the two heroines Aurora and Emily, and readers of Montgomery who know Barrett Browning's novel-poem will understand something more about Emily by considering why Montgomery chooses to encourage simultaneous reading of Emily's career and the career of Aurora Leigh.

In the novel, Emily turns to *Aurora Leigh* shortly after she has said goodbye to Dean. She has been struggling to write – and failing. Then one day the divine flash comes again and she finds her voice. She records her jubilation in her diary:

I flung down my pen and bowed my head over my desk in utter thankfulness that I could work again.
> 'Get leave to work –
> In this world 'tis the best you get at all,
> For God in cursing gives us better gifts
> Than men in benediction.'
So wrote Elizabeth Barrett Browning – and truly ... the work for which we are fitted ... what a blessing it is and what fulness of joy it holds. (102)

Without knowing the exact source of the lines, the reader acknowledges their truth and their appropriateness for Emily. Knowing the source and the story invites another kind of speculation. These lines occur in Barrett Browning's poem just after Aurora has said farewell to Romney Leigh and begun her years of struggle alone as a writer in London. She is at one of the low points of her career emotionally, but she is firm in her resolve and in her desire to do good work. It is as though Montgomery uses the Victorian story to suggest both the determination of the female writer and the blessing of finding and using her own voice. Like Emily's story, the story of Aurora is the story of the female writer's fight for recognition and dignity.

Barrett Browning's four-hundred-page poem tells the story of the young poet Aurora Leigh. Her beautiful Italian mother dies when Aurora is four years old, leaving her to the care of her grief-stricken English father, who has chosen to stay in Italy first with the wife and now with the child rather than return to his disapproving aristocratic family in England. Aurora's beloved father, who has given her a scholar's training with books, dies when she is thirteen, and she is taken to England to live with her father's stern, humourless sister. Aurora learns to love England, though it is so different from her warm Italy, and she revels in her father's books, which she finds in her aunt's home. She learns to write poetry. A solitary young girl, she frequently meets with her cousin, Romney Leigh, who lives at the ancestral home and is to inherit all his aunt's lands on her death. Aurora and Romney argue about life and literature – he thinks only good works can benefit the human race and scorns her love of letters and writing. When she is twenty, he finds her with a fresh wreath of ivy in her hair, her own symbolic consecration to the world of writing and poetry. He is amused. He asks her to marry him, to join him in his good works; she tells him of her own ambitions, and he smiles at her talk of work. He openly dismisses her writing and tells her: 'Keep to the green wreath, / Since even dreaming of the stone and bronze / Brings headaches, pretty cousin, and defiles / The clean white morning dresses' (2.93–6). He has found her book of handwritten poems, and he damns it without even bothering to read it: 'That book of yours, / I have not read a page of; but I toss / A rose up – it falls calyx down, you see! / The chances are that, being a woman, young, / And pure, with such a pair of large, calm eyes, / You write as well ... and ill ... upon the whole / As other women. If as well, what then? / If even a little better ... still, what then? / We want the Best in art now, or no art' (2.141–9).

Aurora will not marry her cousin Romney, and after her aunt dies she takes her very small inheritance and moves to a tiny flat in London where she writes prose and books of poems. Meanwhile Romney goes in for large-scale reclamation of the poor, even turning his ancestral home into an almshouse. All the while Aurora hopes that one day he will acknowledge that she can write and that her pen also has power to heal the hurts of humankind. It is obvious to the reader that Aurora loves Romney and would gladly spend her life with him, but that he scorns her devotion to art and she cannot marry where there is no sympathy with what she conceives to be the best and highest in herself. After years of struggle and hardship, Aurora writes a book with the best that is in her, and it is recognized by critics and readers as a masterpiece. Instead of feeling the elation of success, she feels a restless depression. She is satisfied to have devoted her best energies to art, but is this all there is to life? Is she to have no personal happiness, always to serve? As she gazes at her moonlit Italian garden (she has at last returned to Italy and helps Romney's lost Marian Erle raise her illegitimate child), she is thinking of the starkness of her life despite success – and Romney appears. He has come to tell her how wrong he has been about life and especially about her writing. Her latest book has finally shown him the meaning of life and taught him a humility and joy he had never known before: 'for the book is in my heart, / Lives in me, wakes in me, and dreams in me: / My daily bread tastes of it, – and my wine / Which has no smack of it, I pour it out, / It seems unnatural drinking' (8.265–9). They have both learned deep, hard lessons – he, that a woman can write and that writing itself can unite earth with heaven: 'You have shown me truths, / O June-day friend, that help me now at night, / When June is over! truths not yours, indeed, / But set within my reach by means of you, / Presented by your voice and verse the way / To take them clearest' (8.608–13). She has learned that love is the best thing this earth has to offer: 'Art is much, but Love is more' (9.656). But she also goes further and declares that, in ignoring her woman's need for love, she lost the best part of her human self and thus could not be so great an artist: 'Passioned to exalt / The artist's instinct in me at the cost / Of putting down the woman's, I forgot / No perfect artist is developed here / From any imperfect woman' (9.645–9). But Barrett Browning's point is not that woman should forget striving and art, but that she must not also forget, as man must not forget, that the best on this earth is love, and art inspired by love will carry the strongest and highest this life has to offer. Just as Aurora will not let Romney abase himself to her, so he will not let her negate what she has done. The final feeling of the poem comes back to his tempering words: 'Oh cousin, let us be content, in work, / To do the thing we can, and not presume / To fret because it's little' (8.732–4). As with most of her poetry, Barrett Browning is suggesting that the man and the woman fit together and that neither is complete without the other. But she does go further at moments in this poem and wonder if the life of the common woman with children is not the best life after all. She writes the poem in the first person, telling her story seven years after the initial separation from Romney and, when she catches up to her present, she makes the poem a kind of diary of events and thoughts. Thus we see at the beginning of the poem evidence of the untempered lament we find at the end – she is lonely and despairing when she begins to write and recalls all of her life before returning to Italy. Since the lament at the end is then tempered by Romney's praise of her poetry and assurance that she has been doing the work she was meant to do, it may be misleading to look at the sorrows at the beginning of the poem as though they carry the final thoughts on the debate between types of life. If we believed the early voice, we would hear Aurora telling us that if her cousin Romney had loved her as she had wanted to be loved, she would not have been a poet. And at the end of the poem, she blames herself more than him for their years of unhappy separation: 'He mistook the world; / But I mistook my own heart, and that slip / Was fatal' (9.709–11). Do we hear in Aurora's impassioned plea to Romney (he is blind and does not want to marry her if she is merely pitying him) the true thoughts of the woman, or do we hear the exaggerated wrong she naturally feels in claiming her share in the misunderstanding that has kept them apart?

The irony of the novel-poem is that the woman proves her ability to write, even fights to make her voice heard, and then, having won the ear of him she most longed to convince, is willing to renounce art for love. And here is a crucial point in understanding Barrett Browning's poem and Montgomery's treatment of a similar theme. Aurora may be willing to renounce art, but her true partner will not allow her to make that needless sacrifice – he will help her to temper her rash desire to fling away a vital part of herself in mistaken self-immolation. The fact that Aurora finishes and publishes her story is proof itself that Romney has indeed learned to value her voice and her gift and will not let her silence herself, just as she will not let him devalue the good works he has done for others. The true mate for the poet will encourage her work, and so the loving woman can become an even greater artist. Thus it is that Barrett Browning reinforces the necessity of one sex for the other – mutual help, mutual trust, mutual love are the best of this world.

It is remarkable in how many ways Emily's struggles with life and art parallel those of Aurora. But just as Barrett Browning's poem seems partly inspired by events in *Jane Eyre*[3] and yet focuses on very different issues ultimately, so Montgomery's novel, while echoing Aurora's story, is ultimately very different from Aurora's. The similarities are certainly striking: both poets learned a love of language and literature with a doting father; both were later orphans brought up by stern relatives; both struggle in obscurity for an audience and eventually achieve success; each loves from early years one who, through misunderstanding, is kept from marrying her; each faces an amused contempt for her writing from one whose judgment she prizes above that of all others; in loneliness and despair each questions the path she has taken and wonders if a more conventional one would not have been happier. But there are numerous differences, and none so important as this: the man who scorns Aurora's writing does so sincerely (though ignorantly) and is honestly won to greater vision and love when he can recognize the truth of her poetry. Blind and despairing, Romney listens to Aurora's book read aloud, and his hope of life is restored. Emily's work is dishonestly condemned, and the man who finally acknowledges her talent has not been redeemed or reformed by her visions. There is this difference, too: the man Emily loves does inspire her, and there is no question at the end of *Emily's Quest* that Emily will continue to write after she and Teddy are married. Neither she nor Teddy questions her need to write nor the demands of art. Interestingly, Montgomery's story seems to have split Romney Leigh into two characters (themselves, in turn, similar to Brontë's St John Rivers and Rochester). One is a disapproving man who believes women should inspire men but not through words (Dean), and the other is a loving admirer who accepts her art as her best self (Teddy).

Aurora's struggle is, after all, Barrett Browning's interpretation of the Victorian question: Which life would a woman choose, if she were given a choice? Emily's twentieth-century story puts the choice into different terms (though it comes up with the same answer) – Emily can remain single and write, or she can marry the man she loves, and write – if she chooses the right man. Montgomery's story shows the woman artist recognizing and claiming her own voice and power when she throws off false domination. But reading Montgomery's story with a knowledge of Barrett Browning's makes us appreciate more fully the choices Emily does make and especially Emily's growing restlessness at the end of the novel when she knows that beauty is no longer enough to satisfy her soul. Montgomery obviously endorsed Barrett Browning's conclusions about art and love and the wholeness of men and women. Emily is incomplete as a person without Teddy, just as Aurora is incomplete without Romney (and he without her). Whether this brand of romance is really preferable to (or even fundamentally different from) the irresistible attraction of apparent opposites in *Jane Eyre* is something each reader of Montgomery must work out for herself. Clearly, Montgomery is approving of the position that life is better with love. Perhaps (though I doubt it) Montgomery meant to write the kind of romance John Cawelti describes in which the career woman finds out that, after all, conventional love is better than career.[4] Teddy's support – and perhaps his blandness – does leave readers free to believe that Emily's voice will not be weakened or silenced in a subsequent life with him. And yet, we notice that this wonderfully compatible and mutually supportive love is given at the end of the novel as though Montgomery herself would not dare to picture it but offered it as the fairy-tale release from Emily's lonely struggle. Montgomery gives us alternatives but no solutions for the romantic puzzle many women face.

Just as triumphant quotation from *Aurora Leigh* marks Emily's re-emergence as a writer (Emily, like Aurora at this point in her story, has years of early work ahead of her before she is united with Teddy/ Romney), so other poems Emily draws on in *Emily's Quest* suggest changes in Emily's consciousness. Four more of Emily's favourite writers surface in important moments in the story. Emily has been wondering how she would face Teddy – he wrote to her after his encounter with her spirit on the platform of Liverpool station, and the narrator sets the scene for Teddy's whistle-call to her: 'Emily was reading by the window of her room when she heard it – reading Alice Meynell's strange poem, ''Letter From a Girl to Her Own Old Age,'' and thrilling mystically to its strange prophecies' (106). It is indeed a 'strange' poem, full of tears and burden, as though the young girl, who does eventually caress and forgive the older form of herself, is almost too weighed down by current hardships (and/or shadows cast backwards to her youth from her older self) to be able to see much joy ahead: 'all thy memories moved the maiden, / With thy regrets was morning over-shaden, / With sorrow, thou hast left, her life was laden' (35). How appropriate that Emily should be reading this unsettling poem when she hears Teddy call. The meeting itself, as though to belie the poem's sorrow, is joyful; but we know that, though their brief time here is happy, they have much misunderstanding yet to face. There are always complications where hesitant Teddy and sensitive Emily are concerned, and they have already been through so much misunderstanding.

Soon after the reading of Meynell's poem, Emily again meets Teddy, this time by accident early one morning. Sitting in the rapturous silence and beauty of the dawn, Emily is reminded of Marjorie Pickthall's poem 'Dawn.' 'How dear it was to sit here with Teddy on the banks of Blair Water, under the coral of the morning sky, and dream – just dream – wild, sweet, secret, unforgettable, foolish dreams. Alone with Teddy while all their world was sleeping. Oh, if this exquisite stolen moment could last! A line from some poem of Marjorie Pickthall quivered in her thought like a bar of music – "Oh, keep the world forever at the dawn." She said it like a prayer under her breath' (116). The poem indeed captures Emily's feelings of wonder and rapture with nature and with this isolated moment, stolen from time, with Teddy. Pickthall's lines are full of the images and spirit of Montgomery's own descriptions before and during this same scene. The poem pictures many of Montgomery's favourite themes and moments and suggests how, together, Emily and Teddy understand beauty. In Pickthall we find: 'And hush the increasing thunder of the sea / To murmuring melody'; 'And veil each deep sea-pool in pearlier mist, / Ere yet the silver ripples on the verge / Have turned to amethyst'; 'Check all the iris buds where they unfold / Impatient from their hold, / And close the cowslips' cups of honeyed gold'; 'From forest pools where fragrant lilies are / A breath shall pass afar, / And o'er the crested pine shall hang one star' (44–5). A few pages before this morning meeting, the narrator has described the month of Teddy's visit with these images, perhaps inspired by Pickthall: 'A wonderful month followed. A month of indescribable roses, exquisite hazes, silver perfection of moonlight, unforgettable amethystine dusks, march of rains, bugle-calls of winds, blossoms of purple and star-dust, mystery, music, magic' (108). Then, when Emily quotes the line from the poem, the narrator interprets Emily's perception of the world around her in words that are deliberately reminiscent of the poem: 'Everything was so beautiful in this magical moment before sunrise. The wild blue irises around the pond, the violet shadows in the curves of the dunes, the white, filmy mist hanging over the buttercup valley across the pond, the cloth of gold and silver that was called a field of daisies, the cool, delicious gulf breeze, the blue of far lands beyond the harbour, plumes of purple and mauve smoke going up on the still, golden air from the chimneys of Stovepipe Town where the fishermen rose early' (116). The narrator prepares us for the perfect dawn, pictures it through Emily's eyes (deliberately noting irises and buttercups; purple, silver, gold), and records Emily's quotation from the poem. Clearly Teddy is associated for Emily and for the reader with poetry; he inspires in her a lyric joy of nature, but a nature enriched by her human love for him.

Montgomery's uses of allusion and echo with Emily remind us of Emily's own artistic voice and Teddy's positive effect on it. Shortly before Teddy calls to Emily (while she is reading Meynell), Ilse is visiting and hurls across the room an old copy of *The Rubaiyat of Omar Khayyam*. The narrator makes a point of identifying the book and saying that it had been given to Emily by Teddy when they were in high school (109). The reference serves no other purpose there, it seems, and we may wonder why the title of the volume mattered. Couldn't it just have been any book Teddy had given Emily – Ilse's throwing any gift from Teddy would have made Emily angry. But later in the novel, when Emily finds out from Ilse that Ilse and Teddy are engaged, Emily's words to herself are an echo from Khayyam's (or, rather, Fitzgerald's Khayyam's) yearning, melancholy, but determinedly Epicurean poem. Emily stares into her mirror and says, 'Well ... I've spilled my cup of life's wine on the ground – somehow. And she will give me no more. So I must go thirsty' (176). Fitzgerald's poem is full of the wine of life and the wine of the grape, and though he admonishes all to drink and so to forget care and sorrow and this world's mockery of pain, he ends his rendering of Khayyam's poem (stanza 101, fifth version, 1889) wistfully:

> And when like her, oh Saki, you shall pass
> Among the Guests Star-scatter'd on the Grass,
>   And in your joyous errand reach the spot
> Where I made One – turn down an empty Glass! (157)

Emily's words to her reflection have the self-mocking, self-dramatizing quality of the poem, and it would be characteristic of her artistic and mimetic impulses that she would draw from Teddy's gift to picture her own emptiness without him.

But indirect self-mockery is not Emily's usual way. Like her mentor Mr Carpenter, she speaks most often directly and says what she thinks. And just as in her writing she tries to heal, so in her own constructing of a self, she also is often kindly and reassuring. Especially in spring is she able to rejuvenate herself in sympathy with nature around. We remember that it was in spring that she surprised her family by recovering almost overnight from her terrible fall, when she had been lagging in winter. And though Emily later is to find that the beauty of nature is not enough to fill her soul, she does identify with Wordsworth's praise of nature's restorative and inspiring powers, even when she is estranged from Teddy. Amid sorrow she sees the beauty of April and is reminded, by her 'supernal moment,' the flash, of her own immortality. Of course with nature and immortality she thinks of Wordsworth, and also, true to form as a writer, she selects among her favourites by him 'Tintern Abbey,' the one poem most in tune with her need to look, with a loving eye, backwards and forwards. She tells herself in her journal, as Wordsworth tells his sister in the poem: 'After all, freedom is a matter of the soul. ''Nature never did betray the heart that loved her'' She has always a gift of healing for us if we come humbly to her. Corroding memories and discontents vanished' (158). In the poem, Wordsworth is revisiting the Wye River country, and he recalls his five-years'-younger self and his joy at first beholding the hedgerows, cottages, mountains, and fields. He stored up those pictures to solace him in darker times:

> how oft –
> In darkness and amid the many shapes
> Of joyless daylight; when the fretful stir
> Unprofitable, and the fever of the world,
> Have hung upon the beatings of my heart –
> How oft, in spirit, have I turned to thee,
> O sylvan Wye! (50–6)

And Wordsworth shares his memories and wisdom with his sister:

> Oh! yet a little while
> May I behold in thee what I was once,
> My dear, dear Sister! and this prayer I make,
> Knowing that Nature never did betray
> The heart that loved her; 'tis her privilege,
> Through all the years of this our life, to lead
> From joy to joy ... (119–25)

A childhood favourite of Montgomery, Wordsworth is shown here to be woven into Emily's understanding of her own depressions and transcendent joys, reminding her, in her own times of 'fretful stir,' of the enduring blessing of nature. The descriptive passages of the three Emily books, as with all Montgomery's writing, show the effects of Montgomery's Romantic view of nature; but in the Emily books, the writer Emily not only gives us many of these descriptions themselves, but also – as Montgomery does in her own journals – pays tribute to one inspirer of them. We are never to forget with Emily that she is a worshipper of nature and literature – and a worshipper who also creates.

The three Emily books are storehouses for many of Montgomery's personal treasures. As a rapid reader and keen appreciator of beauty, Montgomery thrived on poetry and later fiction and history; Emily reads and loves many of the same books – and grows and changes in her opinions, just as Montgomery did. We understand Emily and the rich possibilities of her imagination and pen through Emily's monologues, dialogues, and diary entries, and also through the narrator's descriptions and interpretations. In many ways, the Emily books show themselves to be a writer's celebration of writing – Montgomery uses in her creation of them an inspired variety of narrative strategies.

The major ironies of the novels, the novels' internal tensions and compromises and challenges, are suggested by the narrator. The narrator turns our attention to *Jane Eyre* in *Emily of New Moon* and again in *Emily Climbs*, and the narrator brings into our analysis of Emily's adult story Montgomery's beloved feminist novel, Olive Schreiner's *The Story of an African Farm*. In *Emily's Quest* Schreiner's novel seems barely to have a part at all – it is merely mentioned in the story as being the book Emily has asked to borrow from Mrs Kent and in which Emily finds a sealed letter from the dying David Kent to his wife. The letter has been in the book for twenty-seven years, undisturbed, and for all those years Mrs Kent has punished herself for her parting angry words to her husband (he died on a business trip after they had separated in a quarrel). A reader unfamiliar with Schreiner's novel, which the narrator miscalls *A South African Farm* here, would find Emily's discovery and Mrs Kent's subsequent confession dramatic even without being able to compare the two stories. But for those readers who do know the Schreiner novel, Montgomery's choice of it as an instrument of delivery is indeed inspired.

The South African novel, originally published in London in 1883 under the protective male pseudonym Ralph Iron, is an audacious book. It is a book in which a writer and appreciator of language and ideas would delight, for it ignores the conventions of time and character boundaries as it explores, in its first half, the confused consciousness and baffled goodness of Waldo, German work-boy on a Boer farm. Waldo's fumblings for truth and his numbed incredulity at the cruelty inflicted on him make the story's first part poignant and irresistible. But the true audacity of the book is found in the second half, in Lyndall, the beautiful step-niece of the crude Boer farm woman Tant Sannie. Lyndall and Waldo are like the two sides of one brain – where he is befuddled, she is incisive; where she is intolerant, he is all patience. Lyndall's long explanation to Waldo about women's oppression and slavery reads like the best radical feminist writing (the impassioned outbursts of Jane Eyre herself naturally come to mind). But Lyndall, unlike Jane or Aurora, breaks free from her oppression only by sacrificing herself. She refuses to give her complete love (to become a slave in her own estimation) to the selfish dastard who pursues her (and to whom she is irresistibly physically attracted), and she eventually has her baby alone in a small country inn, far from the loving help of Waldo or her cousin Em.

Lyndall's tragic death and the sorrow she leaves for Waldo and the others who have loved her seems at first to have no bearing on the gentler lines of Montgomery's story of Emily. But when we think of Teddy's mother, Aileen Kent, and her part in Emily's story, we understand how the wisdom and passion of Schreiner's book have their parallels in Montgomery's novels.

When Montgomery first read Schreiner's novel in 1897, she was struck by the similarities between the Boer girl Lyndall and herself (*Journals* 1:

197). At the outbreak of the Boer War, Montgomery reread the novel and analysed it: 'It is one of my favorites. It is speculative, analytical, rather pessimistic, iconoclastic, daring – and *very* unconventional. But it is powerful and original and fearless, and contains some exquisite ideas. It is like a tonic, bitter but bracing. Also, many people call it a dangerous book. Perhaps it is so, for an unformed mind – but there is more of truth than pleasantness in many of its incisive utterances' (*Journals* 1: 248). In 1920, when Montgomery had been copying out her early journals and conjuring up the character of Emily, she quotes a long passage from the novel, prefacing it with, 'In Olive Schreiner's *African Farm* – which long ago was one of my wonder books – is a very fine and unforgettable paragraph on love' (*Journals* 2: 370). The quoted passage describes different types of love, and Montgomery, in quoting it, uses italics to highlight the part that has always meant so much to her: 'There is another love that blots out wisdom, that is sweet with the sweetness of life and bitter with the bitterness of death lasting for an hour. *But it is worth having lived a whole life for that hour.*' The quotation continues with an analogy between kinds of flowers and kinds of love, and the quoted passage concludes with these lines: 'There is no flower that has the charm of all – the speedwell's purity, the everlasting's strength, the mountain-lily's warmth; but who knows whether there is no love that holds all – friendship, passion, worship?' (*Journals* 2: 370). Montgomery goes on in the journal to talk about her own experiences: 'I have never loved any man with the whole force of my nature – with passion and friendship and worship. They have all been present repeatedly but never altogether in any of my loves. Perhaps it is as well, for such a love, in spite of its rapture and wonder and happiness, would make a woman an absolute slave, and if the man so loved – the *Master* – were not something very little lower than the angels I think the result, in one way or another, would be disastrous for the woman' (*Journals* 2: 370).

Interestingly, the quoted words are Lyndall's (Schreiner 215, 216), and Montgomery's own response to them is a summary of Lyndall's experience. Lyndall succumbed to the passionate love, refused belatedly to become the slave of a man very much lower than the angels, and died. In the novel, Lyndall shares her thoughts about women with Waldo, her emotional equal, but she talks to the posturing Gregory Rose about love. He cannot understand her then (though he later, inspired by his own tender love for her, disguises himself as a woman and nurses Lyndall until her death and gains some understanding of her). Lyndall's question about whether one love can have 'passion, and friendship, and worship' is a question Montgomery weighed frequently in her own life and debated, albeit subliminally, in her fiction. Emily's 'love' for Dean was without passion (despite the sexual tension generated by Dean's jealous desire for Emily), was almost all friendship, and what there was of worship was riddled with lies. Emily's love for Teddy would seem to have all three, but Teddy, as with so many of Montgomery's male characters, is such a shadowy character that we do not get any sense of his being the inspirer of 'worship.' Could the boy next door inspire worship? And passion coupled with friendship seems to work against the most powerful patterns of conventional romance, where mystery discourages friendship. In her private thoughts Montgomery wrestled with the stereotypes and formulae and patterns her culture endorsed – and the inclusion of *The Story of an African Farm* in her most self-revealing fictional series is a marker of depths, registered but overtly unexplored in her text.

Part of the problem with the passion and the worship parts of Montgomery's characters is found in the conventions Montgomery believed she had to follow. She laments to her journal and to MacMillan (to whom she dedicated *Emily of New Moon*) that she could not write a young girl's romantic experiences as they really are. Having finished the second Emily book she says to MacMillan: 'The second volume of a series, especially if it deals with a very young girl, is the hardest for me to write – because the public and publisher won't allow me to write of a young girl as she really is. One can write of children as they are; so my books about children are always good; but when you come to write of the ''miss'' you have to depict a sweet insipid young thing – really a child grown older – to whom the basic realities of life and reactions to them are quite unknown. *Love* must scarcely be hinted at – yet young girls often have some very vivid love affairs. A girl of *Emily's* type certainly would' (*Letters* 118). If she had trouble restraining the descriptions in the second Emily book, she must have found the curb on the adult in the third almost unbearable. It is too bad Montgomery didn't choose to risk her publisher's and public's condemnation if, indeed, she was at this late point in her career capable of writing the book she thought she wanted to write.

There is unrestrained passion in *Emily's Quest*, but it belongs to

Teddy's mother. She has seemed half-crazed in the first two Emily books, always jealously guarding Teddy, especially against Emily. She stays in her tiny house in the Tansy Patch (did Montgomery know that tansy is a natural abortive?) as though it is her cell, and is usually described with reference to her hungry or wild eyes. Perhaps half-wild Mrs Kent is as close as Montgomery comes to a literary unconscious for Emily; perhaps Mrs Kent's uncontrolled love is a cautionary reminder of the possibly degenerative powers of passionate love unbridled. One is reminded of how critics Gilbert and Gubar argue that mad Bertha Mason Rochester in *Jane Eyre* is Jane's shadowed self, the part of her that could rebel savagely against restraint and domination (336–71). Emily and Mrs Kent have usually avoided each other, for in their few encounters each has been driven to bitter or hurtful words. But when Ilse is engaged to Teddy, Mrs Kent suddenly seeks out Emily. She probes Emily's wound and asks about her love for Teddy. Mrs Kent assumes that Emily will now hate Ilse for taking what is hers, just as Mrs Kent had always hated Emily since she knew Teddy loved her. She tries to enlist Emily's hatred of Ilse, as though she sees Emily and herself as two deserted women, allied by their loneliness and despair. Mrs Kent says: 'I used to hate you. I don't hate you any longer. We are one now, you and I. We love him. And he has forgotten us – he cares nothing for us – he has gone to *her*' (186). When Emily responds to her, we hear Montgomery's echo of Lyndall's discussion of love: 'He does care for you, Mrs Kent. He always did. Surely you can understand that there is more than one kind of love. And I hope – you are not going to hate Ilse because Teddy loves her' (186). Mrs Kent cannot understand that there is more than one way of loving – passionately, exclusively – and she has never read the novel she lends to Emily a short time afterwards.

Emily's echo of Lyndall, and the deliberate mention of the book itself, which Emily reads before she returns it, suggests that to Montgomery, at least, Emily's story is related to Schreiner's book. Certainly Emily is capable of the passion of Lyndall; and Emily's clear-headed appreciations of nature have all the love and warmth of Waldo's ecstasies. Mrs Kent's blind passion and self-destruction are in keeping with Schreiner's pessimism, but Lyndall is never melodramatic or monomaniacal. At the end of their interview, Mrs Kent's sorrow seems beyond help: ' "I want rest – rest," said Mrs Kent, laughing wildly. "Can you find that for me?

Don't you know I'm a ghost, Emily? I died years ago. I walk in the dark"'' (189). Ironically, Emily does bring her rest and release. The letter, tucked in the pages of the novel, tells Aileen Kent that her husband forgave her and loved her. He said on his deathbed (after having read Schreiner's book himself?) that things were clearer to him now and he knew she had not meant the harsh things she had said. Emily is the means of restoring peace to Mrs Kent.

Ironically, the final passages of Schreiner's passionate, powerful novel are about peace and rest. Waldo, sitting in the sunshine, is finally at one with nature and finds the rest that has eluded him since Lyndall's death. He has finally put passion away and can find peace. Schreiner's narrator describes Waldo's search and reward in words that sound very much like Montgomery's and Emily's own: 'He moved his hands as though he were washing them in the sunshine. There will always be something worth living for while there are shimmery afternoons. Waldo chuckled with intense inward satisfaction as the old hen had done; she, over the insects and the warmth; he, over the old brick-walls, and the haze, and the little bushes. Beauty is God's wine, with which he recompenses the souls that love Him; He makes them drunk ... There are only rare times when a man's soul can see Nature. So long as any passion holds its revel there, the eyes are holden that they should not see her ... when the old desire is crushed, then the Divine compensation of Nature is made manifest. She shows herself to you ... Then the large white snowflakes as they flutter down, softly, one by one, whisper soothingly, "Rest, poor heart, rest!" It is as though our mother smoothed our hair, and we are comforted' (Schreiner 284–5). Emily is the instrument for restoring David Kent's forgiveness to his wife, and Aileen Kent finds rest for herself and the courage to tell Emily how she has thwarted Emily's and Teddy's love. In burning Teddy's letter of proposal to Emily, Aileen Kent had thought to keep Teddy to herself, but she now knows that betrayal has brought her no comfort. And perhaps Emily cannot find lasting comfort in Nature – despite her fondness for Wordsworth – because her old passion has not been crushed, and she is not ready to renounce hope entirely. The only lasting peace for Emily, Montgomery's book makes perfectly clear, would be in her own death or in union with Teddy.

We are invited to consider three principal texts – *Jane Eyre, Aurora Leigh,* and *The Story of an African Farm* – in relationship to Emily's career and choices. It is indeed interesting that the most pessimistic of these is all but submerged in the narrative. The echoes are there for those who know Schreiner's novel and its rich cadences, but we are not even told what Emily thinks of the book. Certainly all three books (Brontë's, Barrett Browning's, and Schreiner's) debate women's power and women's place in cultures that misunderstand, scorn, and/or destroy women. By prompting consideration of Emily in relationship to these heroines, Montgomery's *Bildungsroman* or *Künstlerroman* affirms women's voices. Concentrating on the positive and openly supporting the view that a woman can be what a woman has courage to believe she can be, Montgomery makes Emily's writing success an invitation to her female readers to strive for their own goals. And though Emily finds life without Teddy lonely, we see that she can survive without him (knowing that he did love her) and can prosper in her chosen work. The best of all possible worlds, Montgomery does suggest, is to have one's own work and to find the ideal love partner, one who calls out the 'passion, friendship, and worship' that Lyndall describes. But barring that ideal, love in any of its positive and liberating forms is a good thing, provided one has found one's true self and voice (and work) first. Montgomery's Emily books do not sink to romantic formulae, though they use versions of those formulae; instead, Montgomery mixes voices and genres (autobiography, biography, drama, lyric, narrative) and allusions in ways that challenge accustomed boundaries and assumptions of girls' fiction and domestic romance. When we consider Montgomery's (limiting) choices to please publishers, offer happy endings, and concentrate on real but idealized life, we can appreciate how admirably free is Emily Byrd Starr.

Perhaps Montgomery's own support of the teachings of Mr Carpenter account for a number of the unexplored possibilities in Emily's life and career. Recently, Janice Kulyk Keefer has argued that Mr Carpenter's advice to Emily from his deathbed in *Emily's Quest* shows Montgomery's own choices and self-imposed limitations (186–99, 239–51): 'Don't be – led away – by those howls about realism. Remember – pine woods are just as real as – pigsties[5] – and a darn sight pleasanter to be in' (24).[6] Montgomery's choice to stay almost exclusively among the pinewoods and an idealized realism probably limited her ability to expose the most intimate processes of the sensitive and intelligent mind. And these self-imposed limits probably made it difficult to render believably the adult problems an Emily or Ilse (or Montgomery) would work through. No wonder *The Story of an African Farm* must make its impact in Emily's story almost subliminally.

But whatever their limitations in subject matter or perspective, the Emily books are remarkable. In them Montgomery creates an unforgettable heroine whose keen sense of self and love of writing add powerful dimensions to Montgomery's favourite, continuing themes of identity and romance. As the story of a writer, the Emily books make an invaluable contribution to our understanding of a woman artist and the cultural pressures she will – even yet – defy, resist, or embrace if she is to have a voice she knows is her own.

PART III

The Other Heroines

Romancing the Home:
Pat of Silver Bush, Mistress Pat,
Jane of Lantern Hill

All Montgomery's heroines experience powerful love of the physical home – sometimes, as with Anne, several homes. Following the best of nineteenth-century tradition, Montgomery enshrines home as a sacred centre for family and for the developing self. She also borrowed from nineteenth-century novelists the device of suggesting character traits through houses – both in giving houses personalities of their own and in using descriptions of houses to characterize the people who live in them. First Green Gables, then Patty's Place, then the House of Dreams, then Ingleside (and, in the recreated past, the house Windy Poplars) are home centres for Anne, and something about the very structure of each house reflects an important aspect of Anne's life and changes. For Emily, New Moon and then the Disappointed House express who and what she is. The physical house reifies each heroine's perception of beauty, honour of tradition, and sense of self. So it is with the King children at the King farm, with Valancy and her Blue Castle, and with Marigold and her Cloud of Spruce.

Two of Montgomery's heroines carry this love of house and home to extremes and suggest radically different positions in Montgomery's own thinking. For Pat Gardiner, the house of Silver Bush is herself – so closely does she identify with it that the physical house for years replaces the spirit of home it once healthily embodied. For Jane Stuart, the Lantern Hill house becomes an instrument for autonomy – in her happy story, domesticity is a means for blissful self-discovery and affirmation. In these late novels Montgomery deals with an old theme in strikingly different ways. Pat and Jane are similarly besotted with kitchen, garden, furniture, and household rituals, but Pat's story often reads like nightmare and Jane's like fairy tale. Pat's domesticity is unrecognized imprisonment; Jane's is undeniable liberation.

Pat of Silver Bush (1933)

When Montgomery told MacMillan she had finished *Pat of Silver Bush*, she described it as follows: 'It is a story for girls, of the *Anne* and *Emily* type and will probably please that public' (*Letters* 162). She tells him, after it is published: 'I really put more of *myself* into *Pat* than into any other of my heroines' (*Letters* 168). Both comments are intriguing because it is hard to understand them. First of all, Pat is very unlike Anne or Emily. While they are talented, ambitious (Anne at least for a time), and special, Pat is virtually ungifted and determinedly unambitious. Second, if Pat is really like Montgomery, then Montgomery's life in the 1930s must have been bleaker even than her letters to MacMillan suggest.[1] Pat is morbidly afraid of change and is unwilling to let people or things undergo any transformation, however positive. Pat herself is an unintentionally depressing study in unconsciousness and in domesticity turned into self-imprisonment. It is a fitting comment on the heroine, perhaps, that the two most absorbing characters of the Pat books may well be the Silver Bush farmhouse and Hilary Gordon, not Pat herself.

Rather than a self-willed and self-sufficient – or at least determinedly self-searching – heroine (like so many other Montgomery heroines), Pat is a girl and then a woman possessed by her own love of the literal house she lives in and a willing slave to clan traditions. She is a Hestia who constantly feels herself threatened with removal of/from the hearth. The quality of description that in the Anne and Emily books reinforces the perceptive powers of the heroines here in the Pat books reinforces Pat's perverse preference for Silver Bush over almost any human being. Whereas the nature descriptions of the Anne books and the nature and domestic descriptions of the Emily books remind us that the heroines are blessed with surrounding beauty and are successful in their joyful communion with it, in the Pat books, the concentration on beauty is the perverse fuel that confirms Pat in her self-destructive choice of the thing over her soul. Montgomery's nostalgic and yearning raptures over the house and garden and moonlight seem to suggest that Pat is wise to prefer Silver Bush to human comfort – and yet, at the same time, it is perfectly clear that Pat is mistaken not to recognize Hilary Gordon as her destined partner. Pat questions virtually none of the forces that bind her to the home.

Near the end of the introductory chapter, Pat gives us the line that characterizes her life: ' "I *hate* changes," cried Pat, almost in tears' (6). A couple of pages later, the narrator chills us with this reinforcement: 'This was comforting [finding out that a favourite hill cannot be moved] in a world which Pat was already beginning to suspect was full of a terrible thing called change ... and another terrible thing which she was not yet old enough to know was disillusionment' (9). Montgomery makes it clear that everything suggesting change is a terror to Pat. Pat does not want a new baby in the house because it will be an 'intruder,' and even in talking about the baby Pat feels that 'Everything seemed to have changed a little in some strange fashion ... and Pat hated change' (17). When she decides that the new baby will be a Gardiner after all, so why not like it, she munches her toast in comfort and the narrator explains yet again: 'She had had a secret, dreadful fear that she would find everything changed and different and heart-breaking' (28). And then she finds out that her young aunt is going to be married, and the narrator again, only a few pages later, sums up Pat's thoughts: 'Oh change was terrible! What a pity people had to get married!' (39). Pat's fear of change persists right until the very last pages of the second book, and the narrator's reminders are legion.

The first hundred pages or so of the novel reinforce in description, narration, dialogue, and imagined internal monologue all the ways in which Pat associates Silver Bush with loving and approval and home. At seven she croons to herself, 'Oh, I've got such a *lovely* home ... Nobody ... *nobody* ... has such a lovely home. I'd just like to *hug* it' (18). When there is a clan wedding, the narrator shares with us Pat's view of Silver Bush itself in autumn bridal splendour (46). When Pat mourns the loss of Aunt Hazel after the wedding, it is Silver Bush that comforts her (55). After Pat gets lost walking home from the Bay Shore Farm and is rescued by Jingle, she falls asleep happily at Silver Bush, comforted more by the house than by her own mother. Pat suddenly realizes that she should not say anything to mother about her mother's childhood home and thus sees her own love for Silver Bush as part of the natural order of love: 'Mother loved Bay Shore almost as well as she, Pat, loved Silver Bush. Dear Silver Bush! Pat felt as if its arms were around her protectingly as she drifted into dreamland' (68). When Pat performs well in school and gives a dreaded recitation, Silver Bush congratulates her. Pat tells Judy Plum about the approval of her teacher and classmates: 'And when I came home I'm sure Silver Bush smiled at me' (89). And so on.

Pat throws herself into the domestic joy of home. Even her vanity is soothed by such love. At her first party Pat sees her brown skin and straight ginger hair reflected unflatteringly in the mirror beside the ideal pink and white cheeks and curly head of another girl and is at first crushed by a realization of her own lack of beauty. After some of Judy Plum's comforting, she turns to Silver Bush and surrenders remaining vanity to joy of home: 'What did it matter if she had no great beauty herself? She had the beauty of shining meadows ... of moon secrets in field and grove ... of beloved Silver Bush' (145). Judy Plum is a co-worshipper of Silver Bush, of course, and when Pat recovers from scarlet fever and is again up and around, Judy gives her the best of greetings: 'Sure and the house do be glad to see you round it again' (203).

Silver Bush's love and approval and well-being are of primary importance to Pat, but it is not until Bets dies that Pat's love of Silver Bush takes what we can later see to be an unfortunate turn. Rather than the inspirer of joy and the home of her family, Silver Bush becomes the place that must remain constant: 'Silver Bush was all her comfort now. Her love for it seemed the only solid thing under her feet. Insensibly she drew comfort and strength from its old, patient, familiar acres' (231). At the end of the story, Hilary Gordon recognizes what Pat's love of the place has become. In the last paragraphs of this story, he tries to imagine a house he can build for Pat that will be more beautiful than Silver Bush, and the sensitive, canny young man feels the shadow of what the next thirteen years (eleven of them chronicled in the next novel) will prove to be true: 'For a moment he almost hated Silver Bush. It was the only rival he feared' (277). Only when Silver Bush is ashes can Hilary claim Pat to be the mistress of a new home.

Rather than the romantic hero of 'Lara-like glooms' (258) that Pat's immaturity makes her think she wants, Jingle is a 'rather comical knight-errant' (116) who shares all Pat's values. Jingle loves flowers, as Pat does, and naming. He adores houses and determines to be an architect so that he can build places of love and drama and dream. They discover together a 'beauty spot' they name Happiness that has a brook Jingle names Jordan because it 'rolled between' (70). One of their early exchanges in Happiness is emblematic of the depth of their communication. With the loving dog McGinty beside them, Jingle 'took a bit of birch bark from a fallen tree near them and, with the aid of a few timothy stems, made under her very eyes the most wonderful little house ... rooms, porch, windows, chimneys, all complete. It was like magic' (72). Delighted with it, Pat asks how he does it; his reply and their subsequent comments about Silver Bush show Jingle as the perfect partner for Pat: ' "I call them my dream-houses. Some day when I'm grown up I'm going to build them really. I'll build one for *you*, Pat." "Oh, will you really, Jingle?" "Yes. I thought it out last Saturday night after I went to bed. And I'll think of lots more things about it. It will be the loveliest house you ever saw, Pat, by the time I get it finished." "It couldn't be lovelier than Silver Bush," cried Pat jealously. "Silver Bush *is* lovely," admitted Jingle. "It satisfies me when I look at it. Hardly any other house does. When I look at a house I nearly always want to tear it down and build it right. But I wouldn't change Silver Bush a bit" ' (72–3). No wonder the narrator exclaims, 'Canny Jingle! Pat never dreamed of doubting his opinions of houses after that' (73). Jingle continues to add to his plans for Pat's house right through the second Pat book, though he becomes separated from Pat herself and almost loses hope of ever being with her. The house he plans for her is eventually his tangible way of preserving their relationship, and it is to this dream house that he is able to take Pat when Silver Bush is burned.

The scene with Jingle's mother is perhaps the best thing in *Pat of Silver Bush*. The whole is constructed to reveal Jingle's quality of love and spirit. As a piece of narrative, the episode is ingenious – Montgomery uses farce and comedy to undercut sentimentality, and then uses description to heighten the heart-breaking details of Doreen Garrison's indifference to the son she has not seen since his babyhood. Interestingly, motherhood (revered in the later Anne books, enshrined in Emily's rescue of Ilse's mother's reputation) is one sacred cultural force not pictured particularly positively in Pat's life. Pat's mother is virtually absent – Jingle's is shallow and selfish. Nevertheless, Judy Plum as mother substitute and Silver Bush itself are comforting presences to offset the motherless Montgomery's cool or shadowy representations of the biological mother.

The narrator records minutely Jingle's excitement over the prospect of seeing his mother and showing her his and Pat's secret play place, Happiness. He wants to prepare a bouquet for her, and is extremely particular about what flowers are appropriate: ' "Delphiniums are so haughty," said Jingle. "And they've no perfume. Just sweet-smelling flowers, Pat. And a bit of southern wood. You know Judy calls it 'lad's love.' So it ought to go in mother's bouquet." Jingle laughed a bit consciously. But he did not mind if Pat thought him sentimental' (179). Naturally the flower-loving Pat would sympathize perfectly with Jingle's feelings. Jingle wants Pat to be with him, and here is where Montgomery uses humour to counteract sentiment. Rather than setting up both Jingle and Pat as starry-eyed and fresh-faced cherubs, waiting for the inevitable blight of reality, Montgomery emphasizes Jingle's ridiculous glasses and Pat's unruly hair: 'She had put her hair in curlers the night before, to look her best before Jingle's mother, but the result was rather bushy and rampant ... "Standing out round yer head like a hello," said Judy sarcastically' (179–80). Pat worries over her looks and thinks to herself, 'Would Jingle's mother think her just a crude little country girl with a head like a fuzz-bush?' (180). Pat knows that she has been right to worry when 'Mrs Garrison flicked an eye over Pat, who had an instant conviction that her stockings were on crooked and her hair like a Fiji islander's' (181). But Pat is not crushed by the look, for she has already seen Doreen Garrison for the hollow woman she is: 'Tall, slender, graceful as a flower, in a soft fluttering chiffon dress like blue mist; pale, silvery-golden hair sleeked down all over her head like a cap under a little tilted hat of smooth blue feathers: bluish-green eyes that never seemed to see you, even when they looked at you, under eyebrows as thin as a line drawn in soot; a mouth that spoiled everything, so vividly red and arched was it. She might have stepped off a magazine cover. Beautiful ... oh, yes, very beautiful! But not ... somehow ... like a mother!' (180). This magazine image cannot return any of Jingle's love, and when he calls her 'mother,' 'A flash of amazement flickered in Doreen Garrison's restless eyes ... a little tinkling laugh rippled over her carmine lips ... She stooped and dropped a light kiss, as cold as snow, on his cheek' (180–1). When he offers her the precious flowers so thoughtfully chosen, she says, 'Angel-boy, what can I do with such an enormous thing? ... Just put it somewhere, honey, and I'll take a bud out of it when I go' (181). Several pages later, after more slights and disappointments, the scene ends with Doreen Garrison, 'this tarnished, discrowned queen who had so long sat on the secret throne of his heart' (183), flitting down the steps and driving away. The narrator turns us from Jingle to the emblematic flowers: 'His bouquet was lying on the hall table. She had not even remembered to take the bud. The southernwood in it was limp and faded' (183). But Jingle is not entirely crushed, though he suffers the loss of his childhood dream from his mother's coldness. He and Pat burn the letters Jingle had secretly written for so many years to his mother, and beside those ashes he rises phoenix-like, transformed into the young man Hilary Gordon, who vows, 'I'm going to college ... and I'm going to be an architect ... and I'm going to succeed' (186). At the end of the second Pat book, when Pat thinks her own dreams have vanished with the burning of Silver Bush, Hilary will be there for her, as she is here for him, to transform disaster into hope. The sacrificial flame is yet another reminder of the numerous bonds and parallels between the two. But we notice that *he* thinks; he resolves; Pat just supports, sympathizes, remains stereotypically passive. The scenes make wonderful use of humour and contrast, but they do not show us a heroine who has an active will of her own.

Mistress Pat (1935)

The second Pat book, *Mistress Pat*, is one of the saddest books Montgomery wrote. It has clan stories and comic anecdotes and juicy bits of gossip and fanciful descriptions, as do all Montgomery's novels, but so many things the heroine loves go awry that the pervasive tone of the book is grieving. Pat seems fixated on change and decay and death. The antics of Tillytuck, the colourful hired hand, and even the fireside tales of Judy Plum cannot balance the frequent reminders of loss. Most of what Pat dreads eventually happens: Tillytuck comes and then goes; Sid marries the despised and vulgar May Binnie; Gentleman Tom disappears and McGinty dies; Rae gets married and goes to China; Joe comes home only briefly and gets married; Jingle travels and stays away from Silver Bush, Uncle

Tom threatens to marry and change life at Swallowfield,[2] and Judy Plum dies.

Pat's life from twenty to thirty-one is a struggle to ward off change, to cling to Silver Bush as the only immutable source of love and joy. The wrong turning that Pat took after Bets' death in *Pat of Silver Bush* means that, as the years go by and everyone else changes and leaves, Pat holds on more and more desperately to the place Silver Bush, as though it alone can keep her safe and hold the beloved past close enough to touch.

Each of the eleven chapters of the book follows Pat's responses to change. Love of Silver Bush and hatred of change mark every episode. Hilary is away for most of the novel, studying in Toronto and then travelling the world and designing prize houses. As with the younger Pat, here we see that Silver Bush is the standard for taste as well as the beloved: 'She loved her home with a passion. She was deeply loyal to it ... to its faults as well as its virtues ... though she would never admit it had any faults. Every small thing about it gave her the keenest joy. If she went away for a visit she was homesick until she could return to it' (2). Judy sums it up for Rae: 'But Patsy has always had Silver Bush in her heart ... right at the very core av it' (14). Pat herself says to Judy: 'I never want to leave Silver Bush ... I want to stay here always and grow old with my cats and dogs. I love the very walls of it' (71).

When Tillytuck leaves, Pat faces another hated change, and it is interesting that, though she is engaged to David Kirk, she shows her true mind when she whispers to Judy Plum: 'Anyway, we've got Silver Bush and you left' (284). And, of course, in this book of relentless changes, we know that Judy Plum herself will have to die and leave Pat alone with Silver Bush. Judy tells Pat that she knows she has come to her 'journey's ind,' and Pat's response is characteristic: 'however can I ... however can Silver Bush get along without you?' (320).

During the year following Judy's death, the last year of the novel, Pat finds that 'Almost every one she had loved was changed or gone ... the old voices of gladness sounded no more ... but Silver Bush was still the same' (325). One by one Montgomery has stripped away the things and the people Pat loved – even David and Suzanne have left the Long House. Hilary no longer writes to her, and she has no other friends to keep her company. Silver Bush sustains her: 'By spring hope was her friend again and her delight in Silver Bush was keen and vivid once more' (326). And yet her mother watches as Pat goes out more and more often on solitary walks 'among the twilight shadows. They seemed to be better company than she found in the sunlight. She came back from them looking as if she were of the band of grey shadows herself. Mother didn't like it. It seemed to her that the child, on those lone rambles, was trying to warm herself by some fire that had died out years ago' (327). And Pat does seem to be slipping into these shades of the past. When she is left alone on her very last night at Silver Bush, she tries desperately to burst through the 'shut door' that separates her from the past Silver Bush she loves: 'Judy and Tillytuck and Hilary and Rae and Winnie and Joe were all in there and if she could only go in quickly and silently enough she would find them. A world utterly passed away might be her universe once more' (328). Life has seemed to take away all Pat's supports – Judy, Silver Bush, even Hilary – and though Hilary does miraculously appear, rescue Pat from desolation, and even restore her past to her in transforming Silver Bush the place into Silver Bush the inviolable memory, the gloom of Pat's story is not entirely erased. The ending is happy, but the movement of the story has been so relentless that the reader is forced to realize how lucky Pat's rescue is: life is cruel, and only luck (since she will not self-reflect) keeps Pat from becoming a sorrowing shadow herself.

Hilary Gordon is the perfect partner for Patricia Gardiner because he understands her and shares her values – he anticipates her needs, because they are also his needs, and he recognizes the essence of Pat's nature in a way she has not understood it herself. He proposes to her by acknowledging the importance of preserving their past; in the new house 'we'll build up a new life and the old will become just a treasury of dear and sacred memories ... of things time cannot destroy. Will you come to it with me?' (334). The love-starved, homeless Jingle has always cherished in Pat her passion for home. She wrongly identifies with Silver Bush itself and mistakenly believes she can live with and for it alone, but Montgomery has made sure that hope and rescue were always within Pat's reach. Montgomery's two novels may have been written in response to her own depression with the passing of beloved things and the despair over unwelcome changes in her own home and the world around her, but in her fiction, as usual, she provides a happy escape for her characters. Montgomery seldom attacks the status quo head on, and in the Pat books we find Montgomery's own older world symbolized in a beloved Prince

Edward Island farmhouse – a farmhouse that dies because the vulgar, pushy May (the new order?) leaves an oil stove burning in the kitchen when they all go to church. The old world may be blasted into rubble, but the novels promise us the romance of an ideal marriage and an ideal home to counteract the gloomy commentaries on the times. All that is left of the old Silver Bush house, for Pat, is the front door knocker, Judy Plum's beloved cow cream jug that she had brought from Ireland, Judy's hooked rugs, and Judy's picture of white kittens that she had willed to Hilary. But these are enough, if we recognize, with Hilary, that Silver Bush is a romantic symbol of the ideal home; Pat may learn with Hilary that the love of home Silver Bush has inspired in her will enable her to create a new home in British Columbia. Wrested from a specific place, home becomes the spirit of love itself.

But since Pat is unreflective and Jingle is – through her – fulfilling his own needs for a domestic princess, what does the book enjoin us to consider about choice or love of place or quality of life? The nightmare quality of Pat's losses cannot be dispelled in the last-minute rescue. The rescue itself is a reminder of powerlessness. At least Emily Byrd Starr can continue to write even when she knows her life is unfulfilled without Teddy. Poor Pat – without Jingle – wouldn't even have the old kitchen comforts of Silver Bush. So much for self-discovery and self-knowledge. If Montgomery was trying to be ruthlessly realistic about Pat's alternatives, the fairy-tale ending obliterates the potentially thought-provoking quality of the two books' constant and relentless changes. 'Why worry?' the second book's conventionally romantic conclusion seems to say. 'Love will come to the rescue.' But if love had not come, would Pat ever have known herself? Despite the happy ending, Pat seems a victim, not a self-creator. Domesticity is her life, not a part of it.

Jane of Lantern Hill (1937)

Victoria Jane Stuart is afraid not of change but of sameness. She is stifled by a routine she is not allowed to question or bend. And for her initially, home is oppression and her house a prison. In this late, wish-fulfilling novel, Montgomery gives an entirely different treatment of domesticity from that in the Pat books. The gloom in Jane's life belongs to the world of a wicked witch and can be banished by learning to cook and clean. Montgomery uses a passion for home as a basis for a simple, direct story of self-empowerment and self-discovery.

Montgomery's next-to-last (nineteenth) novel, *Jane of Lantern Hill*, is wholly fairy tale; unlike the Pat books it offers a gently exaggerated version of Montgomery's favourite themes and conventions. It is set half in Toronto and half on Prince Edward Island (*The Blue Castle* is the only one of her novels set entirely away from P.E.I.) and suggests that, though Prince Edward Island is undoubtedly the best place on earth, Toronto, when it can be made to remember its ravines and pheasants and wild flowers and blue Lake Ontario, can do to fill in the time away from home. This late novel is an unblushing celebration of domesticity – Jane loves to cook, to manage a budget, to clean house. Even before she ever visits P.E.I., she learns to go on moon sprees. She looks at the moon and imagines herself scouring and polishing it – cleaning it to restore its silver light. Montgomery is not praising domesticity for its own sake, but for what it represents to Jane: discovery of her own powers of creativity and control. Jane, a true Hestian female, learns that tending the hearth is for her tantamount to keeping the heart beating.

Unlike Anne Shirley or Emily Starr, and like Pat Gardiner, Jane has parents, but she has never seen her father, and she and her mother live with Jane's maternal grandmother in a grim Victorian mansion in downtown Toronto. Jane's mother's life consists of one party after another and an endless round of dinners and theatre outings. Grandmother wants Robin Stuart to be bright and sparkling, and the accommodating Robin dresses up and goes out. Grandmother despises Jane, and Jane is not allowed to bother her mother, to bring friends home, to help in the kitchen, or to decorate her own room. In short, grandmother Kennedy keeps the keys, the accounts, and the domestic organization completely in her control. In Jane's upper-middle-class life, being allowed to grow a flower or hang a picture or wash lettuce for a salad would all be considered jobs for servants. Grandmother makes it clear to Jane that any leanings she has to the domestic are signs of her father's low blood. In this repressive atmosphere, the domestic becomes powerful; it symbolizes freedom and autonomy. Jane finds both – on Prince Edward Island.

In Toronto, Jane is very much the ugly duckling or the princess on the glass mountain; she is unable to recognize her own strengths and is powerless to experiment with life. Going to P.E.I. seems a further punishment at first – she will be separated from her beloved though equally powerless mother for three months, and she is going to the sticks. But the wilderness turns out to be an Eden, and 'Dad' is perfection itself – a writer who savours words, relishes beauty and irony, and leaves all the meals and planning to her. Jane, who has never done more than prepare a salad, discovers that she is a talented cook. She conquers the wood stove, arms herself with a cookbook (just as Rilla uses the child-care book to bring up her war baby in *Rilla of Ingleside*), and learns about spices. The house she and her father buy is a child's dream – and the domesticity is, I might add, a child's dream as well. The house is full of dear little nooks and cupboards and has its own garden and fields. Many critics rightly turn to the Emily books for Montgomery's literary autobiography – seeing in the young writer the spirit of the rebellious and misunderstood Maud – and Montgomery herself said that she put much of herself into the character of Pat. I believe we should look to *Jane of Lantern Hill* if we want to see, pressed into one place, all the homey things Montgomery herself loved, as she described them over the years in her letters and her journal. Jane delights in naming, in Bible verses (Montgomery's own favourites), ocean bathing, salt air, P.E.I. Junes, cats, gardening, star-gazing, quilts, buggy rides, driftwood fires, storms, wild strawberries, salt codfish, and a table laden with pies and pickles and chicken. Those loving, descriptive passages about trees, wild flowers, and red roads that characterize *Anne of Green Gables* and the Emily trilogy are here again but this time accompanied by equally lengthy descriptions of the conversations and antics of Island children – real children, not high-minded, sweet, soul companions like Bets Wilcox, or fiery originals like Ilse Burnley. The tauntings Jane gets from the otherwise affectionate Snowbeam children are realistic and amusing – the opening pages of chapter twenty-five are an excellent example of Montgomery's rendering of realistic children's dialogue in this novel.

Jane of Lantern Hill may have too much wish-fulfilment for many readers – Jane ultimately brings her mother and father back together again, and she even picks out the house on the ravine in Toronto where they will live for the winter months (returning to P.E.I. and Lantern Hill for the summer, of course); Jane is good at *everything* she puts her hand to, whether it is driving a tractor, shingling a roof, finding a home for her orphan friend. The only thing she cannot do, it seems, is make good doughnuts. Even when Jane recaptures a tame lion that has escaped from a travelling circus, leads him by the mane into an old shed, and secures him there, the reader is apt to think by this time in the narrative, 'Well, why not? If you're going to have it your own way, why not do a thorough job of it?'

Everything about Jane's story is more straightforward than anything in Pat's. While Pat's maturity and identity and soul are intricately entwined with Silver Bush, Jane's love of home is really an uncomplicated delight in her individual expression of domestic worship. Jane will, no doubt, go on to love many, many houses. Her talent is in recognizing magic and then going to work to create home comforts around it.

Three houses contribute to Jane's understanding of herself and home. First there is the unfriendly Kennedy mansion in Toronto; second, the little house on Lantern Hill that she and her father select; third, the house on the ravine in Toronto, that Jane picks out to be a home for her parents and herself.

The book opens with Jane's disgruntled view of 60 Gay Street, most inappropriately named, she feels, since no real laughter is allowed in Mrs Kennedy's dark chambers. The house sounds as though it should belong to the Wicked Witch of the West: 'It was a huge, castellated structure of brick, with a pillared entrance porch, high, arched Georgian windows, and towers and turrets wherever a tower or turret could be wedged in. It was surrounded by a high iron fence with wrought-iron gates ... those gates had been famous in the Toronto of an earlier day ... that were always closed and locked by Frank at night, thus giving Jane a very nasty feeling that she was a prisoner being locked in' (1–2). No house on old Gay Street would ever think of winking at Jane, for they are all 'dark and dingy,' 'grimy with age,' with 'tall, shuttered, blinded windows [that] could never have thought of winking at anybody' (1). Just as Jane herself is deploring the age and unfriendliness of the place she would so like to be able to love, she overhears two women talking about the shabbiness of the formerly grand street. Their verdict on it is a commentary on the quality of Jane's emotional life with her thwarted mother and hate-filled grandmother. The women say of 60 Gay, 'It's worse than dead ... it's decayed' (4). And even if loyal, loving little Jane could forget her imprisonment in this dusty tomb, grandmother is there to check her. When Jane tries to love the house despite her grandmother, she finds the house as unfriendly and unyielding as the old lady. Jane is realizing, as Pat Gardiner eventually, belatedly realized, that houses may be the people who live in them and care for them: 'She wanted to love it ... to be friends with it ... to do things for it. But she could not love it ... it *wouldn't* be friendly ... and there was nothing it wanted done' (13). Jane's only solace before she meets the orphan Jody next door is in going on moon sprees and in imagining herself to be Alice in the looking-glass world where everything would be the reverse of what it is in her cheerlessly grand Toronto mansion (30). Wise in her eleven years, Jane knows that, 'I don't belong here' (51).

When Jane is forced to go to Prince Edward Island to visit a father she cannot remember, she mourns for the prison-like Gay Street, since it is the only place she knows and since her mother is there. Her effusive, insincere Aunt Irene meets her and takes her to her house, and Jane again instinctively recognizes the quality of spirit through and with the quality of house: ' "Here we are at home, lovey." Home! The house into which Jane was ushered was cosy and sleek, just like Aunt Irene herself, but Jane felt about as much at home as a sparrow alone on an alien housetop' (77).

From the moment she sees him, however, her father is no stranger. In fact, in keeping with the fairy-tale quality of the story, he is the man whose picture she had cut out of a magazine because she had liked his face so much. Her mother had been strangely upset by the picture and, when it had been taken away from her, Jane had mourned for it as though for a dear friend. With this sympathetic, slightly inscrutable, but wholly appreciative man, the fairy-tale book does not need a prince. Jane's father is romantic hero and loving father combined, and together the pair set off to find a house so that they can begin enacting the child-fantasy of virtually undisturbed domestic comfort and communion.

Naturally they share the same standards of beauty and harmony and reject house after house in their quest for the perfect place. And naturally they both recognize the place the minute they see it, though Jane must pretend to talk her father into it in their subsequent discussions. Of course the Lantern Hill house winks at her: 'Jane saw the house first ... at least she saw the upstairs window in its gable end winking at her over the top of a hill ... It squatted right against a little steep hill whose toes were lost in bracken. It was small ... you could have put half a dozen of it inside of 60 Gay' (100). Jane perceives the power of it immediately: 'Magic! Why, the place was simply jammed with magic. You were falling over magic' (103). But what marks this as home, to Montgomery readers, is the description of the view. No matter how lovely, the house would not be complete without a dash of purple and silver in its setting: 'Lantern Hill was at the apex of a triangle of land which had the gulf for its base and Queen's Harbour for one of its sides. There were silver and lilac sand-dunes between them and the sea, extending into a bar across the harbour where great, splendid, blue and white waves were racing to the long sun-washed shore. Across the channel a white lighthouse stood up against the sky and on the other side of the harbour were the shadowy crests of purple hills that dreamed with their arms around each other. And over it all the indefinable charm of a Prince Edward Island landscape' (101–2).[3] Any Montgomery reader knows that the combination of dunes and sea and hills and lighthouse and ethereal colours is meant to be irresistible and at once binds the place and Jane and her father as kindred spirits.

So the sensitive, misunderstood writer and his sensitive, neglected daughter proceed to live out an idyllic fantasy – the dream fulfilment, perhaps, of Montgomery's own childhood yearning for her father and her abiding passions for Prince Edward Island and domesticity. Jane thrives as the 'chatelaine of Lantern Hill' (199), as Pat did as the 'chatelaine of Silver Bush.' On her very first night in it, her friend the moon consecrates her to the place: 'The moon was up and had already worked its magic with the landscape' (112). And she thinks of the contrast between this spirit home and her prison in Toronto: 'how lovely it was to lie in this comfort-able little ''spool'' bed ... and watch the moonlight patterning the walls with birch leaves and know that dad was just across the little ''landing'' from you, and that outside were free hills and wide, open fields where you could run wherever you liked, none daring to make you afraid, spruce barrens and shadowy sand-dunes, instead of an iron fence and locked gates' (112–13). Jane learns to value her own talents and to celebrate her own powers of loving and doing. Back in the prison of Gay Street she can still be refreshed by Lantern Hill because she herself has been strength-ened by self-knowledge. Her attitude to life is now radically different; even life in Toronto is now bearable, because she knows she has a real place and is herself powerful. She has found the truth of the saying, 'Home is where the heart is' (194), but she has also learned that she has the capabilities to transform monotony into cheer and routine into method.

She even develops a quiet sympathy with her old aunt, who loves 60 Gay Street as passionately as Jane does Lantern Hill. Jane's discovery of home has meant her recognition of herself and her conscious, unfearing perception of her surroundings. With the wisdom of Lantern Hill inside her, Jane is now virtually indomitable.

Thus liberated, Jane is able to see magic even in Toronto. While her mother is visiting with a friend, Jane explores some new houses and finds one that beckons to her as Lantern Hill had beckoned: 'Yes, this house belonged to her ... she could see herself in it, hanging curtains, polishing the glass doors, making cookies in the kitchen' (224). In finding the Toronto house, Jane has graduated from appreciator of beauty to active searcher for beauty, and the reader knows that the power in Jane will enable her to find and create 'home' wherever her sturdy and sensitive spirit detects magic. Montgomery's loving description shows us the artist spirit that can relish lake as well as ocean; electric lights as well as lantern glow.

In the very last lines of the novel Jane tells her reunited parents (in her little Lantern Hill room) that she knows a house in Toronto that will be perfect for the three of them. And the last view we have is of the thwarted grandmother, the dethroned wicked witch who will not be able to counter Jane's beneficent spells in the new house: 'Jane thought of the little stone house in Lakeside Gardens. It had not been sold yet. They would buy it. It would live ... they would give it life. Its cold windows would shine with welcoming lights. Grandmother, stalking about 60 Gay, like a bitter old queen, her eyes bright with venom, forgiving or unforgiving as she chose, could never make trouble for them again' (296–7). Jane, after all, is just beginning to explore her own charms.

In the three novels *Pat of Silver Bush*, *Mistress Pat*, and *Jane of Lantern Hill*, Montgomery uses houses metaphorically. But in the Pat books, Pat's dark journey into the soul makes a wrong turning when she believes the place Silver Bush has a power that she does not herself have. In her love of home and place Pat misapprehends herself, failing to see that her love of Silver Bush is what gives it so much power in her life. Judy Plum loves the place, too, but even she does not identify with it as Pat does, and she is eager for Pat to find a worthy partner and have a home of her own. Hilary, the artist-architect, can appreciate the beauty of Silver Bush without being enslaved by it. And so the two Pat books show a painful, sometimes oppressively gloomy process of self-neglect and false perception. Pat must lose Silver Bush in order to be free to appreciate the nurturing powers within herself. And that self-appreciation is well beyond the story.

The passionate love of home and worship of the domestic set Jane free from the moment she begins to experience them. The Toronto house is external to her – it is her jail, not her soul; and even when she finds and loves Lantern Hill and then the Lakeside Gardens house, she sees herself as important to them. She knows that she is the one with the strength and love to transform each house into home. For Pat there is only the one essential place, until she transfers at the end of the story, her misguided and exclusive passion for Silver Bush to Hilary Gordon. The suggestion is that, through Hilary's love, Pat will value herself and their shared home-of-spirit more than she will ever again value a physical place. The far less complex Jane discovers through the houses she loves that life is full of beauty and joy for those sure enough of themselves to see with an open mind and heart. After all, Grandmother Kennedy is a bit like an old and unregenerate Pat Gardiner – she tries to transfix her beloved (both house and daughter) and in so doing is imprisoned by death and decay. In other words, the deep pattern upholding *Jane of Lantern Hill* can be read as a symbolic, wishful retelling of Pat's story. In her last writing years perhaps Montgomery turned away from even hinting at the gloomy obsessions with loss and self-betrayal she had no intention of honestly exploring fictionally, and instead returned to the liberation of fairy tale and archetype she had tapped so successfully in *Anne of Green Gables*. Pat's (wrongly perceived) Silver Bush must be burned to ashes,[4] but Lantern Hill, like Green Gables, is spared to the imaginative landscape, and beckons yet from its romantic spruce and maple grove, probably somewhere close to the Four Winds lighthouse.

A Changing Heroism:
An Overview of the Other Novels

Kilmeny of the Orchard (1910)

Tired out from writing *Anne of Avonlea* (1909) at breakneck speed, Maud
Montgomery was not ready to create a third novel for the Page Company
right away. Instead she decided to take a 24,000-word story she had
already published under the title 'Una of the Garden' and stretch it into a
48,000-word novel. The Page Company was pleased but changed the
heroine's name and the work's title to *Kilmeny of the Orchard*. The
writing in it belongs to formula romance fiction and shows little of the
sophistication or irony we find in *Anne of Green Gables* or even *Anne of
Avonlea*.

Readers curious about turn-of-the-century magazine-quality fiction that
acts out unquestioningly the popular stereotypes for (rising) middle-class
men and women will find a good example in *Kilmeny of the Orchard*.
Montgomery's readers probably enjoyed seeing the new knight errant in
the son of a merchant educated in the liberal arts, trained to achieve, and
at leisure to go on a mission of mercy to help out a less robust college
friend in distress on P.E.I. In this affirmation of middle-class values we
note that Kilmeny represents the best of the old-world stock: 'Thrawn and

twisted the old Gordon stock might be, but it had at least this one offshoot of perfect grace and symmetry' (117). Kilmeny marries the man who is himself the son of a Nova Scotia farmer and we thus find that the new mercantile aristocracy – the wealthy middle class – is firmly rooted in the thrifty strength of the land. The formula Montgomery used in creating *Kilmeny of the Orchard* was one that flattered the middle and the working classes in its suggestion of worth transcending 'taint' and virtue rewarded with material success. Kilmeny may look like the 'Madonnas of old paintings' (61), but she is really a picture drawn by Montgomery's accommodating and flattering pen of the middle-class conception of its own new order of chivalry and righteousness. Montgomery outgrew this formula (had already outgrown it, really), even if she did not put aside all the cultural assumptions encoded in *Kilmeny*.

Those readers who assume that formula romance fiction and fairy tale are always the same (and also that they are equally inferior) should compare the admittedly flimsy construction of *Kilmeny of the Orchard* with the fairy-tale pattern of *Jane of Lantern Hill*. The differences in the treatment of the heroines (leaving age aside) tells almost everything. Beautiful Kilmeny Gordon, mute daughter of a fanatical and twisted mother, is brought up to believe that she is ugly and that all strangers – especially men – are dangerous. She is told that love is a curse and that she must not try to mingle with a wicked and thwarting world. She lives on a secluded homestead on Prince Edward Island, where she makes an old orchard into an enchanted garden, going there to play her violin. Kilmeny's music – all of her own spontaneous composition – speaks the feelings and thoughts she cannot herself utter. And in telling the outline you have told almost all. Kilmeny is beautiful, loving, sweet-natured, and highly principled. The one thing about her that surprises the adoring Eric Marshall is that Kilmeny means what she 'says' when she tells him that she will not marry him unless she can speak like other women. The only changing Kilmeny does in the story is to grow less frank about her feelings after Eric declares his love for her. She supposedly changes before our eyes from a child to a woman because (Prince Charming) Eric kisses her and she becomes conscious of love. And that is it.

Apart from being unbending, Kilmeny is without surprises. The narrator tells us that she writes little notes that show wit and humour, but we are never given any of these, and Kilmeny remains a beautiful picture, even at the end of the story when she screams Eric's name and warns him that Neil Gordon is about to pounce on him from behind and murder him with an axe. Everything is decorous and predictable. Old Mr Marshall takes one look at Kilmeny and pronounces her the perfect wife for his son. In keeping with formula-romance roles, Kilmeny does not have to do anything but look beautiful and act sweet for the world to be hers. She eventually goes off with Prince Charming to live in his commercial palace and leaves her homely, faithful relatives behind, next to the enchanted orchard. Kilmeny is nothing more than her story; she is static. Jane Stuart is also rescued by a Prince Charming and lives part of the year in an enchanted place, but Jane herself changes and grows and learns to think and plan and struggle for what she wants. Jane is human; Kilmeny is not. The enchanted worlds of Lantern Hill and Lakeside Gardens of Toronto become backdrops for Jane's creative powers. Kilmeny remains as unearthly as her music. Formula often uses stereotype; fairy tale, archetype.

Everything about the story belongs to formula. Eric Marshall is good looking, wealthy, young, and in need of 'one quixote thing' (4) to make him perfect. He has never been in love and has made no time in his busy, 'clean,' active life for romance. His father is the gruff but loving patriarch who wants Eric to find a perfect woman for a wife so that he can enjoy grandchildren. Prince Edward Island is pastoral perfection; Eric's landlord and landlady are the perfect kindly gossips; Eric's rival for Kilmeny's affections is a dark, passionate, unscrupulous foreigner (Montgomery's story makes unblushing use of xenophobia and bigotry); Kilmeny's guardians are rough-tongued, God-fearing Scots; Kilmeny's mother was an abused and misunderstood woman who herself became twisted and unforgiving. In formula romance there must be a rival and there must be an apparently insurmountable obstacle to the protagonists' love. Italian Neil Gordon, adopted by the Gordons when his peddlar mother died after giving birth to him and his father deserted him, is the expected hot-blooded murderous rival, and the barrier is Kilmeny's virtuous firmness. Montgomery makes the story pleasing to read and lifts it briefly beyond formula with her loving descriptions of sunset and garden; we are carried along by the lyric passages and by the predictable events.

Today Montgomery's story appears crude in many ways. The racism is disturbing. Neil is described as a 'feline creature basking in lazy grace, but ever ready for an unexpected spring' (39) and as giving vent to 'the untamed fury of the Italian peasant thwarted in his heart's desire' (155). The unchallenged snobbery is off-putting. Old Mr Marshall dismisses the kindly and generous Williamsons thus: 'If Thomas Gordon had been a man like Robert Williamson I shouldn't have waited to see your Kilmeny. But they [the Gordons] are all right – rugged and grim, but of good stock and pith – native refinement and strong character' (253–4). In such a context, Eric Marshall's refusal to be influenced by the possible 'taint' on Kilmeny's birth (Kilmeny's father was a bigamist) is no doubt meant to seem large-minded. Eric and Kilmeny are porcelain dolls.

Interestingly, though Kilmeny is meant to be a paragon, she does not represent the only alternative for women, even within the formulaic thinking of the story. The book begins with a college graduation, and we find at least twenty women, beautiful and brainy, among the men. Eric is good friends with one of the top female scholars, and even Eric's father is pleased to see women taking their degrees. But whether for contrast or as a reassuring touch of verisimilitude, only the frame for Montgomery's story is really modern. The story itself takes its pattern from old-fashioned chivalry and its offspring: the maiden in distress in her own turn saves her rescuer through love.

The Story Girl (1911) and *The Golden Road* (1913)

The Story Girl was a personal favourite of Montgomery. Perhaps it is more closely modelled than her diaries or letters will show on actual episodes with her 'merry cousins' in Park Corner and with Well and Dave Nelson, the two little boys who boarded with the Macneills in Cavendish. And whether based on real events or not, the two books, but particularly the first, capture the flavour of children's interactions and inventions. The five King children – cousins and siblings – the hired boy Peter Craig, the weepy friend Sara Ray, and Sara Stanley herself are breathing, (usually) believable children with tempers and dreams and a love of eating and good times.

But there is more to *The Story Girl*, in particular, than a remembrance of joys past or even an exploration of those precious 'spots of time' of the kind that Wordsworth paints. From the first to the last Montgomery's fourth novel is a celebration of story and the story teller (Coldwell 125–

35) Sara Stanley (the Story Girl) is the most important and colourful person in the group, and it is her fascinating voice and captivating manner that make her central to the children's lives. Through Sara Stanley we find the art of narrative given lavish praise. The other children are always eager to hear one of her stories, and she has a story for just about everything. The heroine of the two books is, thus, the artist who revels in life and creates from it what will take her audience beyond itself.

The two books fit together, *The Golden Road* picking up the narrative exactly where *The Story Girl* leaves it, but the tone and atmosphere of the two is very different, suggesting the contrast between recreation and nostalgia. In *The Story Girl* we witness life; in *The Golden Road* we hear Bev remembering.

Sara Stanley is unquestioningly the centre of life in *The Story Girl*; the boy narrator, Beverley King, and the other characters he quotes frequently remark on her gifts even when she is not herself performing. When the two brothers first meet her they are struck by her voice: 'Never had we heard a voice like hers. Never, in all my life since, have I heard such a voice. I cannot describe it. I might say it was clear; I might say it was sweet; I might say it was vibrant and far-reaching and bell-like; all this would be true, but it would give you no real idea of the peculiar quality which made the Story Girl's voice what it was' (15). And her voice creates the air of romance in all that she speaks: 'The Story Girl's words fell on the morning air like pearls and diamonds. Even her prepositions and conjunctions had untold charm, hinting at mystery and laughter and magic bound up in everything she mentioned. Apple pies and sour seedlings and pigs became straightway invested with a glamour of romance' (24). She makes even the oldest story sound interesting and thrills her listeners with the multiplication table itself (80). And some of the stories are truly delightful – whether they are retellings of Montgomery's own clan tales, as with the story of the courtship of Betty Sherman, or something eerie and new, as with the Proud Princess. Most of the stories are short and poignant.[1] Sara Stanley, in telling them, becomes an old-world minstrel or scop continuing the traditions of her clan and creating new sensations among the young and old. Even Emily Byrd Starr is not more successful than Sara Stanley at the weaving of tales.

In *The Story Girl*, except for a few long descriptions of the usual Montgomery type, Bev makes only brief interjections about adult life or lessons or truths. For example, at the end of an episode concerning Peg Bowen, the supposed witch who is believed to have cast a spell on the children's cat, Bev winds up the chapter succinctly: 'Thus faith, superstition, and incredulity strove together amongst us, as in all history' (269). Or he says about the sermon contest and the wisdom of not asking adult permission: 'You could never tell what kink a grown-up would take. They might not think it proper to play any sort of a game on Sunday, not even a Christian game. Least said was soonest mended where grown-ups were concerned' (278).

But in *The Golden Road* a much older-sounding Bev indulges in frequent asides about youth and waxes philosophic in purple passages. The quick pace and short paragraphs of *The Story Girl* give way to paragraphs and pages of explanation and interpretation. Note, for example, how Bev privileges description over characterization or action in the two opening paragraphs of chapter thirteen, 'A Surprising Announcement':

'Nothing exciting has happened for ever so long,' said the Story Girl discontentedly, one late May evening, as we lingered under the wonderful white bloom of the cherry trees. There was a long row of them in the orchard, with a Lombardy poplar at either end, and a hedge of lilacs behind. When the wind blew over them all the spicy breezes of Ceylon's isle were never sweeter.

It was a time of wonder and marvel, of the soft touch of silver rain on greening fields, of the incredible delicacy of young leaves, of blossom in field and garden and wood. The whole world bloomed in a flush and tremor of maiden loveliness, instinct with all the evasive, fleeting charm of spring and girlhood and young morning. We felt and enjoyed it all without understanding or analyzing it. It was enough to be glad and young with spring on the golden road. (157)

The Story Girl's restlessness is put aside for Bev's remembering, as though he sees no contrast between her discontent and his own nostalgic observation that, 'It was enough to be glad and young.' Would we really rather read his sweetly melancholy memories of springs long past than feel the active, eager chafe of the spirits he is supposedly trying to capture?

A conspicuous instance of insistent describing and remembering comes towards the end of the book with the visit of Sara Stanley's father, the artist. Bev, Sara, and Mr Stanley take a walk in the woods, and Bev's relentless poeticizing must surely grate on even the most determinedly receptive of readers. The Story Girl is silenced in Beverley King's remembering, as though years later he believes he speaks with her fascinating voice. For some of (what I believe to be) the most contrived and self-conscious prose Montgomery ever put into a novel, read the whole chapter 'The Path to Arcady' (321–35). (Emily Byrd Starr would have called it 'fine writing.')

Excess marks even the fun parts of the second novel. The King newspaper, *Our Magazine*, is quaint and funny, but we are given too much of it. Often Sara Stanley loses prominence in favour of a general hilarity. Nevertheless, as with all Montgomery's novels, there are some wonderful scenes. 'Great-Aunt Eliza's Visit' (67–89) is funny; 'The Love Story of the Awkward Man' is well told, supplied to an old Beverley King by an old Story Girl, and the only piece we have from Sara Stanley as a mature woman artist.

When Beverley King lets Sara Stanley and the other children speak for themselves, and when the pace of the narrative imitates the quicksilver movements of a child, both *The Story Girl* and *The Golden Road* are captivating. But when Montgomery allows Bev to intrude and interpret and moralize and generally hold forth, I believe the stories are dull. Nevertheless, while Beverley King is not himself ever an entirely believable person, the others are, and Peter Craig, the hired boy, stands out as one of the most convincing boys Montgomery created. Even if Sara Stanley remains somewhat blurred despite her power and presence, her stories are often crisp, vivid reminders that for Montgomery a heroine was she who found and appreciated drama and beauty in the everyday world around.

The Blue Castle (1926)

Having completed (she thought) the Anne series and having written two of the books about her new dark-eyed heroine Emily, Montgomery turned away from Prince Edward Island, and from childhood and adolescent stories, and wrote the first of her two adult novels. Set in the beautiful Muskoka area of Ontario, which Montgomery had holidayed in and loved, the new novel deals with twenty-nine-year-old Valancy (originally called Miranda [CM 67.5.9]) Stirling, who can endure her drab, pinched, loveless life only because she envisions for herself a romantic blue castle in Spain where she is the honoured and much-sought mistress. Something like *Kilmeny of the Orchard, The Blue Castle* has the shape of a formula romance, but there are enough comic reversals and surprises in the story to keep it from being wholly predictable, and there is as much liberating fairy tale as limiting formula. Its plot undoubtedly belongs to romance fiction: thinking she has only one year to live, Valancy defies her clan and goes to nurse the (social outcast) Cissy Gay, who is dying of consumption. After Cissy dies, Valancy asks the local, mysterious suspected reprobate to marry her, informing him of her impending heart failure. They have an idyllic year, but at the end of it a terrible fright reveals to both of them that Valancy's heart is not so frail as she had believed, and she finds that the doctor had sent her the wrong letter by mistake. A healthy and depressed Valancy returns to her clan, believing Barney does not love her and that she must give him a divorce since she is not going to die. Meanwhile, Valancy has discovered that Barney is really the son of a millionaire who wants his run-away child to come home and marry the girl he had originally been in love with. But Barney really does love Valancy and carries her away from her suddenly obsequious and obliging clan to live a life of travel and woodlore and eternal romance. The sudden fright was one Montgomery borrowed from a newspaper story (*Letters* 154–5), but the appearance of old Doc Redfern, the patent-medicine millionaire, and the happily-ever-after ending certainly belong to formula romance and melodrama. The differences between Montgomery's romance and one of strict formula – such as Colleen McCullough's 1987 novel, *The Ladies of Missalonghi* (which echoes, whether consciously or unconsciously, Montgomery's *Blue Castle* in a startling number of ways)[2] – are found in comedy and in character motivation. We can believe in Valancy in a way we would never dream of believing in McCullough's cardboard Missy.

The opening chapters of *The Blue Castle* are both poignant and funny – Valancy's sudden rebellion turns the chill monotony of her life into comedy. She says what she thinks and, after a lifetime of timidity and fear, laughs at the self-absorption of her clan. This tiny portion of a family dialogue at dinner gives an idea of Montgomery's handling of Valancy's rebellion:

Aunt Alberta, to save her dinner, plunged into an account of how a dog had bitten her recently. Uncle James, to back her up, asked where the dog had bitten her.

'Just a little below the Catholic church,' said Aunt Alberta.

At that point Valancy laughed. Nobody else laughed. What was there to laugh at?

'Is that a vital part?' asked Valancy. (59–60)

Valancy is a heroine because she flings aside restraint, rules, and Deerwood respectability (though not respectability altogether). She follows her own heart where both Cissy Gay and Barney Snaith are concerned, and leaves behind forever the galling imprisonment of being 'one of the Deerwood Stirlings.' As with so many of Montgomery's heroines, however, we see that Valancy's rebellion is not really against morality or the established order but against the petty corruption of the values of the old order. Valancy wants marriage and home life and the security of a husband who responds possessively to the desire of a famous artist to paint her portrait: 'I didn't know what *you* wanted. But I told him *I* didn't want my wife painted – hung up in a salon for the mob to stare at. Belonging to another man' (173). Valancy, we are assured, has been looking for genuine (read that as traditional but not necessarily always conventional) romance and beauty, and she has been heroic enough to recognize them when they were magically disguised in a homespun shirt or log house. Fashionably beautiful cousin Olive, with her pretty curls and complexion, proves to be the ugly stepsister, and Valancy is Cinderella.

But even if Valancy's story is predictable in shape, and Valancy herself is, after her first rebellion, largely conformist in her own desires and expectations, Montgomery skilfully gives the novel some unexpected developments. One of them is to include a description of an 'up back' dance at Chidley Corners, where Valancy is having a wonderful time until a drunken crowd arrives. Swearing and fighting break out, and one of the men forces Valancy onto the dance floor. Montgomery's description of the reeking whisky and the 'girls, swung rudely in the dances ... dishevelled and tawdry' (106) is worth reading in full.[3]

The novel as a whole has quite a few romantic, moonlit moments, and the portion of the story describing Valancy's and Barney's life on Mistawis is really one protracted lyric in Montgomery's best style – the manuscript of the novel shows that Montgomery took great pains with the writing and revising of these numerous descriptive passages.[4] And, as an added twist, instead of just having rapturous descriptions of nature given by the narrator as though through the eyes of Valancy or even Barney, we find Valancy inspired by and quoting her favourite nature writer, John Foster. In fact, it has been John Foster's philosophic and poetic books that have kept Valancy's soul alive for the five years before her heart trouble; she has borrowed them with stealth from the public library, memorizing long passages and savouring every turn of phrase. In a sense, then, many of the nature descriptions in the book are given through John Foster, since those that are not his are given as though through Valancy's or Barney's eyes, since Valancy has been trained by her reading of Foster, and since Barney *is* Foster. Only one-fifth of the novel's descriptions come right from the pages of Foster's *Thistle Harvest*, *Magic of Wings*, or *Wild Honey*, but we feel in many of the outdoor descriptions Foster's (Barney's) desire to find truth or message in the quality of beauty described. Foster's passages and the narrator's descriptions would make an interesting comparative study – in the subtle turnings of their similarities and differences perhaps we would find encoded Montgomery's estimation of what distinguishes the male voice from the female (itself fashioned into an apparently neutral narrator's). Whether Foster or the narrator is speaking, we find in the descriptions an incredibly rich concentration of colours and jewels, reminding us of the highly romantic, poetic infusions in *Anne's House of Dreams*.

Perhaps the most interesting development in the novel has to do with the similarities between male and female, rather than their differences. After all, the love story of Valancy and Barney is a continual discovery of their similarities and sympathies – they know how to talk about poetry and life in the same language, they laugh at the same jokes, they share silences, they love the out-of-doors, she worships John Foster, they both hate society's niceties and expectations. At the outset, when Valancy is still stuck with her mother and cousin, she sees Barney and begins to romanticize his freedom: 'Men had the best of it, no doubt about that. This outlaw was happy, whatever he was or wasn't. She, Valancy Stirling, respectable, well-behaved to the last degree, was unhappy and had always been unhappy. So there you were' (29). We later find that Barney has had a miserable childhood and young adulthood and that he had disappeared from society and civilization because he had turned bitterly misanthropic. His apparent freedom and happiness are recklessness and desperation, and his only solace has been the woods and his John Foster writing. Thus it is that when Valancy and Barney face each other at the end of the novel, we see them as the same: both believe themselves to be unlovable; neither can believe that the other finds her or him worthy. Valancy fears her own unloveliness; Barney, the taint of his father's patent-medicine millions. They are twins. Ironically, this similarity is in the tradition of the finest romance literature, rather than in the conventions of formula romance. In Valancy and Barney we hear, unspoken, the words of Jane Eyre's famous declaration to Edward Rochester: 'equal, – as we are!' (Brontë 222), the most hopeful, ecstatic, and self-persuading words an independent woman can utter.

The recognized equality of spirit and similarity of feeling are what make Valancy's and Barney's story appealing, combining traditional romance and fairy tale. Valancy's story begins with dreams of chivalry, knights, and castles, and she finds an unshaven scapegrace living on a lonely island. Valancy recognizes the chivalry-in-disguise in a moment; unlike Anne Shirley, who cannot see Gilbert as anything but a school friend, or Pat Gardiner who cannot see Jingle, Valancy is willing to accept cheerfully the muddy overalls and rattling car of her chosen knight. But behind the stories of Anne and Valancy is the same conception of romance. Each heroine rebels against her surroundings in order to find her own conception of the romantic: Anne is twenty-two when she finds that her everyday world is every bit as romantic as the world of poetry and chivalry she imagines, and that Gilbert shares her values; Valancy is long past girlhood when the novel begins, and John Foster has already been training her to believe that the everyday world around is as full of glamour and surprise and beauty as any castle in Spain. We remember that, from the time Valancy gets a good look at Barney, her hero changes from the inscrutable and Byronic inhabitant of a castle to the rough-chinned reprobate of 'up back.' Valancy learns quickly as an adult the very same lesson that Anne learns over three novels and ten years of late girlhood: the romancing of the world of nature is a romance that lasts; friendship can be a solid foundation for love.

As a person Valancy ceases to be really interesting once she is married to Barney – she becomes his other self and an almost mute appreciator of the enchanted world of Mistawis. She sheds every spark of bitterness or anger or piercing irony that made her initial break from her clan both entertaining and meaningful. The nature descriptions take over and the comical surprise of Doc Redfern's arrival provides interest, but Valancy and Barney both dissolve into the romance. Their reconciliation scene, where they learn they are the equals they have seemed to be, offers a flicker of interest, and then Valancy and Barney disappear forever into their travels to the Alhambra, a genuine castle in Spain that is now the real-life counterpart for Valancy's imaginary blue castle.

In other words, Montgomery plays with romance convention, seems to overturn it, and then submits to it, as she always did with her promising heroines, who never fully flout the expectations of the surrounding culture but who continue to offer readers a brief vicarious flight of imagined rebellion and escape. Their rebellions are, after all, harmless (as far as the establishment is concerned) since the heroines eventually adopt traditional attitudes and values (and roles). As usual in Montgomery's novels, this returning to the establishment leaves us with a scrap of hope too: beyond the ending of the novel Valancy and Barney may just live the harmonious partnership their story promises – they may even become individuals again. With Montgomery, conventional expectations triumph, but not completely, and that little glimmer of 'might yet be' keeps exacting (and woman-affirming) readers from wanting to throw away what is truly delightful in Valancy's pursuit of romance and self.

Magic for Marigold (1929)

What can a late-twentieth-century reader make of the values implicit in this puzzling book? Montgomery originally published parts of *Magic for Marigold* in the *Delineator* as a series of short stories (Gillen 156), but the episodic quality of the narrative, a standard feature rather than an aberration of Montgomery's fiction, is not the real problem here, although one might wonder about the book's construction and pace when Montgomery devotes two full chapters to the Leslie clan's deliberations about a name for a new baby. Marigold herself belongs to the worlds of poetry, fairy tale, and enchantment, and seems at times a spirit sister of Anne, Emily, the King children, and Sara Stanley. She has an imaginary playmate called Sylvia with whom she spends many delicious hours. One of the most poignant episodes of the book describes Marigold's temporary loss of Sylvia. Grandmother, who disapproves of Marigold's having an imaginary playmate, waits for Marigold's mother to go away on a visit and then tells Marigold that she cannot have the key to the garden door. Marigold does not argue, knowing all too well how stubborn her grandmother can be; but Marigold eats little and gradually becomes so thin and pale and listless that grandmother is alarmed. Montgomery shows the grandmother to be loving but also angry – she does not want to give in to Marigold even when she can see that the child is failing. She is, Montgomery shows, one of those hard, prosaic people who cannot understand others' beliefs and dismisses what she cannot understand. An old friend of hers, a noted psychologist, convinces her that Marigold is dying of a broken heart, and she – very grimly – places the key beside Marigold's breakfast plate. Marigold is at once transported with joy and rushes out to her beloved Sylvia.

Marigold's predicament over the key to the magic door is typical of her powerlessness. And this is the central difficulty with the book. Although Marigold is a winsome and even charming little girl, she is so often consciously helpless against the adults and the children around her. It is not that she is exactly weak-willed; it is, rather, that others are livelier, and she gets caught up with their schemes. In fact, the other children's devilment, though sometimes 'int'resting,' to use Marigold's own favourite descriptor, seems hectic and cruel, and two-thirds of the way through the book we may well wonder why Montgomery stacks one frantic episode on top of another without exploring more of the steady, even tenor of Marigold's own mind and imaginings.

What Marigold learns, evidently with the narrator's approval, is disturbing. Montgomery's recreation of the culture around Marigold is realistic with a vengeance. The French are ridiculed throughout; Marigold learns not only that the French hired man, Lazarre, cannot speak 'correctly,' but that when he gets drunk and gives his wife a black eye his proper punishment is to be scolded like a child by Marigold's great-grandmother. Similarly, a Russian princess who comes to play with Marigold behaves with all the passionate savagery of the stereotyped foreigner (the only bit of humour here is that Marigold thinks Varvara is American rather than Russian). Or there is the episode where devilish Gwennie persuades Marigold to dress up in old clothes from the attic and go to an adult costume party that they have been forbidden to attend. Marigold wears a dress that belonged to her father's first wife, Clementine, a celebrated beauty who died young. Gwennie steps on a ball at the party and goes shrieking to the floor, taking Marigold with her, so that Marigold lands in front of Clementine's mother. The narrator is not in the least sympathetic with Clementine's mother's hysterics at the sight of her dead daughter's dress. Instead, old Mrs Lawrence, of whom we have been told nothing really prejudicial before, is ridiculed by the narrator and reviled by Gwennie: ' "My heart broke – when Clementine died – and now to have it brought up like this – *here* – " people made out between Mrs Lawrence's yoops' (174). Gwennie shouts at her: ' "Shut your face, you old screech-owl," she said furiously. "You've been told Aunt Lorraine had nothing to do with it. Neither had Marigold. It was me found that mouldy old dress and made Marigold put it on. Now, get that through your dippy old head and stop making a fuss over nothing ... you fat old *cow*" ' (174). The narrator merely says, 'Mrs. Lawrence, finding some one else could make more noise than she could, ceased yooping' (175). On the way home Uncle Klon laughs and says, 'I don't believe any one ever told her the truth about herself before' (175), and while we are wondering if the truth is that she is a 'cow,' we find out the one really damning thing about Clementine, the thing that can make Marigold stop feeling jealous of Clementine's beauty. We find out that Clementine had the unpardonable effrontery to have big feet. Is the narrator – is Montgomery – endorsing the treatment of old Mrs Lawrence who may be an obnoxious bore but is here ridiculed for publicly showing her grief? And is Clementine to be pitied and despised and, ironically, forgiven by Marigold for being her father's first wife simply because she had big feet?

The world around Marigold is full of hidden ugliness. Great-grandmother's stories to Marigold reveal the humorous and very disturbing passions and peculiarities of clan members of the past. Some of great-grandmother's confidences to Marigold are in questionable taste in a supposed children's story, though they are certainly the stuff of real life. How do we feel in the late twentieth century – for that matter, how did Montgomery's contemporaries feel – to hear that great-grandmother's husband fell in love with his cousin and that she, his wife, learned that a man will come back to you if you wait: 'They generally come back if you have sense enough to keep still and wait – as I had, glory be' (70).

And perhaps it is the novel's assumptions about male and female that are hardest to accept in the 1990s. There are many lessons along the way, but at the end of the book Marigold receives her 'Chrism of Womanhood' when she learns how to respond to the delightful boy Budge. Marigold tries to be the ideal companion for Budge – she pretends not to mind snakes and toads because she fears Budge would despise her if she did. When Budge begins to neglect her to play with a new boy, Marigold sulks when Budge does come back to her. As Aunt Marigold explains to a grieving Marigold, 'We – women – must always share' (273). So far so good. Aunt Marigold is sharing with her niece and making her feel the importance of women's ways of knowing and being and understanding. But the final sentences of the novel reinforce a very different lesson. Marigold has been encouraged throughout the book to be passive – her playmates show more vitality than she does – and now the book ends with a final endorsement of this passivity. Marigold learns not just to share, but to wait – as her great-grandmother had said – to be ready when the boy decides to whistle his way back again. Marigold has outgrown Sylvia, but if she is generous and forgiving she will have Budge:

Yes, she must share Budge. The old magic was gone forever – gone with Sylvia and the Hidden Land and all the dear, sweet fading dreams of childhood. But after all there were compensations. For one thing, she could be as big a coward as she wanted to be. No more hunting snakes and chivying frogs. No more pretending to like horrible things that squirmed. She was no longer a boy's rival. She stood on her own ground.

'And I'll always be here for him to come back to,' she thought. (273–4).

Perhaps Montgomery meant the final line to show Marigold's sturdiness and reliability. Perhaps others read those last sentences and see Montgomery's praise of individuality and the female. I see instead acknowledgment of the boy's standards as the measure (if she can be a 'coward,' who defines the term and applies it?) and Marigold's failure to measure up as self-acknowledged inferiority. Of course she will be there for Budge – how good of him to come back to such a little coward as herself. Previous episodes, too, have taught Marigold that what little boys really want from little girls is a sympathetic ear and lavish praise. Is Montgomery slyly exposing the foibles of the sexes or is she exposing *and* endorsing them? The latter seems likely.

While the male-female debate is puzzling, other parts of the book are not. Old grandmother (Marigold's great-grandmother) flavours the pages with salt and vinegar – with worldly wisdom and clan scandals. Montgomery was incensed that people wondered if her crusty matriarch had been inspired by Mazo de la Roche's grandmother of the Jalna books (Gillen 169–70) – perhaps she answered them by writing *A Tangled Web*. But it is true that – if a questionable moralist – old grandmother is one of the best characters of the book. In a rare moment of praise, old grandmother tells Marigold about a woman she loved, and gives us one of the best passages of the novel: 'I loved Annabel. She was the only one of the Lesley clan I really loved. A sweet woman. The only woman I ever knew who would keep secrets. A woman who would really burn a letter if you asked her to. It was safe to empty your soul out to her. Learn to keep a secret, Marigold. And she was just. Learn to be just, Marigold. The hardest thing in the world is to be just. I never was just. It was so much easier to be generous' (73).

Unfortunately, for adult readers, old grandmother dies in the first quarter of the book. The book as a whole suffers from the lack of a real heroine. Marigold has her moments, and Montgomery gives us some wonderfully joyous descriptions through the laughing Marigold's eyes – but the potentially sinister world overshadows its uncertain centre. Is old grandmother right about men and women and life in general? Montgomery's unusual book shows us sorrow, cruelty, madness, and unimaginativeness alongside dancing joy, imaginative ecstasy, and loving kindness. The narrator is sometimes surprisingly – and disturbingly – partial and at other times surprisingly removed. If Marigold Lesley is not an inspiring heroine, however, she at least struggles to know herself and revels in the beauty of her home and the Island. And even if we cannot ourselves endorse Marigold's or the narrator's assumptions about women and men and their roles and limitations, we will probably find Marigold and her world 'int'resting.'

A Tangled Web (1931)

Montgomery's second adult novel makes a startling contrast with a children's novel such as *Magic for Marigold*; the passivity recommended for and assumed in Marigold plays virtually no part in the middle-aged world Montgomery depicts in the adult comedy. Marigold learns to be a receiver of confidences and also learns to desire contact with a male action and passion she as a girl evidently lacks. The narrator encodes multiple messages in this assessment of Marigold's response to Budge: 'She liked his scarlet boy-stories better than her rose-pink and moon-blue girl-fancies' (*MM* 267). Both the women and the men of *A Tangled Web* are passionate and misguided – and the narrator of the adult book makes us laugh at almost everyone. Somewhere between *Magic for Marigold* and the writing of *A Tangled Web* Montgomery made a shift in thinking about the essential differences between male and female and their mutual and independent needs. Or perhaps, Montgomery chose to be honest in the adult novel in a way that she did not feel free to be in the children's book.

As always in Montgomery's novels, the quality of romance in *A Tangled Web* reveals the quality of the male and female personalities involved. Only one of the five main stories of the book deals with Montgomery's usual subject – a young girl learning through pain and (varying degrees of) self-reflection to be a woman. Gay Penhallow is in love with good-looking Noel Gibson, and they become engaged. Gay's daydreams are everything we would expect a girl such as Marigold to feel, too. But Gay's romance goes sour – her malicious cousin Nan decides to steal Noel, and does, and Montgomery chronicles Gay's slow realization that her lover is wavering and then false. Interestingly, too, though Montgomery paints Nan as a selfish and heartless woman, she does not lay all the blame with her. Noel comes across as a spineless, self-important man who deserves to be dropped by Nan as well as Gay. Montgomery even allows Gay the luxury of seeing Noel again and realizing for herself what he really is. Thus, even in the one story line that looks most familiar to a Montgomery reader, we find some surprising developments in the thinking of the heroine. She learns to see for herself what her cousin is and also what her young dreams had made her imagine her hero to be.

Donna Dark's romance with Peter Penhallow is a violent and sudden thing. They are both passionate and stubborn people, and Montgomery gives a good scene showing their stormy recriminations and resentments. Donna has decided to give up her morbid mourning for her boy-husband, who was killed in the war ten years earlier, and to elope with Peter. A more conventional romantic telling would have the fiery lovers meeting and blazing through the night to a secret wedding and a honeymoon in South America or Africa. But in Montgomery's adult comedy, Donna and

Peter, instead, behave in perfect consistency with their pride and temper. Donna is cold and rattled from waiting for an hour in the chilly night air, and Peter ignores her physical and mental coolness since he is caught up in his own exuberance and heat; they argue, and Donna gets out of the car with this most realistic admonition to Peter: ' "Go to hell" she said' (203).

Jocelyn and Hugh Dark have never lived together because at their wedding Jocelyn has fallen in love with another cousin and, when she and Hugh arrive at their new home, she tells him what she has just realized and goes back to live with her mother. For ten years she is faithful to her dream of love for a man she has never seen since. Hugh is brooding and faithful, and Jocelyn sickens of life but is true to her own dream. Montgomery does not encourage laughter over their tragedy until the fateful cousin reappears on Prince Edward Island and Jocelyn must see how she deluded herself, throwing away years of happiness for the false infatuation kindled in a glance. So much for love at first sight.

The openly comic romance of the novel is the one Pennycuik creates in deciding he must marry Margaret Penhallow if he is to stay in the running for the jug. Slick, dapper, strutting little Penny imagines he is conferring great honour on the faded Margaret. Little does he know that Margaret has her own dreams. Though she accepts Penny, since to be unmarried is to be despised in her clan, she is thrilled when Penny wants to break the engagement. And here Montgomery makes a wonderful departure from the usual conventions of romance. Margaret finds romance and happiness without adult love or marriage – instead, she is in love with a little house she has secretly named Whispering Winds and wants more than anything to live there with a child to love and raise as her own. Margaret, in other words, suggests that the loving maternal spirit has other ways to fulfil itself than through marriage – especially when the marital option is Penny Dark. Initially believing she has no other way to become mistress of her own house than marriage to Penny, Margaret becomes engaged to him, but 'Margaret felt positive anguish when she realised that marriage meant the surrender of all the mystery and music and magic that was Whispering Winds' (236). Interestingly, too, Montgomery makes Margaret a dressmaker and a poet – she creates beauty for young women to wear and she writes of the love and beauty she sees in the world. When the old copy of *Pilgrim's Progress* that Aunt Becky leaves her turns out to be a first edition worth $10,000, Margaret is free to buy her little house and to adopt the abused child Brian. There she will work in her garden and make dresses and write poetry and love little Brian and be a perfectly happy woman. No other Montgomery novel heroine escapes conventional romance with such success.

All the stories have happy endings; Montgomery's puncturing of romance is an illusion, just as it had been much earlier in *Anne of Green Gables*. The undercutting of sentimentality through the pungent and pervasive cynicism and irony of Aunt Becky and the narrator is in turn undercut by the positive resolution to all the stories. Gay falls in love with Roger, Donna and Peter have a big clan wedding, Margaret gets her house and child, Hugh and Jocelyn are reunited, Big Sam and Little Sam overlook their differences and live together again (though their inclusion in the story and their final reunion is to be regretted, since it occasions one of Montgomery's worst racial slurs),[5] Lawson recovers his memory when the jug shatters against his head, and Aunt Rachel gets real Jordan water for her vial. Montgomery's apparent satire on human foibles and entanglements is really a comedy with wedding bells and treasure for its beleaguered participants.

Even in this adult book that suggests a unifying and equalizing foolishness in men and women, Montgomery reverts to her favoured pattern of irruption, upheaval, and restoration. No one is irrevocably warped by anyone else's cruelty or misapprehensions, but yet the cruelty and misfortunes are there for us to see and remember. We find that Brian's uncle strangles Brian's kitten; Staunton Grundy contemplates the sermon of a man with whom his own wife was always in love. The relations between men and women are the substance of life, the book suggests, but there is no limit to misadventures and also to the discoveries that can be made for new ways to work out old problems. In other words, Montgomery's comic, romantic, adult novel does have the distinction of suggesting that life is full of interesting possibilities and that no single answer or pattern can fit all people and all occasions. Compromise and growth and humour are constantly demanded of those who want to make the best of life.

The character of Aunt Becky, obviously kin to old grandmother of *Magic for Marigold*, is a triumph of humour and acerbity. Her mock obituary, that she reads to the clan at her levee, is the best thing in the book, and one of the best pieces of comic realism Montgomery wrote. The whole of it is worth reading, but part of it suggests how far this book departs from Montgomery's others in assessing the power and position of women as Montgomery probably saw it. Of herself, old Aunt Becky says: *'She longed for freedom, as all women do, but had sense enough to understand that real freedom is impossible in this kind of a world, the lucky people being those who can choose their masters, so she never made the mistake of kicking uselessly over the traces'* (60). Aunt Becky's longing for freedom takes the form of delight in others' slavery – she holds everyone in the clan who cares about it to ransom for the heirloom Dark jug.

This frame story and collective motive is the weakest aspect of the book. The novel begins and ends with the Dark jug, and supposedly everything in the book is initiated by or intimately connected with the jug: Nan would not have been around all summer if her aunt had not wanted to find out who would inherit the jug; Peter would not have seen and fallen in love with Donna or rescued her from the burning Dark house had it not been for the jug, and so on. It is not possible, however, to believe that bold and independent Donna could hesitate to marry Peter because she might lose her chances for the jug, nor is it believable that Penny and Margaret are tempted to become engaged at least partly to stay in the running for the jug. Even as an admittedly ridiculous, deliberately satirical device, the jug is largely unconvincing and ineffective. Montgomery always had trouble constructing a plot, and though the jug cannot be dismissed, since it is the motivator behind and the reason for the stories themselves, we must often ignore it in order to think about the human interactions Montgomery paints so well.

There is no single heroine in *A Tangled Web*, though the novel does focus on females, as do all Montgomery's novels. But the focus here is different from the focus in Montgomery's other stories in that the men and women really do seem to play equal parts in the fabrication, destruction, and reconstruction of romance. We may see through the eyes of Donna and Gay and Margaret and Jocelyn, but we also see clearly what Peter and Roger and Penny and Hugh think. Everyone suffers; everyone changes; everyone gives up some secret dream or delusion and then recovers something of it. For the first time, perhaps because it was an adult novel, but more probably because it came later in her career, Montgomery tries to show women and men as similarly deluded and self-deluding and as equally entangled in a great pattern of events over which they have, paradoxically, both ultimate and little control. When each is true to what she or he really wants, the Dark jug doesn't matter at all. Heroism becomes the ability to see, suffer, and repair.

This novel's assumptions about the interconnectedness of life suggest an essentially female view of the world. If, as Carol Gilligan describes it, men see the world in terms of argumentation and separation, and women see it in terms of interconnection and co-operation, then the principles underlying Montgomery's comedy about equality are essentially female, sporadically feminist. In assessing the difference between men's and women's understanding of structure and connection, Gilligan, too, uses the image of the web: 'Just as the language of responsibilities provides a weblike imagery of relationships to replace a hierarchical ordering that dissolves with the coming of equality, so the language of rights underlines the importance of including in the network of care not only the other but also the self' (173). In Montgomery's scheme the clan acts both as a metaphor for the larger human community and as a microcosm of human interactions and foibles. Montgomery uses conventional romance as a kind of comic, universal touchstone for character and also as a serious initiator of individual self-analysis. Romance is inevitably bound up with finding or establishing a home, and home is a tangible link with the clan as well as an emotional centre for the individual.

This adult novel about men and women and clan life expresses most clearly Montgomery's lifelong view that the (female) principles of co-operation and interconnection best sustain the individual and the community. Men and women will be equally culpable and equally heroic in a culture that values both sexes. And this valuing of women and men, who, in turn, value clan and home, suggests that for Montgomery the ultimate romance begins with a beauty- and community-embracing self.

Epilogue

As an extremely popular writer, Montgomery captures and reflects expectations and dreams of her culture – especially those of girls and women. Montgomery's novels are really fictional biographies, stories that show the patterns of many women's lives, then and now. When we recognize how the boundaries of the novel and of biography are similar, we can understand the importance of the patterns Montgomery repeated. Carolyn Heilbrun, in *Writing a Woman's Life*, says: 'Roland Barthes has called biography ''a novel that dare not speak its name,'' and the understanding that biographies are fictions, constructions by the biographer of the story she or he had to tell, has become clear' (28). The story Montgomery had to tell, in a variety of forms in her fictional biographies, involves romance. Consciously and unconsciously using the life scripts available to her, those formed by her reading and by her surrounding culture, Montgomery shows us how respectable but also imaginative and strong girls and women depart from and ultimately conform to cultural expectations.

Each fictional biography shows how the heroine challenges social boundaries, liberating us by the glimmer of possibilities, and then how each heroine conforms to role and gender prescriptions, usually in marriage or in the romantic disposition to courtship and to marriage. Montgomery's liberating contribution to the conventional romance story – having the friend become the lover – is as far as she dared/chose openly to stretch the pattern of love relationships between men and women. And yet, subtly, insistently, another picture emerges. We find in reading and rereading Montgomery's fictional biographies that the lasting romance is often between a conscious, socially responsible self and nature/beauty/home/honour, and not just between a woman and a man. Perhaps in privileging the individual's perception of beauty and belonging, Montgomery meant to reveal a special freedom within the predictable life patterns she (re)created for her heroines. Perhaps Montgomery believed that conscious romance with nature/beauty/home/honour could transform the culturally conforming (auto)biography into a story of individual, private liberation. Perhaps she offered her readers forms of freedom she herself had struggled to achieve.

In Montgomery's many positive forms of romance, the self has an inner, confident voice as well as public articulation; the conscious self honours faith and trust and bravery; the belonging self enjoys a private home and a sense of community; beauty is all around to the loving 'eye' and kindred spirit; love is a partnership where friends share values and vision. Montgomery's heroines find that romance, like the fragrance of sweet-grass on the sand hills, offers them imaginative refreshment on their various journeys. As readers of the heroines, perhaps we can separate Montgomery's confinements by genre and expectations from her liberations of imagination and perception to see how romance is, ultimately, the power we give to the visions we endorse. We may not accept all the forms of romance that the heroines endure or explore, but we may understand from examining them how Montgomery has encouraged generations of readers to enjoy a love affair with the life she describes.

Notes

Introduction: The Fragrance of Sweet-Grass

1 Montgomery eventually sold some five hundred short stories in Canada and the United States. For collections of Montgomery's short stories, see *The Doctor's Sweetheart and Other Stories*, ed. McLay; and especially the series of volumes being edited by Rea Wilmshurst and published by McClelland and Stewart in Toronto: *Akin to Anne* (1988), *Along the Shore* (1989), *Among the Shadows* (1990).

2 Montgomery's published journals do not include any mention of *Rebecca of Sunnybrook Farm*, but there are certainly a remarkable number of similarities between *Anne of Green Gables* and *Rebecca of Sunnybrook Farm*. See Classen 42–50. But there is also another form of proof for Montgomery's having read the novel. Montgomery sometimes copied into her journals – and from there into her letters – favourite passages from books she was reading or had read. In a letter to G.B. MacMillan, written on 3 December 1905, Montgomery quotes from Emerson: 'In the actual – this painful kingdom of time and chance – are Care, Canker and Sorrow: with thought, with the ideal, is immortal hilarity – the rose of joy; round it all the Muses sing' (*Letters* 16). It just so happens that Rebecca hears this very same passage (223), worded exactly this way, though the words 'Ideal' and 'Joy' are capitalized. What makes this quotation interesting is that in Wiggin and in Montgomery we are reading identical *misquotations* of the original lines of Emerson. In Irwin Edwin's edition of Emerson, we find this wording: 'It is strange how painful is

the actual world – the painful kingdom of time and place. There dwells care and canker and fear. With thought, with the ideal, is immortal hilarity, the rose of joy. Round it all the muses sing' (123). In the Slater, Ferguson, and Carr edition, we find this version: 'In the actual world – the painful kingdom of time and place – dwell care, and canker, and fear. With thought, with the ideal, is immortal hilarity, the rose of joy. Round it all the muses sing' (100). It is fair, I believe, to assume that Montgomery had been reminded of Emerson by her reading of *Rebecca of Sunnybrook Farm* and that Miss Maxwell's misquotation to Rebecca is what came to Montgomery's mind (and pen) when she was writing to MacMillan.

3 Several sources could have inspired Montgomery's use of 'kindred spirit': perhaps she was inspired by the Bible's frequent use of 'kindred' and 'kindreds'; or by Thomas Gray's 'Elegy Written in a Country Churchyard' – 'If chance, by lonely contemplation led, / Some kindred spirit shall inquire thy fate,' (95–6); perhaps by Olive Schreiner's *The Story of an African Farm*: the old phoney Bonaparte goes to the German's cabin 'for an hour of brotherly intercourse with a kindred spirit' (68); but the most likely immediate prompter for the phrase would have been Elizabeth von Arnim's *Elizabeth and Her German Garden*, which Montgomery read (and delighted in) in May 1905 (she began writing *Anne of Green Gables* in June of 1905): 'and I go from room to room gazing at the sweetness, and the windows are all flung open so as to join the scent within to the scent without; and the servants gradually discover that there is no party, and wonder why the house should be filled with flowers for one woman by herself, and I long more and more for a kindred spirit – it seems so greedy to have so much loveliness to oneself – but kindred spirits are so very, very rare' (42).

4 Sometimes, as with *Rilla of Ingleside* or *A Tangled Web*, a book may have more than one heroine.

5 Annis Pratt notes: 'Women's fiction reflects an experience radically different from men's because our drive towards growth as persons is thwarted by our society's prescriptions concerning gender' (6).

6 It is worth noting that Montgomery frequently uses other children or adults as foils for the heroine and for the heroine's conception(s) of romance.

7 Perhaps in assessing Montgomery's heroines and style we should keep in mind what she said in 1899 about her favourite reading: 'I like realistic and philosophical novels in spells, but for pure, joyous, undiluted delight give me romance. I always revelled in fairy tales' (*Journals* 1: 235).

8 In the following chapters, all references to the novels will be given, in parentheses, in the text, using some initials of the title where there is any danger of confusion about which novel is cited. The editions I follow are listed in 'Works Cited.'

9 Åhmansson, vol. 1. This thesis appeared after I had completed my study on Montgomery. It contains many fascinating points about correspondences between Mont-

gomery's life and the writing in *Anne of Green Gables* and *Anne's House of Dreams*. Åhmansson's section 'Lady Anne Cordelia Elaine Shirley and the Elusive World of Romance' (101–14) is of particular interest.

PART I Anne

Romancing the Voice: *Anne of Green Gables*

1 For a recent compilation of materials on *Anne of Green Gables*, see Garner and Harker.
2 It is easy to see from looking at the manuscript for the novel (owned by the Confederation Centre of the Arts in Charlottetown, Prince Edward Island) that Montgomery wrote the opening with ease and speed. There are only slight local adjustments to this lengthy sentence, and later additions of two phrases (CM 67.5.1).
3 Montgomery used Tennyson's poem 'Lancelot and Elaine' as a central device in a 1901 short story about a suicide, 'The Waking of Helen' (*Along the Shore* 243–53).
4 Note that, in explaining the appeal of the 'green-world archetype,' Annis Pratt says, 'nature for the young hero remains a refuge throughout life' (17).
5 For helpful insights on the powers of literary allusion, see the article by Ben-Porat, and also the one by Perri.
6 Annis Pratt says of women: 'Our quests for being are thwarted on every side by what we are told to be and to do, which is different from what men are told to be and to do: when we seek an identity based on human personhood rather than on gender, we stumble about in a landscape whose signposts indicate retreats from, rather than ways to, adulthood' (6).
7 For a comparison of Montgomery with some other leading writers from whom she learned, see MacLulich, 'L.M. Montgomery and the Literary Heroine.'
8 See chapter six of Janice Radway's *Reading the Romance* (186–208). At the end of the chapter we find this chilling reminder of closure: 'even as the narrative conveys its overt message that all women are different and their destinies fundamentally open, the romance also reveals that such differences are illusory and short-lived because they are submerged or sacrificed inevitably to the demands of that necessary and always identical romantic ending' (208).

Romance Awry: *Anne of Avonlea*

1 This use of the child is one of the eight strategies Mary Rubio also describes in the unpublished speech I refer to in the introduction of this study.
2 As Rea Wilmshurst tells us (21), Montgomery is using 'the vision and the faculty

divine' from Wordsworth's *The Excursion*, I.78, and also 'Apparelled in celestial light' from stanza one of 'Ode: Intimations of Immortality.'

3 Wilmshurst (20) identifies 'east o' the sun, west o' the moon' from Norse fairy tale, but she is not, nor am I, able to identify the quotation. In the rest of the passage, we surely hear Emerson's 'rose of joy,' from his essay 'Love,' and numerous biblical echoes in 'market place' and the 'priceless lore.' The phraseology itself suggests biblical paraphrase.

4 Mary Rubio and Elizabeth Waterston give a positive assessment of the several plot lines of *Anne of Avonlea*. See their Afterword (277–82).

5 Lavendar Lewis tells Anne: 'I don't care what people think about me if they don't let me see it' (250); she plays with Shakespeare's use of 'great' and 'greatness' (Wilmshurst notes [21] that the passage is from *Twelfth Night*, II.v.) when she says 'Some are born old maids, some achieve old maidenhood, and some have old maidenhood thrust upon them' (265); she tells the romantic Anne that a broken heart is very like a toothache (267); she tells Charlotta the Fourth, alluding to Micah 4:4, that 'I never want to stray from my own vine and fig-tree again' (327).

6 The 'gay knight riding down' here is probably the Lancelot of 'The Lady of Shalott' as much as the one from 'Lancelot and Elaine.' Notice in part three of the short poem the emphasis on Lancelot's riding down to Camelot. Here are a few lines: 'The gemmy bridle glittered free, / Like to some branch of stars we see / Hung in the golden Galaxy. / The bridle bells rang merrily / As he rode down to Camelot' (82–6).

Recognition: *Anne of the Island*

1 She says: 'My forte is in writing humor. Only childhood and elderly people can be treated humorously in books. Young women in the bloom of youth and romance should be sacred from humor' (*Journals* 2: 133).

2 Philippa borrows from hymns, the Bible, Shakespeare, Ben Jonson, Burns, Dickens, Tom Taylor, and Henri Benjamin Constant (Wilmshurst 22–6).

3 The piece reads like a short story and, since Mrs Skinner calls herself 'Amelia' in one place and 'Sarah' in another, I suspect that Montgomery had written this piece earlier and had forgotten to change the name throughout when she was copying from the short story to the manuscript for the novel.

4 The speaker in the poem sets apart the wonderful days of love from the rest of his lament, with these lines: 'Love took up the glass of Time, and turned it in his glowing hands; / Every moment, lightly shaken, ran itself in golden sands' (31–2).

'This Enchanted Shore': *Anne's House of Dreams*

1 A recent edition of Montgomery's poetry offers a better selection, and arrangement,

of poems: *The Poetry of Lucy Maud Montgomery*, ed. Ferns and McCabe.
2 The short story, where parts of this description and numerous other passages from
the novel also appear, was published in February 1917 in *Canadian Magazine*
under the title 'Abel and His Great Adventure,' and republished in 1979 in
Catherine McLay's edited collection of Montgomery short stories, *The Doctor's
Sweetheart and Other Stories* (124–39). I do not know which was written first, the
novel or the story, but from evidence in the manuscript, I would guess that the
story was written first and then borrowed from for the novel. In the short story
old Abel is talking to a schoolmaster, whom he refers to as 'master.' At one point
he tells him the story about thoughtless city people adopting cats for the summer
and then leaving them to starve. Old Abel says: 'Master, I cried. Then I swore'
(*Doctor's* 129). In the novel, Captain Jim is telling exactly the same story to Anne
and Gilbert, and when he gets to this part, he says: 'Master, I cried. Then I swore'
(*AHD* 74). The manuscript for the novel (CM 67.5.2: 139) shows a page of flaw-
lessly written script with the word 'Master' in it. Given Montgomery's habit of
copying from other pieces into the actual manuscript of a novel, and given that
the word 'master' really makes no sense with Gilbert (much less Anne), it is fair
to guess that the short story came first. Why Montgomery would publish this short
story – in Canada – when her novel was in the works is a mystery. At any rate, in
the short story we find this somewhat shorter version of the description quoted in
my text: 'The early sunset glow of rose and flame had faded out of the sky; the
water was silvery and mirror-like; dim sails drifted along by the darkening shore.
A bell was ringing in a small Catholic chapel across the harbour. Mellowly and
dreamily sweet the chime floated through the dusk, blent with the moan of the
sea. The great revolving light at the channel trembled and flashed against the opal
sky and far out, beyond the golden sand-dunes of the bar, was the crinkled gray
ribbon of a passing steamer's smoke' (*Doctor's* 126). The passage I have quoted
from the novel continues: 'A few dim sails drifted along the darkening, fir-clad
harbour shores. A bell was ringing from the tower of a little white church on the
far side; mellowly and dreamily sweet, the chime floated across the water blent
with the moan of the sea. The great revolving light on the cliff at the channel
flashed warm and golden against the clear northern sky, a trembling, quivering
star of good hope. Far out along the horizon was the crinkled gray ribbon of a
passing steamer's smoke' (*AHD* 29–30). It is interesting to see what Montgomery
edited as she copied.
3 'Will all great Neptune's ocean wash this blood / Clean from my hand? No, this
my hand will rather / The multitudinous seas incarnadine, / Making the green one
red (*Macbeth* II. ii.59–62). Jerry Rubio first pointed out this echo to me after I had
delivered a talk on *Anne's House of Dreams* in 1985.
4 Montgomery herself said (*Journals* 2: 222) that she modelled Captain Jim on the

character in her own early short story 'The Life-Book of Uncle Jesse,' first published in *Housekeeping* in 1909. It has been reprinted in *Along the Shore* 33–47.

5 For a fiery contemporary demand for women's suffrage, see Nellie McClung's, *In Times Like These*. See also Prentice et al. 174–88. It is interesting to note that Montgomery had the vote because of the service of her half-brother, Carl (*Journals* 2: 230).

Heroism's Childhood: *Rainbow Valley*

1 For an interesting assessment of the importance of gossip in lives and literature, see Patricia Meyer Spacks's, *Gossip*.

2 For a fascinating picture of Canadian women before and during the war, see Prentice et al. 107–211.

3 For a helpful summary of the differences in expectations for boys and girls, men and women, that shape our conceptions of romance, see Kreps's chapter 'The Prince' 14–38.

4 Tennyson's popular 'The Lady of Shalott' was well known to Montgomery's contemporaries. In it the Lady weaves at a magic loom until Lancelot comes and breaks the spell. She becomes dissatisfied with her life of dreams and shadows and eventually dies for love. The stanza Montgomery probably echoes here describes the Lady's dawning discontent:

> But in her web she still delights
> To weave the mirror's magic sights,
> For often through the silent nights
> A funeral, with plumes and lights
>   And music, went to Camelot:
> Or when the moon was overhead,
> Came two young lovers lately wed;
> 'I am half sick of shadows,' said
>   The Lady of Shalott (64–72)

5 If we look at the manuscript for the novel (CM 78.5.2), we find that Montgomery takes considerable pains with parts of their story. Some of Montgomery's early trial paragraphs are preserved at the back of the manuscript, on the reverse side of the typescript for *Anne of the Island*. We find among these notes several passages from the Rosemary-John romance, among them (ms notes 29), the interesting description of the trees at night and the surprise of rejuvenation that life holds for us (*RV* 135–6).

Womanhood and War: *Rilla of Ingleside*

1 Parts of this chapter and the chapter on *Jane of Lantern Hill* were from my lecture 'L.M. Montgomery: The Other Heroines.'

2 Montgomery herself wrote a poem entitled 'The Piper' because so many people asked her about Walter's poem. Her poem was published posthumously in *Saturday Night* on 2 May 1942. See Ferns, 39.

Recapturing the Anne World:
Anne of Windy Poplars and *Anne of Ingleside*

1 Montgomery refers to this same passage of Tennyson's *Idylls* in one of her early letters (1 Apr. 1907) to MacMillan discussing love. She says: 'When I was a school-girl I very much admired and believed a line in his poem "Lancelot and Guinevere." "We needs must love the highest when we see it." I don't believe it now. It is *not* true. We must *admire* the highest but *love* is an entirely different matter and is quite as likely to leave the best and go to the worst' (*Letters* 30).

PART II Emily

1 As T.D. MacLulich says, 'In building the Emily series around Emily's artistic development, Montgomery drew on virtually all of her thoughts about writers and writing, so that Emily's story contains the most complete exposition she ever provided of her own ideas about literature' ('L.M. Montgomery's Portraits' 468).
2 See especially these passages: *Journals* 1: 208–28, 240–41, 255, 294, 325; 2: 68, 101, 287–306, 369–70.
3 Alice Munro says that Dean Priest 'may be the nearest that L.M. Montgomery ever got to creating a plausible lover.' She believes that, 'In Jarback's scenes with Emily, there is from the beginning ... a true sexual tension' (358, 359).
4 Confederation Centre CM 67.5.8: 357 (renumbered in red ink as 337)

The Struggle for Voice: *Emily of New Moon*

1 One of Montgomery's overdone descriptions of a sunset is found in an early story 'A Strayed Allegiance,' originally published in 1897 and reproduced in *Along the Shore* 221–40. The offending description (228–9) is also noted by Wilmshurst in her introduction (8).
2 A small comic echo is even found between the dissimilar serving women of the two novels. Ellen Greene tells Emily, 'I've always threaped at your father to send you to school' (*ENM* 22); Hannah tells Jane that the Rivers sisters 'never fell out nor "threaped"' (Brontë 302). Readers may also want to look at Montgomery's hectic

Gothic short story 'The Red Room,' published in 1898 and found now in *Among the Shadows* (181–98).

Testing the Voice: *Emily Climbs*

1 Montgomery describes in her journal the surprise and jealousy with which her success was greeted. She was invited to meet Earl Grey, governor general of Canada, in September of 1910. See *Journals* 2: 10–17.
2 P.K. Page quotes from *Emily Climbs* to comment on Montgomery. Emily says: 'I shall always end *my* stories happily. I don't care whether it's "true to life" or not. It's true to life as it *should be* and that's a better truth than the other.' Page says: 'It may even be a truer truth. And I think L.M. Montgomery knew it' (Afterword, 241–2).

Love and Career: *Emily's Quest*

1 The description of Emily's inspiration echoes the description of Waldo's final understanding of Universal Unity and rest in *The Story of an African Farm*. The narrator describes Waldo's feelings (a passage I quote at greater length later in this chapter): 'Beauty is God's wine, with which he recompenses the souls that love Him; He makes them drunk' (Schreiner 285).
2 Mary Rubio suggests that Montgomery 'hates to marry Emily off to anyone' and turns the novel's ending into farce ('Canada's' 5).
3 Elizabeth Barrett Browning was 'annoyed' by connections made between *Aurora Leigh* and *Jane Eyre*, but the connections have continued to be made (Forster 316).
4 After describing what he calls the Cinderella formula and then the Pamela formula, John G. Cawelti says: 'Another more contemporary formula is that of the career girl who rejects love in favor of wealth or fame, only to discover that love alone is fully satisfying' (42).
5 In her wholehearted endorsement of Carpenter's view of idealized realism, perhaps Montgomery forgot that she had already used the pinewoods-pigsty contrast in the words of Emily in *Emily Climbs*. Emily is comparing three books that Dean has lent her: 'One was like a rose garden – very pleasant, but just a little too sweet. And one was like a pine wood on a mountain – full of balsam and tang – I loved it, and yet it filled me with a sort of despair. It was written so beautifully – I can *never* write like that, I feel sure. And one – it was just like a pig-sty. Dean gave me that one by mistake. He was very angry with himself when he found it out – angry and distressed' (*EC* 29).
6 Montgomery's own assessment of contemporary literature and realism is recorded in a letter to MacMillan (10 Feb. 1929) in which she remarks on his gift-book to her,

The Key above the Door: 'There is a wonderful freshness as of wind in heathery fields about it quite out of the common rut of modern fiction with its reeking atmospheres of brothel and latrine' (*Letters* 138).

PART III The Other Heroines

Romancing the Home: *Pat of Silver Bush, Mistress Pat, Jane of Lantern Hill*

1 Mollie Gillen notes that with the Depression and her own thoughts, the 1930s were gloomy for Montgomery: 'Her own generation had seen wrenched from its pedestal and hurled to ruins everything that had been believed immovable' (168).
2 The episode with Mrs Merridew (*MP* 104–11) is distressing to read. Montgomery's unexamined weight prejudice, probably as common then as now, makes the intended humour sound cruel to the ear attuned to this prejudice.
3 The hills with 'their arms around each other' is reminiscent of the wonderful trance-scene description in Tennyson's *In Memoriam*, where 'the trees / Laid their dark arms about the field' (95.15–16, 51–2).
4 The original for Silver Bush is the Campbell homestead, now called Silver Bush, in Park Corner, Prince Edward Island. It not only still stands, but also houses the Anne of Green Gables Museum and is open to visitors during the summer and fall. It is from Silver Bush that the L.M. Montgomery newsletter, *Kindred Spirits of P.E.I.*, is published four times a year (first started in spring 1990).

A Changing Heroism: An Overview of the Other Novels

1 It is interesting to find in Montgomery's scrapbooks, owned by the Confederation Centre of the Arts in Charlottetown, P.E.I., some of the original magazine and newspaper clippings from which Montgomery later drew stories for *The Story Girl* and *The Golden Road*. In the scrapbook for 1890–1900 (CM 67.5.15), for example, we find a three-column story by Lauron Hooper called 'When Kissing Came into the World,' clearly the original for Sara Stanley's 'How Kissing was Discovered' (*SG* 185–90).
2 For months after a Canadian journalist noted the similarities between *The Blue Castle* and *The Ladies of Missalonghi*, the controversy and speculation about possible borrowing by McCullough from Montgomery enlivened news in Canada, Britain, and Australia. McCullough said that she had read *The Blue Castle* and admitted that there were echoes of it in her book. The controversy died down, but *The Blue Castle* came back into print and remains there.
3 It is interesting to note that very little is added or changed in the manuscript for this Chidley Corners experience (CM 67.5.9: 218).

4 Many of the descriptive passages were added later to the manuscript. For example, at the beginning of chapter thirty-one, dealing with Valancy's and Barney's autumn and winter on Mistawis, we find almost continuous description. By comparing the manuscript and the printed text, we find that of the (approximately) 930 words of the first twelve printed paragraphs, 545 words were added in revisions (CM 67.5.9: 341). (The numbering of the manuscript at this point becomes chaotic, and much of the lyrical chapter thirty-one is heavily marked in red ink.)

5 The whole story of Big Sam and Little Sam is irksome, but their squabble over a naked statue will offend many readers of the 1990s. Big Sam thinks the statue is obscene and Little Sam keeps it, even though Big Sam moves out. As a conciliatory move, Little Sam finally paints it bronze. Big Sam's comments are the final words of the novel: ' "Then you can scrape it off again," said Big Sam firmly. "Think I'm going to have an unclothed nigger sitting up there? If I've gotter be looking at a naked woman day in and day out, I want a white one for decency's sake" ' (TW 324).

Works Cited

Åhmansson, Gabriella. *A Life and Its Mirrors: A Feminist Reading of L.M. Mont-gomery's Fiction*. Vol. 1. Stockholm: Uppsala 1991

Alcott, Louisa May. *Little Women*. New York: E.P. Dutton 1948

Arnim, Elizabeth von. *Elizabeth and Her German Garden*. London: Virago 1985

Ben-Porat, Ziva. 'The Poetics of Literary Allusion.' *PTL: A Journal for Descriptive Poetics and Theory of Literature* 1 (1976): 105–28

Brontë, Charlotte. *Jane Eyre*. Ed. Richard J. Dunn. 2nd ed. Norton critical ed. New York: Norton 1987

Brooke, Rupert. *The Complete Poems of Rupert Brooke*. London: Sidgwick and Jackson 1933

Browning, Elizabeth Barrett. *Aurora Leigh and Other Poems*. Intro. Cora Kaplan. London: Women's Press 1978

– *Poetical Works*. 5 vols. Vol. 2. New York: Dodd, Mead 1885

Browning, Robert. *The Poems of Robert Browning*. London: Oxford UP 1928

Brownstein, Rachel M. *Becoming a Heroine: Reading about Women in Novels*. London: Penguin 1984

Cawelti, John G. *Adventure, Mystery, and Romance: Formula Stories as Art and Popular Culture*. Chicago: U of Chicago P 1976

Classen, Constance. 'Is "Anne of Green Gables" An American Import?' *CCL: Cana-dian Children's Literature / Littérature canadienne pour la jeunesse* 55 (1989): 42–50

Coldwell, Joyce-Ione Harrington. 'Folklore as Fiction: The Writings of L.M. Montgomery.' *Folklore Studies in Honour of Herbert Halpert*. Ed. Kenneth S. Goldstein and Neil Rosenburg. St John's, Nfld: Memorial U of Newfoundland 1980. 125–35

Culler, Jonathan. *On Deconstruction: Theory and Criticism after Structuralism*. New York: Cornell UP 1982

Edwards, Lee R. *Psyche as Hero: Female Heroism and Fictional Form*. Middletown, Conn.: Wesleyan UP 1984

Eisler, Riane. *The Chalice and the Blade: Our History, Our Future*. San Francisco: Harper and Row 1987

Emerson, Ralph Waldo. *Essays: First Series. The Collected Works of Ralph Waldo Emerson*. 3 vols. Intro. Joseph Slater. Text est. by Alfred R. Ferguson and Jean Ferguson Carr. vol 2. Cambridge, Mass.: Belknap P of Harvard U 1979

– *Essays by Ralph Waldo Emerson*. Intro. Irwin Edman. New York: Thomas Y. Crowell 1961

Epperly, Elizabeth R. 'Greetings from Two of L. M. Montgomery's Grandchildren: Interview with Dave and Kate Macdonald.' *Kindred Spirits of P.E.I.* (Spring 1990): 4–5

– 'L.M. Montgomery and the Changing Times.' *Acadiensis* (Spring 1988): 177–85

– 'L.M. Montgomery: The Other Heroines.' Unpublished lecture given for P.E.I. Island Lecture Series, 3 Apr. 1989, Charlottetown, P.E.I.

– 'L.M. Montgomery's *Anne's House of Dreams*: Reworking Poetry.' *CCL: Canadian Children's Literature / Littérature canadienne pour la jeunesse* 37 (1985): 40–6

Ferns, John. ' "Rainbow Dreams": The Poetry of Lucy Maud Montgomery.' *CCL: Canadian Children's Literature / Littérature canadienne pour la jeunesse* 42 (1986): 29–40

Fitzgerald, Edward. *The Rubaiyat of Omar Khayyam*. New York: Walter J. Black 1942

Forster, Margaret. *Elizabeth Barrett Browning: A Biography*. New York: Doubleday, 1989

Fowler, Alistair. *Kinds of Literature: An Introduction to the Theory of Genres and Modes*. Cambridge, Mass.: Harvard UP 1982

Garner, Barbara Carman, and Mary Harker. '*Anne of Green Gables*: An Annotated Bibliography.' *CCL: Canadian Children's Literature / Littérature canadienne pour la jeunesse* 55 (1989): 18–41

Gilbert, Sandra. 'Soldier's Heart: Literary Men, Literary Women, and the Great War.' *Speaking of Gender*. Ed. Elaine Showalter. New York: Routledge 1989. 282–309

Gilbert, Sandra, and Susan Gubar. *The Madwoman in the Attic: The Woman Writer and the Nineteenth-Century Literary Imagination*. New Haven: Yale UP 1984

Gillen, Mollie. *The Wheel of Things: A Biography of L.M. Montgomery*. Don Mills, Ont.: Fitzhenry and Whiteside 1975

Works Cited 263

Gilligan, Carol. *In a Different Voice: Psychological Theory and Women's Development*. Cambridge, Mass.: Harvard UP 1982

Gray, Thomas. *The Complete Poems*. Ed. H.W. Starr and J.R. Hendrickson. Oxford: Clarendon P 1966

Heilbrun, Carolyn G. *Writing a Woman's Life*. New York: Ballantine 1988

Jacobus, Mary. *Reading Woman: Essays in Feminist Criticism*. New York: Columbia UP 1986

Johnson, Sonia. *Wildfire: Igniting the She/Volution*. Albuquerque, NM: Wildfire 1989

Katsura, Yuko. 'Red-Haired Anne in Japan.' *CCL: Canadian Children's Literature / Littérature canadienne pour la jeunesse* 34 (1984): 57–60

Keats, John. *Selected Poems and Letters*. Ed. Douglas Bush. Boston: Houghton Mifflin 1959

Keefer, Janice Kulyk. *Under Eastern Eyes: A Critical Reading of Maritime Fiction*. Toronto: U of Toronto P 1987

Kreps, Bonnie. *Subversive Thoughts, Authentic Passions: Finding Love without Losing Your Self*. Toronto: McClelland and Stewart 1990

McClung, Nellie. *In Times Like These*. Toronto: George J. McLeod 1917

McCullough, Colleen. *The Ladies of Missalonghi*. London: Arrow 1987

MacLulich, T.D. 'L.M. Montgomery and the Literary Heroine: Jo, Rebecca, Anne, and Emily.' *CCL: Canadian Children's Literature / Littérature canadienne pour la jeunesse* 37 (1985): 5–17

– 'L.M. Montgomery's Portraits of the Artist: Realism, Idealism, and the Romantic Imagination.' *English Studies in Canada* 11 (Dec. 1985): 459–73

Meynell, Alice. *The Poems of Alice Meynell*. Complete ed. London: Burns Oates and Washbourne 1924

Miller, Judith. 'Montgomery's Emily: Voices and Silences.' *Studies in Canadian Literature* 9.2 (1984): 158–68

Moi, Toril. *Sexual/Textual Politics: Feminist Literary Theory*. London: Routledge 1985

Montgomery, Lucy Maud. *Akin to Anne: Tales of Other Orphans*. Ed. Rea Wilmshurst. Toronto: McClelland and Stewart 1987

– *Along the Shore: Tales by the Sea*. Ed. Rea Wilmshurst. Toronto: McClelland and Stewart 1989

– *The Alpine Path*. Don Mills, Ont.: Fitzhenry and Whiteside 1975

– *Among the Shadows: Tales from the Darker Side*. Ed. Rea Wilmshurst. Toronto: McClelland and Stewart 1990

– *Anne of Avonlea*. 1909. Toronto: Ryerson 1942

– *Anne of Green Gables*. 1908. Toronto: Ryerson 1942

– *Anne of Ingleside*. New York: Grosset and Dunlap 1939

– *Anne of the Island*. New York: Grosset and Dunlap 1915

– *Anne of Windy Poplars*. New York: Grosset and Dunlap 1936

- *Anne's House of Dreams.* 1917. Toronto: McClelland and Stewart 1922
- *The Blue Castle.* 1926. Toronto: McClelland-Bantam 1988
- *Chronicles of Avonlea.* 1912. Toronto: Ryerson 1943
- *The Doctor's Sweetheart and Other Stories.* Ed. Catherine McLay. Toronto: McGraw-Hill Ryerson 1979
- *Emily Climbs.* 1925. Toronto: McClelland-Bantam 1983
- *Emily of New Moon.* 1923. Toronto: McClelland and Stewart 1925
- *Emily's Quest.* 1927. Toronto: McClelland-Bantam 1983
- *The Golden Road.* 1913. Toronto: Ryerson 1944
- *Jane of Lantern Hill.* Toronto: McClelland and Stewart 1937
- *Kilmeny of the Orchard.* 1910. Toronto: Ryerson 1944
- *Magic for Marigold.* 1929. Toronto: McClelland-Bantam 1988
- Manuscripts of Montgomery's novels, owned by the Confederation Centre of the Arts in Charlottetown, Prince Edward Island. CM 67.5.1, 2, 8, 9, 15; CM 78.5.2
- *Mistress Pat.* Toronto: McClelland and Stewart 1935
- *My Dear Mr. M.: Letters to G.B. MacMillan.* Ed. F.W.P. Bolger and Elizabeth R. Epperly. Toronto: McGraw-Hill Ryerson 1980
- *Pat of Silver Bush.* Toronto: McClelland and Stewart 1933
- *The Poetry of Lucy Maud Montgomery.* Ed. John Ferns and Kevin McCabe. Don Mills, Ont.: Fitzhenry and Whiteside, 1987
- *Rainbow Valley.* 1919. Toronto: McClelland and Stewart 1923
- *Rilla of Ingleside.* 1920. Toronto: McClelland and Stewart 1921
- *The Road to Yesterday.* Toronto: McGraw-Hill Ryerson 1974
- *The Selected Journals of L.M. Montgomery Volume I: 1889–1910.* Ed. Mary Rubio and Elizabeth Waterston. Toronto: Oxford UP 1985
- *The Selected Journals of L.M. Montgomery Volume II: 1910–1921.* Ed. Mary Rubio and Elizabeth Waterston. Toronto: Oxford UP 1987
- *The Story Girl.* 1911. Toronto: McGraw-Hill Ryerson 1944
- *A Tangled Web.* 1931. Toronto: McClelland and Stewart 1972
- *The Watchman and Other Poems.* Toronto: McClelland, Goodchild, and Stewart 1916
Munro, Alice. 'Afterword.' *Emily of New Moon.* New Canadian Library ed. Toronto: McClelland and Stewart 1989. 357–61
Mussell, Kay J. 'Romantic Fiction.' *Handbook of American Popular Culture.* Ed. M. Thomas Inge. 3 vols. Vol 2. Westport, Conn.: Greenwood 1980. 317–44
Noddings, Nell. *Caring: A Feminine Approach to Ethics and Moral Education.* Berkeley: U of California P 1984
Perri, Carmela. 'On Alluding.' *Poetics* 7 (1978): 289–307
Pickthall, Marjorie. *The Complete Poems of Marjorie Pickthall.* New ed. Toronto: McClelland and Stewart 1936

Pratt, Annis, with Barbara White, Andrea Loewenstein, and Mary Wyer. *Archetypal Patterns in Women's Fiction*. Bloomington: Indiana UP 1981

Prentice, Alison, Paula Bourne, Gail Cuthbert Brandt, Beth Light, Wendy Mitchinson, and Naomi Black. *Canadian Women: A History*. Toronto: Harcourt Brace Jovanovich 1988

Radway, Janice A. *Reading the Romance: Women, Patriarchy, and Popular Literature*. Chapel Hill, NC: U of North Carolina P 1984

Roper, Gordon. 'New Forces: New Fiction (1880–1920).' *Literary History of Canada: Canadian Literature in English*. Ed. Carl F. Klinck, et al. 2nd ed. 3 vols. Vol. 1. Toronto: U of Toronto P 1976 274–97

Ross, Catherine Sheldrick. 'Calling Back the Ghost of the Old- Time Heroine: Duncan, Montgomery, Atwood, Laurence, and Munro.' *Studies in Canadian Literature* 4 (Winter 1979): 43–58

Rowe, Karen E. ' "Fairy-born and Human-bred'': Jane Eyre's Education in Romance.' *The Voyage In: Fictions of Female Development*. Ed. Elizabeth Abel, Marianne Hirsch, and Elizabeth Langland. Hanover, NH: UP of New England 1983. 69–89

Rubio, Mary. 'Canada's Best-Known Children's Writer: L.M. Montgomery (1874–1942), A Writer for All Ages, Times, and Cultures.' International Research Society on Children's Literature. Salamanca, Spain. 9 Sept. 1989

Rubio, Mary, and Elizabeth Waterston. 'Afterword.' *Anne of Avonlea*. New York: Signet 1987. 274–85

– 'Afterword.' *Anne's House of Dreams*. New York: Signet 1989. 277–86

Russell, Ruth Weber, D.W. Russell, and Rea Wilmshurst. *Lucy Maud Montgomery: A Preliminary Bibliography*. Waterloo, Ont.: U of Waterloo Library 1986

Schreiner, Olive. *The Story of an African Farm*. 1883. Intro. Doris Lessing. New York: Schocken 1976

Scott, Sir Walter. *The Lady of the Lake*. Intro. Henry Morley. London: Cassell, 1908

Shakespeare, William. *The Complete Signet Classic Shakespeare*. New York: Harcourt Brace Jovanovich 1972

Smith, Dorothy E. *The Everyday World as Problematic: A Feminist Sociology*. Toronto: U of Toronto P 1987

Sorfleet, John Robert, ed. *L.M. Montgomery: An Assessment*. Guelph, Ont.: Canadian Children's P 1976

Spacks, Patricia Meyer. *Gossip*. New York: Knopf 1985

Tausky, Thomas E. 'L.M. Montgomery and "The Alpine Path, So Hard, So Steep." ' *CCL: Canadian Children's Literature / Littérature canadienne pour la jeunesse* 30 (1983): 5–20

Tennyson, Alfred, Lord. *The Poems of Tennyson*. Ed. Christopher Ricks. London: Longmans 1969

Urquhart, Jane. 'Afterword.' *Emily Climbs*. Toronto: McClelland and Stewart 1989. 330–34

Wachowicz, Barbara. 'L.M. Montgomery: At Home in Poland.' *CCL: Canadian Children's Literature / Littérature canadienne pour la jeunesse* 46 (1987): 7–36

Waterston, Elizabeth. 'Lucy Maud Montgomery: 1874–1942.' *The Clear Spirit: Twenty Canadian Women and Their Times*. Ed. Mary Quayle Innis. Toronto: U of Toronto P 1966. 198–220

Waterston, Elizabeth, and Mary Rubio. 'Afterword.' *Anne of Green Gables*. New York: Signet 1987. 307–17

Whittier, John Greenleaf. *The Poetical Works of John Greenleaf Whittier*. Ed. William Michael Rossetti. London: Ward, Lock [nd]

Wiggin, Kate Douglas. *Rebecca of Sunnybrook Farm*. 1903. New York: Scholastic 1988

Wilmshurst, Rea. 'L.M. Montgomery's Use of Quotations and Allusions in the "Anne" Books.' *CCL: Canadian Children's Literature / Littérature canadienne pour la jeunesse* 56 (1989): 15–45

Wordsworth, Dorothy. *Journals of Dorothy Wordsworth*. Ed. Mary Moorman. Oxford: Oxford UP 1971

Wordsworth, William. *The Poetical Works of William Wordsworth*. Ed. Paul D. Sheats. Cambridge ed. Boston: Houghton Mifflin 1982

Index

Index 271